THE BILLY BOY

To my wonderful parents, Hugh and Nan Anderson, sadly they are no longer with us, and to my wife, Jenny, who in all the years we have been together has always stood by me come what may. Her presence has made my life complete.

THE BILLY BOY

THE LIFE AND DEATH OF LVF LEADER BILLY WRIGHT

Chris Anderson

MAINSTREAM
PUBLISHING
EDINBURGH AND LONDON

First published in Great Britain in 2002 by
MAINSTREAM PUBLISHING COMPANY (EDINBURGH) LTD
7 Albany Street
Edinburgh EH1 3UG

ISBN 1 84018 639 9

A catalogue record for this book is available from the British Library

Typeset in Allise and Berkeley
Printed and bound in Great Britain by
Creative Print and Design Wales

Contents

Acknowledgements

This book could not have been completed without the help of a number of people from both sides of Northern Ireland's political divide. Although many of them did not identify themselves with Billy Wright's politics or modus operandi, they nevertheless realised that certain issues surrounding his death required clarification and investigation. Their kind advice and assistance to me over a four-year period proved invaluable. Their encouragement to keep going in the face of the numerous obstacles placed in my path by officialdom gave me the impetus to complete this book. I hope *The Billy Boy* serves to repay their faith in my ability to complete the course.

There were times when it would have been easy to give up and to admit defeat. In particular, over the past 12 months a number of unnerving incidents made me stop and ask myself if it was safe to pursue the unanswered questions surrounding the death of Billy Wright. Computers suddenly connecting up to the telephone system without being prompted to do so combined with telephone lines inoperative for protracted periods of time without apparent cause or explanation – it all happened. Twice within a three-month period in early 2002 my computer systems were stripped of their content. First, the hard disk on my main PC was completely destroyed. Second, in a more selective intrusion, only the content of my Internet system and e-mail program on my laptop was removed. Fortunately, no information relating to my work on the book was stored on either the main PC or the laptop.

Perhaps the most frightening incident was a phone call to my wife by someone purporting to be from the Post Office. The caller, who my wife described as having an English accent, asked for me by name and when informed that I was not present politely enquired when I would be expected home as they had a registered package for me, which they wished to deliver in person. Puzzled by the call itself and alerted by the absence of an official notification of any such package (it is normal practice for a postal official, when failing to deliver registered mail, to notify the recipient of when and where the item can be collected), my wife became concerned at the persistent nature of the enquiry as to when exactly I would return home. She contacted me and made me aware of the situation. Subsequent enquiries with the Post Office, the local sorting office, Parcel Force and other local carriers failed to uncover any registered package addressed to me. The package has yet to be delivered.

If anything, the above incidents only served to harden my resolve to finish the book. Having done so I must thank a number of people. Firstly, I must acknowledge the help and assistance given to me by Billy Wright's family. In particular to his father David, sisters Jackie and Connie and his ex-wife, Thelma. They provided me with so much useful information and detail that I would otherwise have struggled to obtain. Throughout the four years I have known David Wright, I have come to respect his honesty and integrity. In the face of what can only be described as contemptuous treatment by British Prime Minister Tony Blair and his administration, David Wright has always maintained his self-respect and refused to indulge in petty point-scoring tactics. Likewise the media profession has been less than kind to the Wright family. The contrast in the coverage of the issues of concern relating to the murder of Billy Wright have received far less media coverage than other similar controversial killings. David Wright has always treated me as a personal friend, something I value greatly.

A special thanks is due to Kelvin Boyes, whose pictures appear in this book; Gerry Morriarty, Suzanne Breen and the staff of the Belfast office of the *Irish Times*; John Devine and Dominic Cunningham of the *Irish Independent*; John Cassidy, Stephen Gordon, Donna Carton, Christian McCashin, Stephen Dempster, Ivan Little, Mervyn Jess, Merion Jones and Mick O'Kane. A special word of thanks is also due to Olivia Ward of the *Toronto Starr* who suggested I take on this project in the first place. Thanks also to Tim Pat Coogan, who opened doors and encouraged me as I started off in this profession and who has now written the foreword to this book.

To Jeffery Donaldson MP for his help in pursuing specific issues in relation to Billy Wright's death over the past three years. Others equally deserving of thanks are: Jane Winter of British Irish Rights Watch; Paul Mageehan, of the Committee on the Administration of Justice; Laurence McGill, consultant engineer and John MacAtamney, solicitor; Emma O'Neill who worked so hard on the legal aspects of the book; Billy Wright's former associates who provided me with eyewitness accounts of the murder and of his life both inside and outside the Maze. To all his former associates, especially the late Mark 'Swinger' Fulton – thank you. To all who helped in any way with this project and who out of necessity must remain anonymous – my thanks. To my good friend 'Junior' (Mercer), whose encouragement when times got tough was much appreciated.

In this book, the majority of the quotes from Billy Wright are contained on an audiotape of Wright himself. The tape was given to me by a senior loyalist figure in mid-1998 and I still have the tape in my possession. Other quotes from Billy Wright have come through personal conversations I have had with him.

My only regrets are, despite numerous requests to the IRSP (Irish Republican Socialist Party), I never managed to obtain a face-to-face interview with Christopher 'Crip' McWilliams. Likewise, the PUP failed to respond to a request for an interview in relation to this book. My thanks also to Jackie Mahood, who gave me a detailed insight into a number of important issues concerning Billy Wright and his politics.

Most importantly of all, my heartfelt gratitude to my wife Jenny who sacrificed so much to keep me going and allowed me to fulfil my obsession. Her support has been the difference between success and failure. To all my children, especially Steven, Mark and Kathryn, who endured the upheavals of family life as I struggled to complete this project, thanks for putting up with me. A special thanks to Steven who prepared the final floppy disc copy of this manuscript for me.

In closing, I would say to my critics, of which I expect there will be plenty, I have not intended this book to be a glorification of paramilitaries, nor have I intended it to eulogise Billy Wright. Its objective has been to show what can happen to Catholics or Protestants in Northern Ireland once they have outlived their usefulness or become obstacles to political progress. Murder is murder no matter who the victim is. Questions need to be answered in relation to the murder of Billy Wright. What he was or was not is irrelevant where truth and justice are concerned. Perception must not be allowed to prevent the truth about his death being made known. I trust the majority of those who take the time to read *The Billy Boy* will agree that in this instance the truth has yet to be exposed and others have yet to be brought to justice.

Chris Anderson,
October 2002.

Foreword by Tim Pat Coogan

Chris Anderson has written a most important book. There is a good deal of republican literature available, but with honourable exceptions such as Martin Dillon's *Shankill Butchers*, *Stone Cold* or, in another genre, Frank McGuinness's play, *Observe the Sons of Ulster Marching to the Somme*, little in the way of exposition of the loyalist mind.

By any stretch of the imagination, Billy Wright could be regarded as the embodiment of that mindset. He is very important in the context of contemporary Irish history. One can take him as an exemplar of how loyalists viewed Catholics and/or republicans, as a case study in how the security forces collude with loyalist paramilitaries, or simply how a ruthless man reacted to the storms of Irish history which broke upon him.

And Billy was certainly ruthless. My own abiding memory of him is of the partially blanked out figure in the famous Channel 4 interview in which he defended the killing of a Catholic widow's son. The lady in question, he said, might be innocent herself of any IRA involvement, indeed, so might her son, but the widow would certainly know the names and addresses of a number of IRA activists or sympathisers who were likely to kill loyalists, and her crime was that she did not pass these on to the authorities. That interview will be a valuable piece of the history of our times one day.

Billy Wright's attitude to the IRA was contemptuous: 'I met very few brave IRA men, to their own shame. Ninety per cent of their senior officers left the battlefield; they ran away, they headed south. That's the nature of them – they want to kill, but they don't want to be killed.'

Many nationalists would also regard the Orange terrorists as similarly cowardly. Capable only of the murder of soft targets, operating only when protected by the security forces, this great hatred little-room syndrome is one of the features, and the conflicts, of the problem.

One wonders how much Billy Wright actually knew about the IRA, about matters like discrimination and gerrymandering. The IRA to him seems to have been something which welled up in the South and attacked the North. In the North itself, his view of his activities was: 'We were taking on the IRA and giving them a headache and I think that's what made mid-Ulster [UVF] stand out. We fought the Provies and had no quarrel or disagreement with the Catholic community. I genuinely believe that we were very, very successful and they know that we hammered them into the ground. It was the east Tyrone brigade which was carrying the war in the whole of the North, including Belfast. East Tyrone were decimated, the UVF wiped them out.'

That self-applied gloss on his own activities would hardly comfort the families of the innocent Catholics who died in the murder triangle. To them, the name Billy Wright is synonymous with anti-Christ. Not a man who on his own terms firmly believed 'that the loyalist people have the right to resist and to defend themselves'.

This sense of righteousness amongst loyalists is part of the settler ethos. The natives are by definition treacherous and disloyal, resisting the forces of civilisation and enlightenment. In Portadown, the militias of the righteous ones traditionally have the right to enter homes 'to search for arms', wrecking furniture and, inevitably, destroying any spinning wheels found in Catholic homes.

Not only did the settlers have the right to defend their turf, they could also legitimately destroy any economic threat to 'their' linen industry. Out of this background of bible, and bashing, there grew a mindset which was easily manipulated by the security forces to their own ends. Men who felt it was their bounden right and duty to 'stiff a Teague', when given intelligence, in some cases weaponry, and a clear passage to and from their victims' homes, had the additional merit in the eyes of the counter-insurgency experts of leaving no smoking guns behind them.

One of the important features of Chris Anderson's book is his exposition of the manner in which these forces decided that Wright, who in the eyes of the 'securocrats' had progressed from smoking gun to loose cannon, should himself be assassinated.

There were a number of reasons for this. One, that Wright, whose unenviable exploits had earned him the equally unenviable title of

'King Rat', also suffered from the disability of having above-average intelligence, and was becoming a dangerous power in his own right. The second was that the infamous 'shoot-to-kill' policy demanded that the ever-growing list of Catholic victims demanded some balancing Protestant sacrificial offerings. Wright was the biggest one around.

Anderson, in a telling passage, describes how the late Harold McCusker MP was first made aware by Wright that a shoot-to-kill policy was in operation, and that it was about to be applied to Wright himself. Wright seems to have been on a hit-list from 1981–2 onwards. His death in prison was merely the carrying out of a long-ordained sentence.

Whatever he had done himself, Wright did not deserve to die as he did. He was in the care of the State, and should have been protected. Instead he appears to have been set up for the INLA hit men. One can only speculate as to what Wright's role would have been had, as someone obviously feared he might, he benefited under the terms of the Good Friday Agreement and been released from prison.

On the evidence of his career, one can hardly speculate that it would have been benign. But who knows. Though his attitude to 'the enemies of Ulster' was clearly malevolent, he might have evolved into a political figure with something to contribute. This is speculation. What is certain is that there are lesser Billy Wrights aplenty in the six counties. I was watching some of them marching recently during the 2002 12th celebrations in Belfast.

They were a chilling sight. The low foreheads, the tattoos, the heads shaven for forensic purposes so that they would not leave hairs at the scene of a crime or 'operation'. But they were there, and they have to be reckoned with. And here we come to one of the most important parts of Anderson's book. Amongst those who reckon with them are the leaders of the unionist political community.

I have always made a distinction between unionism as a political culture, which I hold to be deficient because of its 'not-an-inch' approach, and its failures to measure up to the challenges posed by contemporary economic trends and Catholic demography, and Protestantism.

The mass of the Protestant people of Northern Ireland are decent and peace-seeking. But they lack leadership. There is a leadership deficit in the unionist community which cannot articulate the Protestant need for security and at the same time, guide Protestants towards change.

The three principal strands of unionism are the Protestant religion, the British heritage and supremacy. I would fight for their entitlement to the first two, even though there is very little enthusiasm in the United Kingdom mainland for their attention to Ulster Unionist British heritage. But supremacy has no more place in modern, west-European political philosophy than it had in Boer South Africa.

However, as Anderson graphically describes, on one notable occasion, Billy Wright forcefully demonstrated his belief in the rightness of that supremacist attitude – the 1996 Drumcree controversy, during which in a very real sense Billy Wright made it possible for David Trimble to win the political horse-race for the then vacant unionist leadership riding on the back of King Rat.

Wright had a digger, a petrol tanker, explosives and armed men ready to smash through the Drumcree barricades if the Orangemen were not allowed to march. He made these facts known to David Trimble and Trimble in turn informed the authorities of what was planned, with the result that the Chief Constable decided to allow the procession.

It was the greatest capitulation to militant loyalism since Roy Bradford walked out of the power-sharing executive in 1974 following a visit to his ministerial office by the then UVF leader, Ken Gibson. Both episodes illustrate the power paramilitaries exert on unionist decision taking.

Wright and Drumcree also served to highlight the dilemma for loyalism posed by the fact that although he claimed to have eliminated the IRA and republicanism in east Tyrone, that the Catholics still went on inconveniently increasing in number with the result that once 'traditional' marching routes like Drumcree are now Catholic housing estates, containing Catholic voters who support Sinn Fein.

The loyalists cannot live with the Catholics, but as someone said of women, nor can they live without them. The truth is that we all – Catholic, Protestant, Dissenter and the Dublin 4 type who wants nothing more than a giant pair of scissors with which to cut along the dotted line on the map separating the six counties from the 26 and send all the Northerners out to sea – must live together.

The Billy Boy illustrates for us both the Wrights and the wrongs.

Tim Pat Coogan

Introduction

*My son was the last person to be executed at Her Majesty's
pleasure. Executed – for that's what he was.*

David Wright

David Wright, father of murdered Loyalist Volunteer Force (LVF)
leader, Billy Wright, used those powerful and emotive words to me
during a conversation that took place between us back in October
1998. A few days earlier, at Downpatrick Crown Court, three Irish
National Liberation Army (INLA) prisoners – Christopher 'Crip'
McWilliams, John Kennaway and John Glennon – had been convicted
of the murder of Billy Wright. Judge Brian Kerr sentenced all three men
to life imprisonment. The murder trial itself was remarkably brief. It
lasted a little over a day and a half. Few new facts about the murder
came to light during the trial of the three INLA prisoners. All three
pleaded not guilty to the charge of murdering Billy Wright, but
strangely offered no evidence in their defence.

Throughout the duration of the trial, David Wright and his two
daughters listened impassively to the Crown case. Just a few feet in
front of them – almost within touching distance – sat the three
accused. On a number of occasions during the trial, the INLA
prisoners smirked and joked with each other. It was a public display
of contempt by the dissident republicans for the British justice system.
It also showed the value all three men placed on human life.

However, for David Wright the trial proved to be a turning point.
Indirectly it provided him with information to reinforce his belief that
the 'hidden hand' of the State had orchestrated his son's murder.

During the lunch recess on the first day of the murder trial David
Wright was standing at the main doorway of Downpatrick Courthouse.
A few moments earlier he had had a brief conversation with Mr John
Creaney, Crown Counsel. Creaney, in the presence of others, had told

David Wright that in his opinion the three accused would be found guilty as charged. The remark did little to instil in David Wright the belief that the full facts of his son's killing were being presented to the Court. 'I told Creaney I didn't need a gown and wig to reach that conclusion. I also told him I could drive a coach and horses through the Crown case. I instinctively knew certain relevant facts were being hidden and kept out of the public domain,' David Wright told me.

Later, as he stood with his daughters in the entrance hall of the courthouse, a number of men entered the building and brushed past David Wright. Although the men were dressed in civilian clothes, they were all prison officers from the Maze who had been called to give evidence in the murder trail. As they made their way across the hallway, one of them stopped, turned, and walked back to where the Wright family were standing. As the prison officer passed David Wright he thrust a small piece of green paper into his hand. The movement went unnoticed by police officers and court officials standing nearby.

A short time later David Wright went into a cloakroom adjoining the courtroom. Inside he opened the small piece of paper and read the following words:

> Mr Wright, please ask *your lawyers* to contact solicitors [of Co. Antrim]. Ref the suppression of statements by the D.P.P. Don't use your own telephone.

This particular note was given to David Wright by prison officer Brian Thompson. Although he had provided a statement to the RUC, Thompson was not listed as a witness at the trial of the three INLA killers. Thompson believed the authorities were deliberately suppressing his evidence, which included a direct reference to the standing down of the watchtower guard and the warnings given to prison management. Concerned by this, Thompson alerted David Wright to the fact that he had made a statement regarding 27 December 1997 to his solicitors and the RUC, which had not been used.

David Wright contacted the solicitors by telephone and they confirmed the existence of the Thompson statement. However, to date the content of the statement has never been made public.

That small piece of paper was dynamite and proved to be a catalyst for David Wright. It served to convince him that the authorities were deliberately withholding the full facts about the death of his son. It was the impetus, which saw the 67-year-old grandfather embark on a campaign to have a public inquiry held into the circumstances of his son's murder inside the Maze Prison, a jail which was allegedly the most secure prison in Western Europe.

Since then David Wright has continued to campaign for a public inquiry to be established into the death of his son. He has unearthed, disseminated and collated specific and detailed information about the murder, which he says exposes serious inaccuracies and untruths in the British government's official version of how his son died. On two occasions he has endured the harrowing ordeal of visiting H Block 6 at the Maze Prison to view at first hand the murder scene and its surroundings. Those visits in particular only served to further convince David Wright that his son's murder had been state orchestrated.

At the time of his death aged 37 in 1997, Billy Wright was an extremely influential loyalist figure. He was the leader of the loyalist paramilitary grouping, the LVF, which held sway in the staunchly loyalist heartland of Portadown, Co. Armagh. Wright had been involved with loyalism from the age of 15 when he joined the Young Citizens' Volunteers (YCV) – the junior wing of Northern Ireland's largest paramilitary organisation, the Ulster Volunteer Force (UVF).

The LVF had been formed in 1996 following an acrimonious split with the UVF over the organisation's political strategy and its failure to support the Orange Order protest at Drumcree, a few miles outside Wright's hometown of Portadown. Until that point in time Billy Wright had been clearly identified as the UVF commander in the mid-Ulster area. The UVF's mid-Ulster Brigade was one of the organisations most potent and ruthless. It had a long and bloody history in the loyalist war against republican terror groups. However, by the summer of 1996 Wright and the majority of his mid-Ulster colleagues were vehemently opposed to the embryonic peace process and the strategy of fringe loyalist political parties such as the Progressive Unionist Party (PUP). This stance was in direct opposition to UVF strategy at the time and led to the UVF standing down its mid-Ulster Brigade. The Belfast command of the UVF gave Wright 72 hours to leave Northern Ireland or face 'summary justice'. Wright defied the order, split with the UVF and formed his own breakaway organisation, the LVF. The move brought Wright and the LVF into direct conflict with the UVF and its leadership in Belfast.

In March 1997, Billy Wright was sentenced to eight years imprisonment on a charge of threatening to kill. Initially he was held at Maghaberry Prison, Co. Antrim before being transferred to HMP Maze in April that year. He had been in the Maze for just over eight months when his killers struck on 27 December 1997.

There is no disputing who killed Billy Wright. The three Irish National Liberation Army (INLA) inmates, Christopher 'Crip' McWilliams, John 'Sonny' Glennon and John Kennaway, have been convicted of the murder. The INLA also claimed responsibility for the shooting.

However, there are a number of very serious and disturbing factors concerning the murder of Billy Wright, which have yet to be answered satisfactorily. They include:

- The decision by prison authorities to house INLA and LVF prisoners in the same H Block within the Maze Prison.
- The decision by prison authorities to transfer two of the murderers, John Kennaway and Christopher McWilliams from Maghaberry Prison to the Maze despite both men having been involved in a hostage-taking incident during which the two men used a smuggled weapon, and despite the INLA having issued specific death threats against Billy Wright on this particular occasion.
- The failure of the prison authorities to act on warnings about the insecurity of the roof areas at H Block 6 and the possibility of attack.
- The apparent ability of the INLA inmates to gain access to weapons and wire cutters despite the progressive introduction of enhanced security measures at the Maze from May 1997.
- The fact that a breach in the wire remained undetected by prison staff.
- Prisoners were given the names of both INLA and LVF prisoners due to receive visits on 27 December 1997.
- A crucial security camera used to scan the roof area of the H Blocks, including H Block 6, had been out of action on the day of the murder.
- A prison officer, on duty in the watchtower overlooking the murder scene, had been removed from his post twice on the day of the murder, including the time of the murder.
- LVF prisoners were not allowed access to their exercise yard on the morning of the murder, but INLA prisoners had access to their yard.
- Unusually, the INLA prison visits bus was parked adjacent to the LVF wing with the LVF prison visits bus parked next to the INLA wing.

● The failure by police to question INLA prisoners in the Maze until four weeks after the murder.

● The failure by the Coroner to call key witness to give evidence at the inquest into Billy Wright's murder.

These crucial factors, along with vital information revealed here for the first time, have led David Wright to conclude that his son's murder was 'state arranged, state sponsored and state sanctioned, in collusion with some of those in prison management'. Those suspicions are now shared by an increasing number of people and human-rights groups. It is clear that a number of serious questions surrounding the murder of the LVF leader have not been adequately answered despite a police investigation, a murder trail, an inquest and an investigation by a senior English prison official. In such circumstances only a public inquiry can fully establish the truth. The Wright family are entitled to know that truth.

Any state collusion in the murder of Billy Wright must be exposed and remedied. The failure by the authorities to do so only serves to weaken further public confidence in the administration of justice and rule of law in Northern Ireland. Without that confidence there is little hope of our tortured and troubled province ever becoming a stable society.

1. The Loyalist Evolves

I accept that if I die in ignominy and shame, as long as a nucleus of Ulstermen know the truth then I don't mind.

Billy Wright

William Stephen Wright was born on 7 July 1960 in Wolverhampton, England. He was the only son in a family of five. His father, David, originally from Portadown, Co. Armagh, had left Northern Ireland as a young man and had been working in England for some time. The family had eventually settled in the English Midlands where Billy Wright and three of his sisters were born and spent the early years of their lives.

Billy Wright's family were well known in Portadown, both in business and political circles. His great-grandfather, Robert Wright, had established a thriving business in the Co. Armagh market town and was heavily involved in local politics with Portadown Urban District Council. He also held the position of Royal Commissioner for 27 years. Billy Wright's grandfather, also known as Billy, had inherited his father's business acumen as well as the interest in local politics. In the late 1940s Wright's grandfather was elected to the local council in Portadown. In 1947 he topped the poll in the local elections and became the first independent councillor to be elected in Northern Ireland. However, to stand as, and be elected, an independent councillor was viewed as nothing less than an open act of defiance against the controlling Ulster Unionist Party who dominated Portadown Council at that time.

However, Billy Wright's grandfather recognised the social and economic injustices to which Northern Ireland's nationalist community were subjected. He objected to the widespread and common practice of discrimination against Catholics in housing and employment. He tried to fight those same injustices at a local level but encountered the full force of unionist opposition and bigotry. Portadown was and still is to this day, synonymous with Ulster unionism and the Orange Order. In the 1940s very few, if any, would have dared to take on the unionist establishment head to head. In Wright's eyes the Ulster Unionist Party was symptomatic of the malaise affecting politics in Northern Ireland at that time. However, one man could not break the Unionist stranglehold on local government in Portadown. After Unionist councillors opposed his policy that local houses should be allocated on a points basis (at that time councillors voted on the allocation of houses) he became disillusioned with politics in Northern Ireland. Wright had supported the allocation of a house to a former soldier married to a local family. Unionist members of the council opposed Wright en bloc and allocated the house to their own nominee. Following the meeting to allocate the house, one senior Unionist councillor turned to Wright and said: 'You can hang your points system on that decision.'

The family's experiences with the Ulster Unionist Party and the Orange Order left a lasting impression on them. Fifty years after his father had taken on the establishment in Portadown, David Wright said: 'My father used to say you could buy the best Orangeman for the price of a bottle of stout on the Twelfth of July morning.'

In later life Billy Wright himself would learn that the Orange Order and unionism in general had progressed little since his grandfather's sortie into local politics.

After spending the first four years of his life in England, Billy Wright's family returned to Northern Ireland and Portadown in 1964. A few years later, aged seven, following the failure of his parent's marriage, he went to live with a foster family, the McMurrays, in the village of Mountnorris close to the republican heartland of south Armagh. In later life Wright said he had been happy during his time in Mountnorris. He attended the local primary school where a Mrs Flack, a member of the Alliance Party, taught him. During his time at Mountnorris school, Billy Wright studied Irish history, learning about Irish culture and mythology from an Irish perspective. Here he was made aware of the centuries of 'English wrongs' towards Ireland. He later claimed it was unique for Protestant children to be taught in this manner in the 1960s. At that time, the majority of state schools would have been teaching the 'Anglicised' version of Irish history. According to Wright, the teaching he received from Mrs Flack helped awaken and develop his awareness of the political situation in Northern Ireland.

During his time in south Armagh, Billy Wright made many friends within the local Roman Catholic community. Although brought up in the strong Presbyterian faith, attending church twice on Sundays, he mixed freely with the local nationalist children. He later said he saw nothing wrong with that, claiming that the two cultures – unionism and nationalism – were entwined in the area. On Sunday afternoons, Wright and his friends walked the short distance to the village of Whitecross to the only shop that opened on Sunday. Although a Catholic family owned the shop, it served both sections of the community. Following a trip to the shop, Wright and his friends would watch the Gaelic football match at the local Gaelic Athletic Association (GAA) ground. The sport had no political connections for Wright at that time. He described it as just a game. However, despite claims to the contrary, he never admitted to taking part in the sport himself.

At the age of 11, Billy Wright left Mountnorris primary school and transferred to the local secondary school at Markethill a few miles away. Former classmates described him as quiet but articulate and intelligent. Staff at Markethill secondary school had high hopes for the small, blond-haired lad who showed a passion for learning. However, dark forces were at work in Northern Ireland in 1971. The violence, which had erupted across Belfast and Londonderry in 1969, had spread to other areas of the province. South Armagh was one of the areas and later became synonymous with murder and mayhem, earning itself the nickname, 'Bandit Country'.

At this point in his life, Billy Wright said he gradually became aware of the activities of the IRA. Brought up to respect law and order and the forces of the Crown, he slowly became aware of what was happening around him as the security forces began to take casualties at the hands of republican terrorists. The area in which he lived was on the periphery of Bandit Country and Wright claimed he became increasingly concerned at the lack of protection afforded to the Protestant families of the area. That concern developed over the next few years as the IRA expanded its campaign against the security forces. Aged 15, Billy Wright had worked part-time on a number of the Protestant farms close to Mountnorris and Whitecross. A number of the farmers were members of the Royal Ulster Constabulary Reserve (RUCR) or the locally recruited Ulster Defence Regiment (UDR), a part-time unit of the British Army. In April 1970, the UDR had been formed to replace the controversial 'B

Specials'. However, throughout its 20-year history the UDR remained an anathema to Irish nationalists and republicans. By the time it was amalgamated into the Royal Irish Regiment in 1991, nearly 200 members of the UDR had been killed in terrorist-related incidents. Of that figure a sizable number had been killed in the south Armagh area. Most of the UDR soldiers had been off duty when they were attacked. As he worked on the farms Wright noticed that when they were out in the open fields some of the men patrolled the area where they were or stood guard until the day's work was complete. Such was the threat to the local community at that time and the background in which the adolescent Billy Wright was growing up.

At the age of 15 Billy Wright left Mountnorris and moved back to Portadown to live with his aunt. The incident, which was to lead to his departure, was trivial but an indication of events to come. Wright had painted a 'UVF' slogan on a wall of the local primary school. When he had been told to remove it he refused to do so. He decided to leave the area and move back to Portadown.

In 1975, Portadown had strong loyalist paramilitary connections. Both the UVF and the UDA were active in the area and had carried out a number of terrorist attacks against the Catholic community in the mid-Ulster area. The previous year, in May 1974, at the height of the loyalist strike, which brought down the power-sharing executive at Stormont, a number of bombs exploded in the centre of Dublin and Monaghan in the Irish Republic. The attacks, the worst in the history of the Troubles, killed 33 people and injured hundreds of others. At the time, responsibility for the bombings in mid-Ulster was laid at the door of the UVF. Since then suspicions of security-force involvement in the attacks have persisted. However, in recent years the UVF has always maintained it carried out the Dublin and Monaghan attacks unaided. In July 1975, three members of the Miami Showband were killed after the minibus in which they had been travelling was stopped at a bogus army checkpoint near Newry, Co. Down.

The musicians died when the UVF's mid-Ulster unit mounted the fake roadblock on the main Belfast to Dublin road south of Banbridge. The apparent intention of the UVF appeared to have been to put a bomb into the band's minibus and have it explode as they travelled towards their homes in the Irish Republic. However, the device exploded prematurely as two UVF members were loading it into the vehicle. Three members of the Miami Showband – Fran O'Toole, aged 29, Brian McCoy, aged 33, and Anthony Geraghty, aged 23 – were killed in the explosion. Two UVF men – Harris Boyle from Portadown and Wesley Somerville from Dungannon – also died in the attack. Later two other members of the UVF were convicted of the Miami Showband killings and were sentenced to life imprisonment.

On 31 July 1975, the night the UVF gang launched its attack on the Miami Showband, Billy Wright was sworn into the paramilitary group's junior wing, the Young Citizen's Volunteers (YCV). He had just turned 15 when he took his first steps into the world of the loyalist paramilitaries in mid-Ulster.

Billy Wright had never been attracted to either the UDR or the RUCR. For him the real army of the Protestant people was the Ulster Volunteer Force. As far as he was concerned it was the only organisation which held the moral right to defend the Protestant population of Northern Ireland. Since 1966, when the UVF re-emerged as an organisation, Wright's belief was that the UVF had been assumed into the Protestant culture in Portadown, Co. Armagh. For him the sense of Protestantism was stronger in the mid-Ulster area that in any other area of Northern Ireland. However, he never felt compelled to join the Orange Order. Portadown is interlinked with Protestant history down through the years. It is arguably Northern Ireland's most loyal town. It is, in the eyes of local loyalists, perhaps the last bastion of traditional 'Protestantism' in Northern Ireland. The town displays its Protestant heritage at every opportunity. It revels in its history and Protestant culture, which is displayed wherever possible.

In 1641, almost 100 Protestant men, women and children were massacred by Manus Roe O'Cahan, a native Irish rebel, in the River Bann at Portadown during the rebellion of that year. The scene of the massacre is graphically depicted on the banner of one of Portadown District's many Orange lodges: Johnston's Royal Standard, LOL No 99 portrays, 'Drowning the Protestants in River Bann, 1641'. The Orange Lodge, in a constant reminder of the treatment meted out by the Irish rebels to Portadown Protestants almost four centuries ago, carries the banner on every 'Twelfth' parade.

In September 1795 following the Battle of the Diamond, just a few miles from Portadown, the Orange Order was formed. Ten months later the first Orange 'Twelfth' Demonstration was held near the Co. Armagh town. A few months later, on 21 August 1796, Portadown LOL No 1 became the first District Orange Lodge to be formed in the history of the Orange Institution. So strong have the town's links to the

Protestant religion and the Orange Order been over the years that it has become known as the 'Orange Citadel'. This is the town Billy Wright returned to at the impressionable age of 15.

There is little doubt that in the mid-1970s there were individuals within the loyalist paramilitary organisations in Portadown on the look-out for potential recruits such as Billy Wright. It was all too easy to indoctrinate the impressionable mind of a 15-year-old youth with tales of the UVF, the Battle of the Somme and the threat from the IRA and 'Fenians'. The men who recruited Billy Wright and many more like him into the murky world of the paramilitary bear a heavy responsibility. Many of them are still alive and walk the streets of Portadown in relative safety. Many of those they recruited and indoctrinated are dead and buried, their lives prematurely ended by their involvement with paramilitaries. That was the price they paid whilst others grew accustomed to a lifestyle they could only have dreamed of before the advent of the Troubles.

However, Billy Wright's fledgling career as a loyalist paramilitary was cut short in 1975 when he was arrested by the RUC and taken to Castlereagh Holding Centre. While in detention he later claimed he had been beaten by police officers and forced to sign a number of statements admitting involvement in paramilitary activities in the mid-Ulster area. He was subsequently charged with possession of firearms and received a six-year jail sentence. He was sent to HMP Maze where he was held on the Young Person's (YP's) wing on H Block 2. This particular wing in the Maze Prison housed both loyalist and republican prisoners, all of whom were under 21 years of age. Some time after he arrived at the Maze Prison, Billy Wright joined the Blanket Protest.

The Blanket Protest, although primarily associated with republican prisoners, also involved a number of loyalist inmates at the Maze. In September 1976, Kieran Nugent, a member of the provisional IRA, was the first prisoner convicted of a terrorist crime not to be accorded special-category status. When he entered the Maze, Nugent refused to wear prison uniform and, instead of standing naked in his cell, wrapped himself in a blanket to distinguish himself from those prisoners convicted of non-terrorist-related offences. These prisoners became known as ODC's – ordinary decent criminals. The Blanket Protest over the restoration of special-category status would eventually lead to the 1981 hunger strikes.

However, after a period of time Wright was ordered to give up the protest when the UVF leadership decided participation was being viewed as supporting the Provisional IRA in its campaign for the return of the special-category status. After he came off the Blanket Protest, the 17-year-old Wright became a wing commander, serving the remainder of his time at the Maze on H Block 2. During his time on H Block 2, Wright lived in close proximity to republican prisoners, the majority of whom came from the south Londonderry area and Strabane. Like Wright, all the republican prisoners on the YP wings of H2 were under the age of 21. The time he spent alongside the republican prisoners had a lasting effect on Billy Wright. It was here that he formed his first opinions of the republican movement and many of the impressions he formed during that time were to remain with him for the rest of his life. Wright remarked that he had noticed how quickly loyalists would accept the truth when it was proven to be the truth, while republicans, on the other hand, he said, were more than reluctant to accept anything other than what they themselves had set out to be correct.

In one graphic account of his time on H Block 2 Wright recalled how, as he was about to be released from the Maze, he had been standing beside a republican prisoner who was on the Blanket Protest. The man had not washed for over a year and the stench of urine was overpowering. Despite the prisoner's appalling physical appearance, Billy Wright said he experienced an atmosphere of pure history. He is quoted as having said: 'I knew the significance of what I was witnessing. Here was a movement that would inflict on itself so much violence for its own ideology that what would it not do to other human beings? I knew then it had to be resisted.'

He went on to say: 'Anyone or anything that would trust republicans with the lives of over one million Protestants were fools. Republicans were prepared to do whatever it takes to have their own way.'

Billy Wright felt anger and resentment towards the British state for his imprisonment. As far as he was concerned, he was being punished for being a 'soldier' and defending his people. It made no difference to him that he was a 'soldier' of the UVF and not of the State. In his eyes the State had failed in its responsibility to defend his people, the Protestants of Northern Ireland, from attack by republicans. In light of that failure he had felt compelled to take up arms on behalf of his people. Wright was never ashamed of his involvement with, or his support for, the Ulster Volunteer Force.

Billy Wright was released from the Maze Prison in October 1982 after serving three and a half years of his six-year sentence. Before he left the Maze he received a lecture from one of the Maze governors, who, Wright said, was universally hated and despised by prisoners and staff alike within the jail. The governor said he had no doubt that Wright would return to the Maze in the near future. Wright said he and the governor had left the meeting hating each other.

As Wright emerged from the steel fencing and rusting barbed wire of the Maze and into the car park area, his girlfriend and his aunt met him. In an open act of defiance against the authorities, Wright turned, looked up at a British Army observation tower on the perimeter fence of the prison and shouted, 'Up the UVF'. As he did so, he said, his girlfriend and aunt had looked on in total disbelief.

Following his release from the Maze Prison Wright tried to steer his life away from the direction of the paramilitaries. At this stage he was involved in a steady relationship with Thelma Corrigan, from Annaghmore, near Portadown. The Corrigan family had also suffered at the hands of republican terrorists. In October 1976, Thelma Corrigan's father William had been shot dead as he was returning to his home at Meadowview, Annaghmore, Co. Armagh. His son Leslie was very seriously wounded in the attack and died two weeks later. Both men had been returning home after visiting William Corrigan's mother in the nearby Co. Tyrone town of Moy. As they got out of their car, gunmen, who had been hiding in a hedge directly opposite, opened fire, killing William Corrigan instantly. A man was later convicted of the killing.

Immediately, after his release from the Maze, Billy Wright travelled to Scotland where he had been found a job by one of his sisters who was working in the hotel trade. He remained there for two months before officers from the Metropolitan Police based at Scotland Yard, London, arrested him. Wright was detained in Scotland for a period of eight days before he was served with a court order, which excluded him from England, Scotland and Wales. He was subsequently deported back to Northern Ireland where he immediately re-involved himself with the mid-Ulster unit of the Ulster Volunteer Force.

In December 1980, Wright was arrested and remanded in custody on the word of the first loyalist 'super-grass', Clifford McKeown. Wright was charged with murder, attempted murder, possession of explosives with intent and the possession of firearms. He was detained at Belfast's Crumlin Road Prison for ten months. He was released from prison in October 1981 after McKeown refused to give evidence in relation to any of the charges against Wright. Within three months Wright was back in jail, having been arrested after members of the British Army's SAS regiment opened fire on a number of men attempting to remove weapons from a loyalist arms dump.

Describing the incident Billy Wright said: 'Members of the mid-Ulster Brigade of the UVF went to an arms dump in the south Armagh area and while trying to acquire the weapons were attacked by the SAS. Three of them were arrested, one man escaped. I was accused of being that man. I was then remanded in custody for a period of 14 months. I went to trial and was acquitted.

'It came out at the trial that 400 rounds had been fired at him [the man that escaped] by six SAS soldiers. Having spoken to the volunteers who were convicted, they assured me that it was basically a 'wipe-out' had it not been for the fact that someone got away which could have witnessed it. The soldiers on the ground at that time believed that person to be Billy Wright and that where they thought Billy Wright was, they basically just emptied their rifles.

'During the trial . . . after the trial it was brought to the attention of the Judge that one of the soldiers, a sergeant, had threatened to take Billy Wright's life even during the course of the trial.'

Wright went on to say: 'After I was acquitted, [I was told] that I should immediately leave the country and that if I couldn't afford it it would be paid for because I was to be executed by the British.'

This is the first indication Billy Wright had that he was quickly becoming a major thorn in the side of the security forces and the British establishment.

However, it was not only the Special Air Service which was targeting Billy Wright for assassination in 1982. At that time he had also become the target of intense police scrutiny, especially by the specialist undercover RUC anti-terrorist unit E4A. During a period of detention at Gough Barracks, Armagh, in 1982, Wright was informed of a plan to kill him. That plan, Wright claimed, was part of the infamous shoot-to-kill policy adopted by the RUC at that time and which claimed the lives of a number of nationalists in north Armagh.

Wright said: 'During detention in Gough Barracks I had been made aware through a source that I was to be executed by E4A. I left Gough Barracks and drove immediately to the late Harold McCusker's house, the MP. [McCusker was the Ulster Unionist MP in Portadown. He died of cancer in 1991.] I walked down the driveway, I rapped his door, he let me in. I informed him that I had a reliable source that had told me that the RUC . . . and this was in 1982 . . . I believe, that the RUC were about to embark on a shoot-to-kill policy and that I and another well-known loyalist, known as Robert John Kerr, were to be executed in suspicious circumstances to allow or to show signs of neutrality in a shoot-to-kill policy.

'Harold McCusker wrote to the Chief Constable. He replied, basically saying that it was a load of nonsense. I was then remanded in custody for possession with intent. I was in custody for a short period of time and six republicans were executed in the north Armagh area. Harold McCusker came to see me in jail. He asked me not to divulge that I had been with him prior to all these shoot-to-kill incidents or that I had knowledge that a shoot-to-kill policy had indeed taken place. I know that I was to be executed by the security forces as far back as 1981/82.

'It soon became apparent to the late Harold McCusker that what I had told him prior to any of the shoot-to-kill had been honest and truthful. Indeed, it wasn't only to take place against republicans, it was to take place against loyalists and that I was the most likely target – I and another, Robert John Kerr. It subsequently came out at a trial involving a Mr McKeown, that McKeown had been asked by the CID in Portadown to set up a robbery and to set up Robert John Kerr to be shot dead by the police. So one can see from far back that the security forces had taken a keen interest in me and that they had conspired to murder me.'

The Robert John Kerr to whom Wright referred was well known in loyalist circles in the mid-Ulster area. Kerr died in bizarre circumstances just outside Newry, Co. Down, in November 1997. He was killed instantly as he stood beside a boat, being towed on a trailer, which exploded suddenly. A number of loyalists have since questioned the official version of how Kerr died.

Billy Wright's revelations in respect of the alleged RUC shoot-to-kill policy in 1982 confirmed in his mind the belief that as far as the State was concerned, unionists were fair game. He believed his death was to be used as a sort of balancing act alongside the shooting of republican terror suspects. It would, so to speak, even up the score. Wright maintained that by shooting him the security forces would be displaying 'impartiality': they would show they were prepared to take out terrorists on both sides. In doing so it would have proved difficult for either side, loyalist or republican, to accuse the RUC of acting solely against one particular side of the community. The death of Harold McCusker has prevented the full corroboration of Billy Wright's accusations. Fifteen years later, in 1997, Billy Wright's open opposition to the embryonic political process had become even more of a threat in the eyes of the authorities. A threat that by the end of that year had been finally removed.

2. The Mid-Ulster Brigade

It was during his time in custody during 1982 that Billy Wright's interest in Christianity began to develop. In jail he began to read the Bible on a regular basis. He said he had a great desire to know more about the Bible and the teachings of Jesus Christ. In turn he began to study theology and developed a desire to understand the teachings of the Christian faith. Through his study of the Bible and theology he said he recognised the moral struggle he faced between remaining a paramilitary or renouncing violence and becoming a committed Christian. He also recognised the cynicism he would face from others should he decide to commit himself to the Christian faith. However, although he continued his studies in jail he did not become a committed Christian until after his release from custody.

Since his death in 1997, a number of individuals have claimed they brought Billy Wright to an acceptance of Christianity through their own personal faith. That is not the case, as Wright himself said: 'I found Christ alone.'

Some four months following his release from custody, Wright had been sitting alone in his home in Portadown. He described how his mind at that time was bombarded with problems. He had a Bible by his side and decided to open it. The first verse he read was: 'I can do all things through Christ, who strengthens me.'

At that point Billy Wright said he took that verse as a personal promise to him from God. He accepted Christ and became a practising Christian for the next three years of his life. However, unlike many born-again Christians, Wright did not feel attracted to the Free Presbyterian Church and its leader, the Reverend Ian Paisley. Although he admired Paisley's spiritually, Billy Wright did not agree with Paisley's involvement in politics. He never described himself as a 'Paisleyite'.

For three years, from 1982–5, Billy Wright studied and preached the Christian gospel across Ireland. He delivered the message of Christianity in the staunchly republican town of Castlewellan, Co. Down, as well as in many other local towns in Northern Ireland. Perhaps surprisingly, he also travelled to Co. Cork, where he preached to passers-by in the centre of Cork city. However, in 1985, the year he was married, Billy Wright was driven back into the world of the paramilitaries following the signing of the Anglo-Irish Agreement.

British Prime Minister Margaret Thatcher and Irish Taoiseach Garret Fitzgerald signed the Anglo-Irish Agreement at Hillsborough Castle on 15 November 1985. The Agreement established that any change in the status of Northern Ireland would only come about with the consent of the majority of the people of Northern Ireland. However, it failed to say precisely what the status of Northern Ireland was at that point in time. The Agreement also established an inter-governmental conference to deal regularly with security and legal matters, political matters and the continued promotion and development of cross-border co-operation with the Irish Republic.

Following the signing of the Agreement, Margaret Thatcher said: 'I went into this agreement because I was not prepared to tolerate a situation of continuing violence.'

However, not all Thatcher's political associates agreed with the Anglo-Irish Agreement. Thatcher's personal friend and cabinet colleague, Ian Gow, resigned in protest claiming the involvement of the Irish Republic in a consultative role in the running of Northern Ireland would prolong and intensify the province's agony. Within hours of the signing of the Agreement, the loyalist paramilitary group, the Ulster Freedom Fighters, declared the members of the Anglo-Irish Conference and Secretariat to be 'legitimate targets'.

The Anglo-Irish Agreement provoked a backlash from within the loyalist community and compounded the belief that a British betrayal of the province was imminent. Thatcher became the target of unionist range and anger. Locally, loyalist anger focused directly on the Northern Ireland Office at Stormont.

On 18 November 1985, Harold McCusker MP spoke in the House of Commons about his feelings on the Anglo-Irish Agreement.

'I never knew what desolation felt like until I read this Agreement last Friday. Does the Prime Minister realise that, when she carries the agreement through the House, she will have ensured that I carry to my grave with ignominy the sense of the injustice that I have done to my constituents down the years – when, in this, their darkest hour, I exhorted them to put their trust in the British House of Commons, which one day would honour its fundamental obligation to them and treat them as equal British citizens? Is it not the reality of this agreement that they will now be Irish-British hybrids and that every aspect – not just some aspects – of their lives will be open to the influence of those who have coveted their land.'

The anger and violence, which soon followed the signing of the Anglo-Irish Agreement, spluttered on for months as loyalists staged a series of protests across Northern Ireland. On 31 March 1986 violence erupted on the streets of Portadown following the banning of an Apprentice Boys parade in the town. There were serious clashes between loyalists and the RUC. Several people were injured in the rioting as police fired a number of plastic baton rounds in an attempt to restore order. The following day, 1 April, the violence in Portadown continued and 39 police officers and 38 civilians were injured in the disturbances. The security forces fired a total of 147 plastic baton rounds. One of the injured, Keith White, died on 14 April 1986, two weeks after a RUC plastic baton round struck him. At the time of his death he was 20 years of age. He was the first member of the Protestant community to be killed as a result of being struck by a plastic baton round. The death of Keith White was instrumental in propelling Billy Wright back into the UVF.

Wright said he had made a conscious decision to return to the UVF. Later he was to say he had let Christ down. 'I made a conscious decision. I fell on my knees and apologised to God. But I felt contempt for the British government, hatred for the IRA and longing for justice for Northern Ireland Protestants.'

Wright said the violent scenes that followed the signing of the Anglo-Irish Agreement had showed that the RUC were prepared to assist in the downfall of their own people. He believed the only way to counteract that was through open resistance. He went to the Shankill Road in Belfast where he met a very senior member of the UVF who shook hands with him and told him it was great to see him back within the structure of the organisation. For the next several months, Billy Wright played a major role in the reorganisation of the UVF's mid-Ulster Brigade. According to one of his former UVF associates, Wright was alarmed at the state of the UVF in Portadown: 'Billy didn't like what was going on. There were too many people looking after themselves and lining their own nests at the expense of the organisation. He believed the UVF was there to defend the Protestant people, not to exploit them for individual gain.

'At that time the leadership in mid-Ulster had had its day and was long overdue for a change. However, certain individuals had the ear of influential people in the Belfast command and were until then able to count on them for support. But things changed once Billy got going: finances, discipline, welfare – it was all in put in order. He had the ability to organise and get things moving and it didn't take long for the message to get through – the days of the existing leadership of the mid-Ulster UVF were numbered and they knew it.'

By 1988, Billy Wright had re-organised and completely restructured the UVF's mid-Ulster Brigade. Out went the old guard, sidelined by Wright. In came a younger, more militant leadership, under the control of Billy Wright. In the space of just two short years he had completely overhauled the UVF in Portadown. In 1989, the UVF unleashed the full force of its terror campaign against the IRA and its supporters in the mid-Ulster area. That campaign involved taking the war to the enemy, the republican movement, and hitting them where it hurt most: in their own heartland. That campaign was to last a total of seven years and it took a heavy toll on the IRA units in north Armagh and east Tyrone. In 1996, reflecting on the UVF campaign in mid-Ulster, Billy Wright said: 'There is not a death I regret. Every single one of them people, with a few exceptions, were directly or indirectly involved in murder.

'We were taking on the IRA and giving them a headache and I think that's what made mid-Ulster stand out. We fought the Provies and had no quarrel with the Catholic community.

'I genuinely believed that we were very successful, and that might sound morbid but they know that we hammered them into the ground and we didn't lose one volunteer. Indeed, members of the security forces have said that we done what they couldn't do, we put the east Tyrone Brigade of the IRA on the run.

'It was the east Tyrone Brigade which was carrying the war in the whole of the North, including Belfast. East Tyrone were decimated, the UVF wiped them out and that's not an idle boast.'

Among the military operations carried out by the UVF's mid-Ulster Brigade during their seven-year military campaign was the 1991 murder of Gervais Lynch, who was shot dead at his home in the village of Magheralin near Lurgan. His parents discovered Gervais Lynch's body when they returned home after attending a Saturday-night mass at a local chapel. Three high-velocity bullets had killed him. A car used in the attack had been stolen in Lurgan the day before the murder. In October the previous year the UVF had also claimed responsibility for the murder of 19-year-old Denis Carville from Parkview Street, Lurgan. The teenager was shot dead as he sat with his girlfriend in a car at Oxford Island, a Co. Armagh beauty spot near the town of Lurgan. As the young couple were sitting in the car a gunman approached and asked their identities. The gunman opened the door and asked Denis Carville his religion and the name of his local priest. On hearing Denis Carville's response, the gunman told the youth to look away. He then shot him in the head at point-blank range. The UVF claimed the killing under the cover name of the Protestant Action Force (PAF). The murder was believed to have been an act of retaliation for the murder of UDR soldier, Colin McCullough, shot dead at Oxford Island a few weeks earlier.

On 3 March 1991 the mid-Ulster Brigade of the UVF carried out one of its most successful operations against the IRA when it attacked Boyle's Bar in the village of Cappagh, Co. Tyrone. A concerted gun attack on the bar by a number of UVF gunmen left four Catholics dead. It later emerged that three of the victims – John Quinn, Dwayne O'Donnell and Malcolm Nugent – were members of the IRA. The three IRA men died when UVF gunmen opened fired on their car, which had pulled up outside Boyle's Bar. The three republicans were going to the bar after having watched a local Gaelic football match. It appears as though the gunmen had been preparing an attack on the bar when the car and its occupants stopped outside at around 10.30 p.m. Instead of continuing with the original attack, the UVF gunmen turned on the car, killing three of its occupants and wounding a fourth.

The survivor of the gun attack later described what had happened when the gunmen struck. He said as they pulled up outside Boyle's Bar, Malcolm Nugent had shouted: 'There's something wrong, John, there's something wrong.'

Nugent had noticed one of the gunmen standing in the roadway. The survivor recalled how he had looked up to see a silhouette of the gunman in the car headlights. The gunman was wearing a balaclava and carrying a rifle. Within seconds the gunman opened fire on the car and its occupants. In a frantic attempt to escape, John Quinn managed to get the car into reverse gear. However, the vehicle only managed to travel a few yards before coming to a halt. Quinn was then fatally wounded and died within seconds.

After the gunmen had finished firing on the car they turned their attention to the bar. A fourth man, Thomas Armstrong, was shot dead as one of the gunmen fired through an open window of the pub. A local priest who later visited Boyle's Bar described the scene as a 'real massacre'. In a statement admitting responsibility for the attack, the UVF said it had not intended to shoot Thomas Armstrong. It claimed the operation was not sectarian but had been carried out against the IRA command structure in east Tyrone.

The UVF attack on Boyle's Bar, Cappagh, has given rise to numerous allegations that the security forces colluded with the UVF to carry out the attack. Local residents argued that the UVF must have had some form of assistance in avoiding the strong security presence in the east Tyrone area. The British government challenged the allegations and called on those making them to produce evidence of collusion.

In October, the Channel 4 programme *Dispatches* covered the Cappagh killings alleging security-force involvement in the attack. A section of the programme was based upon the evidence of Jim Sands, a former resident of Portadown, who claimed to have attended school alongside Billy Wright. Sands told the programme's makers that Billy Wright had been an active participant in the Cappagh killings. He claimed Billy Wright had been driven from Portadown to Dungannon in preparation for the attack on Boyle's Bar. He was then taken on in another car to the intended target in Cappagh some miles away. Sands claimed Wright took part in the gun attacks and had to be pulled into the car because of his reluctance to leave the murder scene itself. Sands also stated Wright did not want to go because he wanted to make sure all the Fenians were dead. In a newspaper article published in November 1991, Wright dismissed suggestions that the UVF had been assisted by the security forces in carrying out the Cappagh operation. He said: 'Republicans always claim that there is security-force collusion after something like Cappagh yet per ratio the RUC have brought to book more loyalists than republicans. The loyalists have paid a dearer price at the hands of the security forces. There is not one shred of evidence of collusion. We have aborted three out of every four operations because of security-force activities.'

Likewise, and in contradiction of what Jim Sands alleged, there is not a shred of evidence that confirms the presence of Billy Wright in Cappagh at the time the gun attack on Boyle's Bar took place. On the contrary, there are at least four eyewitnesses who have testified to Wright's presence at a family function almost 60 miles away.

Billy Wright described the Cappagh attack as the best carried out by the mid-Ulster Brigade of the UVF. He believed the attack proved that the loyalist paramilitaries had the capability and the intelligence required to enable them to take the war right into the republican heartlands of Tyrone and north Armagh.

Later that month, Wright was arrested and questioned after loyalist gunmen opened fire on a mobile sweet-shop in the nationalist Drumbeg housing estate in Craigavon, Co. Armagh, killing three people. In the attack, UVF gunmen shot dead 19-year-old Eileen Duffy and 16-year-old Katrina Rennie. Both teenagers were working in the mobile shop when the killers struck. The gunmen shot both girls in the head at close range. Another victim, Brian Frizzell, aged 29, was also shot dead. Frizzell was approaching the shop as the attack took place. One of the gunmen told him to lie down and then shot him where he lay. The UVF claimed the killing under the cover name of the Protestant Action Force. Responsibility for the killings has been placed on Billy Wright. An RUC officer later told a relation of one of the victims that Wright had carried out the killings. Once again there is no evidence which puts Billy Wright at the scene of the killings in the Drumbeg estate, Craigavon.

On the night in question, 28 March 1991, Wright had been at his home in Portadown. His wife had decided to attend a church service that evening and Wright had asked his father, David, to help him look after the children. During the course of the evening Wright and his father were sitting in the lounge discussing politics. Billy Wright was nursing his youngest child when he noticed a police Land Rover pull up outside the front of the house. David Wright recalled: 'Billy said to me, "Da, we've got company," and he handed the baby over to me. He opened the front door and a police sergeant said, "Can we talk to you for a minute?" Billy took them into the kitchen and closed the door. They had been there for some time when there was increased activity outside. The door of the kitchen opened and the police officers left hurriedly. Billy came in and said to me, "There's been a hit somewhere locally. The message came over the radio as they were talking to me." By the time Billy sat down the police were away.'

The police had come to warn Billy Wright that they had intelligence which indicated the IRA were about to make an attempt on his life within the next 48 hours. As they were doing so they received the message that there had been a gun attack on the mobile shop in Craigavon. However, despite the fact that the RUC had been in his house when the attack on the mobile shop took place, the police returned the following morning and arrested Billy Wright in relation to the deaths of Eileen Duffy, Katrina Rennie and Brian Frizzell. Wright was taken to Gough Barracks where he was held for seven days before being released without charge.

In January 1992, the UVF shot dead Kevin McKearney, aged 32, as he worked in the family's butcher shop in Moy, Co. Tyrone. Just before closing time the gunmen walked into the shop and opened fire at close range, killing Kevin McKearney instantly. The dead man's 70-year-old uncle, Jack McKearney, was fatally wounded in the attack and died the following month. UVF sources said the family had been a target because of its 'IRA connections'. Two of Kevin McKearney's brothers, Sean and Patrick Oliver (Padraig) McKearney, died whilst on 'IRA active service' in 1974 and 1987. Sean McKearney died along with another IRA member when the bomb they were transporting exploded prematurely. Both men were members of the IRA's east Tyrone Brigade. Padraig McKearney was one of eight members of the IRA shot dead by members of the British Army's SAS Regiment at Loughgall, Co. Armagh, in May 1987. The eight men, all members of the IRA's east Tyrone Brigade, died as they attempted to attack the RUC barracks in Loughgall. Padraig McKearney, a former escapee from the Maze Prison, had been involved in previous IRA attacks on a police station at the Birches, a few miles outside Portadown. Later the same year, Kevin McKearney's father-in-law, Charlie Fox, and his mother-in-law, Teresa Fox, were also shot dead by the UVF at their home just outside Moy, Co. Tyrone. A loyalist source in mid-Ulster said the concerted action taken against the McKearney family was part of the strategy of 'taking the war to the front door of the republicans'.

He said: 'The message we were sending out to the IRA was quite clear: if we can't get you, then we will get your nearest and dearest. We hit them where it hurt them most, their own families. In the early 1990s the IRA in east Tyrone began to hurt. They were now experiencing the same pain as they had inflicted on the Protestant community for years and they didn't like a taste of their own medicine.'

On 29 October 1993, UVF gunmen shot dead brothers Gerard and Rory Cairns at their home at the Slopes, near Bleary, Co. Armagh. Shortly after 8 p.m. two gunmen, dressed in black boiler suits and wearing balaclava masks walked into the Cairns' home through the unlocked back door. Three members of the Cairns family were in the house when the killers entered: 22-year-old Gerard, a lorry driver, 19-year-old Rory, a joiner, and their 11-year-old sister, Roisin, the youngest member of the family. The family, along with their parents, Eamon and Sheila, had spent the evening holding a birthday party for Roisin.

Gerard and Rory Cairns had been sitting in the lounge watching television as the gunmen entered. Roisin, who was in the kitchen, thought the attackers were part of some Halloween trick played by some of her brother's friends. One of the gunmen motioned to Roisin to be silent. The other ran into the lounge where Gerard and Rory were sitting. He then signalled the other gunman to follow him. Both gunmen were armed with automatic rifles. They then stood in front of the Cairns brothers and opened fire, killing both instantly. Rory Cairns was shot through the head and three times in the body as he sat in a chair. Gerard, who had attempted to stand up, was hit three times in the body and fell to the floor. The two gunmen then ran back out through the kitchen before making their escape into the darkness of the October night.

As 11-year-old Roisin Cairns ran into the lounge of the family home she saw Rory sitting in the chair, his eyes closed. She turned to her brother Gerard lying on the floor. As his eyes were open she asked him what was wrong with Rory. She did not realise both her brothers were dead. Roisin then ran to a neighbour's house for help.

The killings didn't end with the deaths of Gerard and Rory Cairns. In August 1994, only weeks before the loyalist paramilitaries announced their ceasefire, the UVF killed Kathleen O'Hagan, a mother of five. She was shot dead at her remote farmhouse in the Sperrin Mountains in Co. Tyrone. Kathleen O'Hagan was seven months pregnant when she was killed. UVF gunmen forced their way into the farmhouse and shot her dead. Her husband Paddy, a former republican prisoner, returned home where his children, who had been in the house when the gunmen struck, met him. One of the children said: 'Mammy's dead. Mammy's in heaven. Bad boys came and broke the glass. They've shot Mammy and she's in heaven.'

Following the shooting, the UVF said that had Paddy O'Hagan been in the house at the time of the attack they would have shot him as well. In a statement issued prior to Kathleen O'Hagan's funeral the family said they blamed the security forces and loyalist paramilitaries for the murder of the 38-year-old mother of five.

On 13 October 1994, the Combined Loyalist Military Command (CLMC) announced it was declaring a cessation of all military operations from midnight that night. The CLMC said the permanence of the loyalist ceasefire was dependent upon the continued cessation of all nationalist/republican violence. It said the sole responsibility for a return to war lay with the republican movement. The CLMC also paid homage to all its fighters, volunteers and commandos, who it said had paid the supreme sacrifice. The CLMC went on to say:

In all sincerity, we offer the loved ones of all innocent victims over the past 25 years, abject and true remorse. No words of ours will compensate for the intolerable suffering they have undergone during this conflict. Let us firmly resolve to respect our differing views of freedom, culture and aspiration and never again permit our political circumstances to degenerate into bloody warfare.

In mid-Ulster, the ceasefire announcement was not altogether welcome. In the eyes of the UVF's mid-Ulster Brigade they had effectively brought the IRA in north Armagh and east Tyrone to its knees. Billy Wright believed his strategy had hit the provisional movement hard. He believed that when the republican/nationalist community in mid-Ulster began to feel the pain and hurt of a concerted UVF campaign against them, they quickly moved to talk peace and negotiate a settlement. He claimed that the mid-Ulster UVF's strategy of taking the war directly to republicans had demoralised them.

He said: 'I met very few brave IRA men, to their own shame. Ninety per cent of their senior officers left the battlefield; they ran away, they headed south. That's the nature of them – they want to kill but they don't want to be killed. The difference between them and us is that loyalists have nowhere to run. At the end of this phase of the campaign, it appeared that all the big names within terrorism were loyalists. I was here all along, I never moved from home and I'm staying here.

'My attitude is very simple towards the IRA. They worked on the principle of their enemy's honesty. They looked at the security forces and they analysed how far the security forces would go. The IRA learned to kill when it wanted to and then withdraw. That was no way to fight a war.'

There is no doubt that the UVF in mid-Ulster carried the war to the IRA during 1989–96. Blame for most of those killings has been laid at the door of Billy Wright himself. Various media commentators speak with unquestioned authority when they say Billy Wright killed upwards of 40 men, yet they have failed to produce any evidence to support their claims. He has been placed at the scene of numerous murders but has never been charged in relation to any of them. He has been accused of working for RUC Special Branch and British Intelligence at the same time. First and foremost he was a UVF man to the backbone, he never considered himself to be anything else. Since his death the media have had a field day with Billy Wright. They have helped create the myth that is now known as 'King Rat'. As far as Billy Wright was concerned, in 1994 he was in an indefensible position. And he knew it.

3. Defiance and Drumcree

By mid-1994 Billy Wright's name had become indelibly linked with loyalist terror. He had been given the nickname 'King Rat' by a Sunday newspaper and Wright himself admitted he was not prepared for the amount of publicity he received. He said he took no pride whatsoever in the title of 'King Rat'. His family life had suffered as a result of the continued attention of the security forces. The police and army raided his home 21 times in one year. There had also been a number of attempts on his life by the IRA. Wherever he went he was a focus of attention.

A former associate of Wright said: 'It only took Billy to drive through the Moy or Blackwatertown once for the local republicans to go to ground for a fortnight. If he was seen in a republican area, the local IRA ran for their lives. That was Billy's reputation in 1994. His reputation alone was a positive weapon in our campaign against the IRA itself.'

Wright was also forced to give up his greengrocer's shop in the centre of Portadown because of increasing police raids on the premises. The raids were often timed to coincide with the busiest shopping times in the Co. Armagh town. Police officers would often enter the shop when it was full of customers, forcing the customers to leave as they carried out a search operation. As a result of the continuous RUC activity customers took their business elsewhere in Portadown, effectively forcing Wright and his father David to close down – at a considerable financial loss. There were occasions when Wright and his family members were stopped and questioned by police and army. On one occasion, as Wright and his father were driving along Church Road in Portadown, they were followed by a car, which pulled out to overtake them. The passenger window of the overtaking car was open and the muzzle of a gun was clearly visible.

Fearing an attempt on his life, Wright shouted to his father to get down on the floor of the car. As he did so the overtaking car cut across the front of Billy Wright's car and forced it into the hedge. Fearing the worst, David Wright said he looked up to see three armed police officers standing in front of the car, two of them pointing rifles at his son. David Wright later described the events of that night as frightening and alarming.

On one occasion, Wright had parked his car in the loyalist Edgarstown area of Portadown as he was attending a social function in a nearby lounge bar. During the evening a local woman, who lived directly opposite the bar, looked out the window to see two men standing beside Wright's car. As she continued to watch, one of the men got down onto the ground and placed a package under the car. Both men then ran and jumped into a car, which had been sitting waiting at the end of the street. The car sped off in the direction of Loughgall. Alarmed at what she had seen, the woman sent her husband across to the bar to warn Wright about what had happened. At the same time she also telephoned the local RUC to alert them. When the security forces eventually arrived and examined Wright's car, it was discovered that a booby-trap explosive device had been placed underneath it.

On another occasion, Wright had been staying at his aunt's house in Portadown's loyalist Brownstown estate. He had parked his car overnight on the roadway outside the house. The next morning Wright became suspicious about the vehicle and the local RUC were called to the scene. After examining the car, the RUC declared it safe. As Wright attempted to open the car a booby-trap device exploded underneath the car. Although shrapnel hit him, miraculously Billy Wright escaped any serious injury. When it exploded, the booby-trap device was sufficiently powerful to blow the engine block out of Wright's car, over a roof and into the back garden of a house. In another failed attempt on Wright's life, a prominent IRA gunman – believed to be responsible for a series of sectarian murders in the north Armagh area – and two other IRA volunteers took over a house opposite the one where Billy Wright was living at that time. According to a republican source, the plan was to stake out Wright's house overnight and shoot him dead as he emerged the following morning. However, after almost 48 hours of waiting, Wright failed to show and the IRA aborted the murder attempt. The IRA later discovered that Wright was on holiday during the time they had planned to kill him.

Following the announcement of the loyalist ceasefire in October

1994, Billy Wright openly supported the UVF peace policy. However, his overall faith in the process began to dissipate. He quickly became sceptical of the political direction being taken by the leadership of the Ulster Volunteer Force in Belfast. He was also highly critical of the role given to the Dublin government in the internal affairs of Northern Ireland. Wright and his mid-Ulster unit began to publicly voice these concerns, an action which brought them into conflict with the UVF leadership. At this point in time a new side of Billy Wright began to appear: the political thinker. He had his own views on what direction the UVF should be taking at that time in relation to the political process. Those views and opinions were contrary to those held by other senior members of the UVF. Wright soon became disillusioned with the UVF's political policies, believing them to be too Marxist in outlook to be representative of the working-class loyalist. He believed he lived in an area of vital importance to the peace process. Mid-Ulster needed stability and Billy Wright believed that what the UVF leadership was putting forward at that time would not provide that stability. He also became aware that in the hours prior to the announcement of the loyalist ceasefire, the UVF command had sanctioned a military operation to proceed in Belfast. The operation was subsequently compromised and four UVF volunteers were arrested. Angered at the UVF command decision to allow the operation to continue after they had already agreed to the ceasefire, Wright began to openly question the UVF's position.

Billy Wright's opposition to the political process was compounded in 1995 when he read the Framework Document drawn up by the British and Irish governments. A copy of the document had been secretly given to Wright before its scheduled publication. He could not accept what was contained in the governments' proposal because he felt it gave the Irish government far too great a say in the internal affairs of Northern Ireland. Wright made his views on the Framework Document known to the UVF. The situation took a turn for the worse in July 1995 when the focus of loyalist opposition to the embryonic peace process centred on the Orange Order's Drumcree Church Parade.

On Sunday, 9 July 1995, the Orangemen of Portadown District were prevented from walking along the nationalist Garvaghy Road after their annual church service at Drumcree Parish Church. The move incensed members of the Orange Order across Northern Ireland. Thousands of Orangemen and their supporters gathered at the Co. Armagh church and a tense standoff developed between them and the security forces.

Amongst those angered at the decision to prevent the Orange Parade returning to Portadown via the Garvaghy Road were Billy Wright and the UVF's mid-Ulster Brigade. As the security forces attempted to prevent large numbers of Orangemen gathering at Drumcree, Wright and his UVF brigade took steps to ensure that they did get through to the protest site at the Co. Armagh church.

On Monday, 24 hours after the Orange Parade had been halted at Drumcree, a crowd of over 50,000 gathered in a field behind the picturesque church where politicians Ian Paisley, David Trimble and Jeffrey Donaldson addressed them. Later the same night police officers at Drumcree came under attack from the crowd and a number of plastic baton rounds were fired at the protesters. Throughout the night there were a series of running battles involving the security forces and members of the Orange Order.

The Drumcree standoff continued until Tuesday, 11 July when at 10.30 a.m. the Orangemen of Portadown District marched down the Garvaghy Road and back to their Carlton Street headquarters in Portadown town centre. MPs David Trimble and Ian Paisley were at the forefront of the parade as it made its way back from Drumcree and into Portadown. As the parade reached its final destination, Billy Wright stared at the two jubilant politicians and shouted across to his father standing nearby: 'Da, they'll never do that again.' Wright meant that after the nationalist community in Portadown saw the very public triumphant pictures of Trimble and Paisley, there would be a concerted campaign to prevent a repetition of the Orange Order parade along the Garvaghy Road. He was correct.

The following day, the Orange Order's annual Twelfth of July Celebrations, an Orange District from Ballynafeigh was prevented from marching along a section of the Ormeau Road in Belfast. When news of the situation in Belfast reached Portadown, Billy Wright and his two young daughters had been visiting his father. On hearing the news Wright immediately left and drove to the Ormeau Road in Belfast to support the stance adopted by the Orangemen. However, when he arrived at the bridge where the security forces had blocked the route of the Orange Parade he discovered that the UVF in Belfast had not come out in support of the Orangemen. The failure of the UVF to support the Orange Order's right-to-march issue in Belfast and Portadown only served to widen the rift between the mid-Ulster Brigade and the organisation's command structure on Belfast's Shankill Road.

The following year the rift between the mid-Ulster Brigade and the

UVF command had deteriorated to almost open warfare. Wright and his mid-Ulster unit were in total opposition of the UVF's political strategy. Wright had openly accused the organisation's leadership of having sold out the Protestant population and in doing so ensured themselves a political future and steady income.

'By 1996 the UVF in mid-Ulster was stronger than anywhere else, even Belfast. We were vibrant and determined to resist the British government's attempts to persuade the loyalist people to accept the political process. We knew the government intended to push the political process through and in doing so would render the loyalist paramilitaries useless. The Framework Document is nonsense and those that drew it up knew it could not be acceptable to unionists. As a result of this document there is more anger in mid-Ulster now than ever there was,' he said.

Wright and his supporters believed the leadership of the UVF had literally 'sold out' the loyalist people, who had supported them for years. The current Brigade Staff of the UVF had, in Wright's eyes, completely abandoned the original concept of the organisation. As far as mid-Ulster was concerned the UVF had been formed in 1912 to defend the Protestant people from the threat of Home Rule and an eventual 32-county Irish Republic. Now it appeared as though the UVF had carried out a complete U-turn and by backing the political process was ensuring the Irish Republic would play a pivotal role in the future of the North. That role, mid-Ulster believed, would eventually lead to the destruction of the Northern Ireland state. It had to be resisted at all costs. In July 1996, the situation between the mid-Ulster UVF and its Belfast command reached boiling point. Once again the Drumcree Orange Parade was to play a significant role in the events, which were to lead to the UVF standing down its mid-Ulster unit.

On Sunday, 7 July 1996, the Portadown Orangemen were once again prevented from completing the return leg of the annual Drumcree Church Parade along the controversial Garvaghy Road. The decision to halt the march was taken two days earlier, on Friday, 5 July, by the then Chief Constable of the RUC, Sir Hugh Annesley.

In reaching his decision the Chief Constable, speaking to senior RUC officers, said: 'I greatly regret that despite all the efforts of the RUC, and many others, it has not proved possible to resolve the conflicting views, especially about the Orange Order Parade along the Garvaghy Road. Following extensive consultation I have concluded that to allow the Orange Order Parade along the Garvaghy Road would be likely to occasion serious public disorder. Accordingly, I have earlier this morning given directions that conditions are to be imposed on the organisers to prohibit this part of the proposed route.'

The Chief Constable said he hoped all those involved in the Drumcree Parade would peacefully comply with the legal requirements which were to be imposed upon the Orange march. The Chief Constable's decision to ban the Orangemen from the Garvaghy Road area was made public the following day. The security-force preparations for the Orange Parade were immense. Units of the British Army erected a barbed-wire cordon across the fields in front of Drumcree Parish Church. Police officers swamped the area in readiness for any possible confrontation with the Orangemen. The army also established a field hospital close to the police lines. Arrangements were made to have thousands of meals prepared for the members of the security forces on duty at the Co. Armagh church. A few miles away, at Mahon Camp, the British Army's 3 Brigade Headquarters in Portadown, thousands of troops were on standby. Live television pictures of Drumcree, transmitted by CCTV cameras, were beamed directly into the command room at Mahon Camp.

At 10.30 a.m. the Portadown Orangemen left their Carlton Street headquarters on the outward leg of the Drumcree Parade. As the Orangemen arrived at the Co. Armagh church the RUC secured both ends of the Garvaghy Road. Police Land Rovers also blocked the small bridge just down from the church on the road leading towards the nationalist Ballyoran housing estate. At 12.40 p.m., their church service concluded, the Orangemen marched down the roadway to the police lines where they were prevented from proceeding any further. Drumcree Two was well and truly under way.

During the course of the day the numbers of Orangemen and their supporters increased dramatically at Drumcree. Fast-food vans and stalls mushroomed in the field beside the church, eager to supply the crowd with a plentiful supply of burgers and hotdogs. Music and announcements were relayed to the crowd via a loudspeaker system organised by the Orangemen. Elsewhere at Drumcree the Portadown Orangemen had established a command centre in a room of the local church hall. Here they 'directed' their Drumcree strategy. At one stage of Drumcree Two, the Orange Order had considered bringing the entire Twelfth demonstration into Portadown should the parade not be allowed to march down the Garvaghy Road. However, by the first night of the 1996 Drumcree standoff the initial relaxed atmosphere had been superseded by an air of menace. Throughout the night a crowd of several thousand pelted the security forces with stones, bottles and fireworks. As the violence continued at Drumcree, Michael McGoldrick, a student from Lurgan working as a taxi driver, was shot dead just a few miles away. Blame for the killing was immediately laid at the door of the mid-Ulster UVF.

However, there is considerable debate over who actually sanctioned the murder of 31-year-old Michael McGoldrick. The media has always placed responsibility for the killing on Billy Wright – something the loyalist leader always denied. Recent interviews with senior loyalists have provided new information on the McGoldrick killing. They have said the murder was not sanctioned by Billy Wright but by UVF personnel in Belfast.

One senior LVF/loyalist associate of Billy Wright said: 'The initial plan was to hijack a number of Catholic-owned taxis in the Portadown area. They would then be taken to various locations where the cars would be burnt but the drivers released unharmed. The idea was to send a clear message to the Catholic community in the Portadown and Lurgan areas: if the Orangemen can't walk down the Garvaghy Road then you won't be allowed to work in any of our areas. That was the plan; the shooting of any taxi driver was never ever discussed.

'It's always been the same with the UVF in Belfast. Once you stand up to them or question their authority they start using black propaganda. You are either a drug dealer, a child molester or a tout. They try to discredit you within your local community and set you up for assassination. That's what they did with Billy Wright. They tried to discredit him by saying he was a drug dealer who was working for MI5. If that's the case, where's the so-called fortune that Billy made from drugs? When Billy Wright was murdered there was no fortune: all he had was what was in his prison bank account, so that puts the drugs empire into perspective.'

The senior loyalist went on to say that in July 1996 the UVF leadership was becoming increasingly alarmed at the growing support for Billy Wright which was developing in many areas of Northern Ireland. He said they recognised that Wright had become identified with those who opposed the political process. He was also openly supporting the Orange Order's protest at Drumcree, something the UVF had initially refused to do. The UVF feared Wright's uncompromising views. The senior loyalist went on to say that Wright viewed the Drumcree situation as more than just a parade down a road in Portadown. Instead he looked on it as a direct attack on the Protestant way of life and culture. Wright believed that Drumcree had to be supported. If the protest failed to succeed he believed it would have a knock-on effect for other similar parades across Northern Ireland. Wright was making it clear that as far as he was concerned there could be no possible compromise on the Drumcree issue. The Portadown Orangemen must be allowed to complete their march along the Garvaghy Road. A failure to do so would mean the beginning of the end for the Protestant faith and culture.

Although an initial supporter of Ulster Unionist Party leader David Trimble, by Drumcree 1996, Wright's support for Trimble was clearly on the wane. Initially, Billy Wright believed that Trimble could be the leader to revitalise the Unionist Party and the unionist people. However, in the light of Trimble's changing attitude on Drumcree, Wright soon began to harbour doubts about the Unionist leader's long-term strategy. The two men came face to face at Drumcree 1996. Trimble, who had been engaged in a process aimed at resolving the Drumcree impasse, arranged via an intermediary to speak with Wright. The two men met in the church hall at Drumcree.

Trimble later said: 'There were some people who did not like the idea of taking part in a process of this nature and I found it necessary to persuade Wright. It was clear to me that I needed to neutralise him because he was going around opposing the planned talks so I had a conversation with him about the way in which we were trying to resolve the issue in a conciliatory way.'

At the conclusion of their meeting Billy Wright made it abundantly clear that he had serious misgivings about Trimble's conciliatory approach to the Drumcree dispute. These doubts were further compounded when Billy Wright became fully aware of what the resolution to the Drumcree dispute entailed. It was proposed that in return for the Orange Order Parade being permitted down the Garvaghy Road, nationalist residents would be allowed a reciprocal parade through the centre of Portadown on St Patrick's Day. Wright was incensed at the suggestion and let Trimble know as much in blunt terms.

On the Tuesday of the 1996 Drumcree standoff, a heavy mechanical digger and a slurry tanker had been moved into the fields close to Drumcree Church. A short time after their arrival a number of men began fixing heavy metal plates to the digger, making it 'armour plated'. When David Trimble tried to intervene, he was unceremoniously told what to do and the work continued uninterrupted. Rumours began to circulate around the Drumcree area that the UVF intended to use the armoured digger to force a way through the barbed wire entanglements in front of the police lines.

Once the lines had been breached, they would then use the slurry tanker as a mobile flame-thrower and spray the security forces with a mixture of petrol and sugar. The rumours sent a wave of panic through the security forces and specialist units were quickly drawn up to combat the alleged threat. However, although they were never used, the presence of the heavy digger and the slurry tanker at Drumcree was sufficient to make RUC Chief Constable, Sir Hugh Annesley, re-assess his original decision to ban the Orange Parade from the Garvaghy Road.

Another factor, which was taken into account by the RUC Chief Constable, arose out of a meeting between Billy Wright and David Trimble. According to a former close associate of the loyalist leader, it became clear during this meeting that the mid-Ulster Brigade of the UVF would not accept any compromise whatsoever on the Orange march.

The former associate said: 'During Drumcree 1996, I was present at a meeting between Billy Wright and Ulster Unionist leader David Trimble. They were discussing developments in the talks held at Ulster Carpet Mills, which involved the Garvaghy Road residents, Church leaders, the Orange Order and the security forces. The talks were aimed at resolving the Drumcree Parade problem.

'Trimble, who had taken part in the Carpet Factory talks, told Billy that it had been decided that the Orangemen would return to Portadown by the same route they had used to march out to Drumcree: the Dungannon Road. In other words, what Trimble was telling Billy was that it had been decided that the Orangemen would concede the Drumcree route down the Garavghy Road and go home with their tails between their legs. Well, Billy wasn't having it and he told Trimble to take a message back to the Chief Constable of the RUC. That message was clear and left nothing in doubt. He said that if the security forces didn't get the parade down the Garvaghy Road then he would. There was no compromise in Billy's stance; he was flaming at the very suggestion that the Orangemen would go back the way they came. Trimble was left in no doubt that Billy meant what he said. Billy left him to carry the message back to the RUC. It wasn't long after that before the decision was taken to put the Orange Parade down the Garvaghy Road.'

A similar version of that meeting at Drumcree was recalled by Wright's father, David, who said his son had discussed the Trimble meeting with him within days of it taking place. David Wright said: 'Billy told me there was no way he was accepting what David Trimble was proposing. As far as Billy was concerned that Orange Parade was only going in one direction: down the Garvaghy Road. As far as Billy was concerned the Drumcree Parade was not simply about Portadown, its outcome would affect every Orange Parade in Northern Ireland. Drumcree didn't just belong to the Portadown Orangemen, it belonged to the Protestant people of Northern Ireland.'

Billy Wright's presence and the potential threat to peace posed by the UVF in mid-Ulster was noted by the security chiefs in charge of the Drumcree operation. RUC Chief Constable Sir Hugh Annesley travelled to Portadown where he viewed the situation at first hand. Having assessed the situation at Drumcree and across Northern Ireland, the Chief Constable gave the go ahead for the Orange Order Parade to go down the Garvaghy Road.

On 11 July 1996, the security forces eventually forced the Portadown Orange Parade down the Garvaghy Road. The move provoked serious trouble in the area and throughout the province. The police recorded over 8,000 incidents. The security forces had fired over 6,000 plastic baton rounds in an effort to control the trouble. One hundred and fifty police officers and almost two hundred civilians were injured in the violence. One man, a Roman Catholic, died when an army vehicle in Londonderry crushed him.

David Wright said that as far as he was concerned, Drumcree 1996 and the politics that followed on from it ensured his son was living on borrowed time. He said his son's actions at Drumcree had been in defiance of the UVF leadership in Belfast who preferred to leave the standoff to the Orangemen. He said his open opposition of David Trimble had also been noted. He said the confrontation between the two men at Drumcree had ended what little respect Billy had left for the Unionist Party leader. The fact that Wright and the mid-Ulster UVF had also been blamed for carrying out the McGoldrick murder also ensured that the considerable weight and power of the British administration would be brought to bear against him.

David Wright said: 'Billy and the UVF leadership were on a collision course, there was no doubt about that. They accused him of breaking the 1994 ceasefire agreement over the McGoldrick murder and his open support of Drumcree angered them. But Billy couldn't accept why the UVF leadership would not support their own people. They accused Billy of not wanting peace. Nothing was further from the truth. Billy wanted peace as much as any other man in Northern Ireland. Show me any man who doesn't want peace. But, unlike the UVF leadership at that time, Billy had principles and he didn't agree with the price the Protestant people were being asked to pay to achieve that peace. However, he eventually paid the highest price possible for those same principles. Billy Wright lost his life because of Drumcree.'

David Wright said following the events at Drumcree in 1996 that his son became a 'political roadblock on the path to peace'.

'He was a roadblock that had to be removed at all costs. Billy was articulating an argument the British government and the UVF didn't want to hear. He had to be removed at all costs and that's where it all started. Politics cost my son his life. Billy's stance against the political process and against David Trimble was attracting more and more support on a daily basis. The British government recognised this. They knew he was the main threat to their long-term strategy for Northern Ireland so they took a deliberate decision to take him out of the equation. From July 1996 my son was a marked man as far as the UVF and the British were concerned.'

In the summer of 2001 a senior figure in the Orange Order told David Wright of a meeting which had taken place between senior members of the Orange Order and high-ranking members of the RUC. The meeting took place in the latter part of 1996, following the Drumcree Two standoff. The senior Orangeman recalled how, during the course of the meeting, one of the RUC officers remarked: 'Billy Wright was part of the Drumcree problem in 1995 and 1996. He won't be part of the problem in 1997.'

The same senior Orangeman promised to provide David Wright with a signed affidavit of the police officer's remark. To date, neither he nor either of his two companions have put pen to paper. However, the significance of the RUC officer's remarks was not lost on David Wright. David Wright, while accepting that the officer may have been referring to the imprisonment of Billy Wright, believes it was a direct reference to a plan to remove Billy Wright on a permanent basis.

4. Expulsion and Imprisonment

In August 1996 the relationship between the mid-Ulster UVF and the organisation's Brigade staff on Belfast's Shankill Road had reached breaking point. In openly supporting the Orange Order's Drumcree protest Wright had deliberately defied a direct order from the UVF Brigade staff, which stated that no members of the organisation were to become involved with Orange Order protests anywhere in Northern Ireland. Wright viewed this Brigade order as a complete abandonment of the fundamental loyalist position of the UVF. He continued to promote his own political views, which were at total variance with those of the UVF's command. Wright reiterated his total opposition to a political process, which he believed would eventually lead to a 32-county Irish Republic. It was now clear to the UVF Brigade Staff that they would be unable to bring Wright and his mid-Ulster unit into line with the policies promoted by the UVF and its political wing, the Progressive Unionist Party. Billy Wright was now a major problem for the UVF and the Northern Ireland Office.

Yet, despite being portrayed as being 'anti-peace', former close associates of Billy Wright said he wanted peace more than most. However, he also knew when that peace arrived he was living on borrowed time. An insight into what Billy Wright was thinking at that time can be seen in a diary he compiled during his last period of imprisonment. The diary reveals Wright's feelings about the Orange Order, Ulster Unionist leader David Trimble, the political process and the Progressive Unionist Party. He wrote:

> The stabilisation of our country through a just, democratic process held many challenges for loyalists, yet held no fears.

Indeed, a harmonious, peaceful Ulster could be regarded as a victory, for it was for that purpose that so many of our people died for and languished in jails for.

So the one question must be, why do so many loyalists and unionist people resent the current process? Of course you could take the Progressive Unionist Party approach and sentence them to death or threaten mass exile.

Nevertheless, their fears are real. Likewise their love of Ulster, and it is incumbent upon all those who have influence to deal with those fears. As loyalists and unionists we are all aware, that sections of the people have resented aspects of the State and that one section in particular even refuses to recognise the State.

However, the prison diary also showed that Billy Wright was capable of looking beyond the narrow political confines of Northern Ireland and turning his mind to the expanding influence of the European Union. He wrote:

As we watch the decentralisation of government and the development of government through regionalisation throughout the United Kingdom we must do so with an eye on a centralised Europe. A Europe in which the United Kingdom will undoubtedly see its future. However, within the context of the United Kingdom one can sense and indeed see evidence that some regions hold more importance than others and some are regarded as a hindrance.

Clearly, Billy Wright had no doubts as to which particular category the British government would place Northern Ireland into. He also had harsh words for the Ulster Unionists and in particular party leader David Trimble. Once optimistic that Trimble would become the type of leader that the unionist people needed and who had been absent for decades, Wright had changed his opinion and now was in open opposition of Trimble and the political direction in which he was taking the Ulster Unionist Party. Under a heading, 'A Powerful Reality', Wright wrote:

I am often struck by the sheer pompous arrogance of the Official Unionists [Ulster Unionists]. They strut about the political stage needing only an umbrella and bowler hat to make them really believe they are truly English politicians. Not so boys. This is Northern Ireland, just in case you haven't noticed.

You see, Davey T [David Trimble], it was people power at Drumcree put you where you are and it was you that put the people where they are today. And, where are they? Locked into a process they can't win. You're at the table, blackmailed through paragraph 42 of the Framework Document. [The British and Irish governments would work together for the good and to bring peace and reconciliation to Northern Ireland and the Republic.]

You've given recognition to Dublin interference in our country by allowing their involvement before the removal of their illegal claim. You have helped, in spite of your words, to legitimise Sinn Fein/IRA, knowing that by doing so you helped disenfranchise two hundred thousand unionist people, and what have you achieved – NOTHING!

You see, Davey T, the real political reality, in spite of your niceties, is that the day and hour that the Provos broke into the activity of the multi nationals at the Baltic Exchange, causing global ramifications and threatening the very existence of the British economy, Ulster was doomed. That's the reality, Davey boy!

Now provide the unionist people with an ability to do likewise south of the border, Davey T, and we guarantee you the southern government's conversion to unionism will be as quick as a bang!

Shocked, Davey T? No more shocked than the people who thought you were strong.

The scathing attack on the Ulster Unionist leader by Billy Wright shows how Wright felt at the apparent weakening of Trimble's hard-line stance following his election as party leader in September 1995. Following their conversations during the 1996 Drumcree standoff, Wright formed the opinion that Trimble would inevitably give ground in any future negotiations on the political process.

A former associate and confidant of Billy Wright said: 'After Drumcree 1996, Billy didn't want anything to do with Trimble. He told me the fact that an Ulster Unionist leader had been prepared to sell out the Drumcree Parade showed that he was prepared to compromise and seek the easy way out of a difficult problem. To be honest, Billy was disgusted with Trimble.

The animosity between Billy Wright and David Trimble was never resolved. After the loyalist leader was shot dead by the INLA inside the Maze Prison, the Ulster Unionist leader tried to call at Wright's home at the Manor in Portadown. Members of the Loyalist Volunteer Force prevented him from doing so.

The decision to stand down the mid-Ulster Brigade of the UVF was taken during a meeting of the Combined Loyalist Military Command in August 1996. The meeting took place at a social club in Monkstown, on the outskirts of Belfast. Although the UVF have claimed that the decision on the mid-Ulster issue was only taken during the course of the meeting, a number of those present disagree. They claim that it became evident during the course of the CLMC meeting that the UVF Brigade Staff had already decided to disband its mid-Ulster unit some time before the actual meeting.

One UVF man who was present in the Monkstown social club said a number of the organisation's members had been tipped off about the mid-Ulster decision in advance and deliberately absented themselves from the meeting. He said: 'They knew the score and deliberately stayed away from the CLMC meeting. Those that were there were shocked and surprised at the decision. Unlike those who had stayed away we had no idea this was going to happen. There were a few who were unhappy at what was going on as they respected Billy Wright as a good UVF man. But, with a few exceptions, nobody said much in the way of objections.'

The mid-Ulster UVF was disbanded because of 'treason' and a breach of the 1994 loyalist ceasefire. Its leader, Billy Wright, was given 72 hours to leave Northern Ireland or face death. The announcement shocked many loyalists who recognised that the UVF in mid-Ulster had been the cutting edge of the paramilitary group. There was a simmering resentment in many loyalist quarters that although many senior UVF men had openly sided with the organisation's leadership on the matter they respected Wright's leadership skills and organisational ability. They also recognised that he had literally taken the war directly to the republican movement in mid-Ulster. However, out of a need for self-preservation they decided that in this instance discretion most certainly was the better part of valour.

David Wright went to see his son just hours before the UVF exclusion order was due to come into effect. He walked from his home in the centre of Portadown to his son's home on the edge of the loyalist Rectory Park estate. David Wright recalled: 'I went to see Billy on the last Saturday of August and the exclusion order was to come into effect at midnight. I said to him, "Son, what are you for doing?" and he said, "Daddy, I'm not moving; I haven't done anything; I have disagreed with the UVF on the politics and I maintain that what I have read in the Framework Document and I see what is coming about – the organisation [the UVF] is going in the wrong direction.'"

Billy Wright defied the UVF exclusion order and death threat and remained in Portadown. Within days of the UVF issuing its death threat, Wright's supporters organised a mass rally in Portadown's Brownstown Park. Thousands of people took part in the rally. It was viewed as an open show of support for the defiant Billy Wright and his political views. The UVF had not anticipated that Wright would command so much respect in the mid-Ulster area. He was not just an isolated hard-line fanatical paramilitary one-man band – he clearly had support. A great deal of that support came from within the mid-Ulster Brigade of the UVF. Rural paramilitaries differ from their urban colleagues. The rural UVF men are often much more active than their city counterparts and they also disliked being controlled from Belfast. In the country loyalist paramilitaries felt they were under greater threat from republican attack than those in the city. The UVF's Brigade staff were taken aback by the size of the Brownstown Park rally. Among those who stood alongside Wright on the platform that night were the DUP's Reverend William McCrea and the leader of the Portadown Orangemen, Harold Gracey. As he addressed the crowd, Billy Wright, dressed in a black suit and collar and tie, told his supporters: 'Here I stand in the land I love, condemned to death by the people I love.'

There was no doubt that Wright was sincere when he expressed those words. He not only felt betrayed by the organisation he had joined at the age of 15, he also felt let down and betrayed by those he had formerly considered to be his friends. However, he had indicated his clear intention to carry on and within hours had moved to form his own paramilitary group in the Portadown area: the Loyalist Volunteer Force.

Many of Wright's former UVF colleagues moved across with him to the newly formed LVF. Among them was Mark 'Swinger' Fulton, who, like his friend, Billy Wright, had joined the UVF at the age of 15. However, there were elements of the mid-Ulster UVF, which remained loyal to the Belfast Command. They included a number of prominent figures who had been in the UVF for a considerable time. Wright believed that a number of his former colleagues had opted to remain with Belfast not on principle but for economic reasons. Some of the UVF men were in business and frequently carried out work in the

Belfast area. Unless they remained loyal to the Belfast command, then the chances of that work continuing were greatly reduced. Wright recognised that factor but felt aggrieved that his former friends should act in such a manner. Men that had been former comrades in arms now became bitter rivals for control of the mid-Ulster area. In the months that followed a bitter feud developed between the LVF and the UVF in the mid-Ulster area. Ultimately, and for as long as Billy Wright remained alive, the LVF held sway in Portadown.

Slowly, Billy Wright was becoming isolated and marginalised as the UVF continued to portray him as a renegade drug dealer who opposed the political process and peace. Wright knew he was also under intense surveillance by RUC Special Branch and the British Intelligence services. During one meeting I had with him he told me that it was his belief that within six months to a year he would either be imprisoned for a lengthy time or dead. He was proven to be correct on both counts.

Throughout the latter half of 1996, Billy Wright continued to claim that the leadership of the UVF and its political wing, the Progressive Unionist Party, was out of step with fundamental loyalist thinking. He said the UVF had denied their very faith and culture by refusing to support the Orange Order Drumcree protest. He said that by setting aside their faith and culture the UVF/PUP could no longer be justified in calling themselves loyalists. Wright argued that there was a self-belief within the UVF that Belfast and only Belfast should control the organisation. As far as Billy Wright was concerned that was unacceptable and there had to be an equal representation of all sections of Northern Ireland on the UVF Brigade staff. He felt that unionism, as it had been known, was dead and gone. He believed there was no longer a requirement for the dull and staid politics of traditional unionism and that it must be replaced by a more vibrant style of politics, which was truly representative of the unionist people. Billy Wright's outspoken views only served to make him more and more of a hate figure. Clearly he was becoming a major obstacle on the path to peace. That obstacle was quickly drawn to the attention of the British government and Prime Minister John Major.

In October 1996, a group of senior loyalists travelled to London for discussions with Major at 10 Downing Street. During the course of the meeting it is alleged the subject of Billy Wright and the situation in mid-Ulster were discussed. Certainly, towards the end of 1996, Billy Wright had become a major thorn in the side of the British authorities. His open opposition to David Trimble, in the heart of Trimble's Upper Bann constituency, was proving to be a constant embarrassment to the Unionist leader. There were concerns too within the Northern Ireland Office that Wright was attracting growing support for his political views. As far as the embryonic political process was concerned, Billy Wright was becoming more and more of an overall problem. A problem that as far as the authorities were concerned had to be resolved sooner rather than later.

In January 1997, Billy Wright appeared in court charged with threatening to shoot 42-year-old mother of four Gwen Reed from Portadown. The charges related to an assault in the Corcrain and Redmondville housing estates of Portadown in August 1995. Wright was accused of threatening to kill Reed in an effort to prevent her giving evidence against some of those involved in the assault. Despite the fact that she had two convictions for deception, the judge, Lord Justice McCollum, said he believed that in giving her evidence to the Court, Reed had been a scrupulously honest witness. However, he went on to describe Billy Wright as an inscrutable witness. Lord Justice McCollum said he found Wright's evidence quite unconvincing and as such he had no hesitation in rejecting it. His Lordship also rejected the evidence of other defence witnesses describing one female witness as unworthy of belief and another as having the demeanour of an untruthful witness. At the end of the trial, Billy Wright and two other accused were found guilty as charged.

Wright had been on continuing police bail prior to the case being heard. However, shortly before the case opened he had surrendered his bail and entered prison of his own free will. In March 1997, Lord Justice McCollum delivered his reserved judgement and Billy Wright was sentenced to eight years imprisonment for threatening to kill Gwen Reed. At the time of Wright's trial Gwen Reed was living outside Northern Ireland under the RUC's Witness Protection Scheme. She has not returned to Northern Ireland since that time. As the sentence was being handed down Billy Wright was not in the dock. Earlier he had asked to be escorted away after protesting his innocence. At one stage he told the judge, 'I want nothing to do with this.'

Comment has been passed in relation to the length of the term of imprisonment imposed on Billy Wright. A number of observers consider the term of eight years to be excessive given that there was no violence on the part of the defendant accompanying the threat to Ms Reed. If one is to research sentences in threats to kill cases over a period of years in such a context it would appear the sentence of eight years given to Billy Wright is almost certainly the longest ever sentence handed out for such an offence.

On his arrival at Maghaberry, he was immediately placed under a 23-hour lock-up regime. Prison management later said they took the decision to restrict Wright's movements within the prison because of the threat to his life posed by other loyalist and republican organisations. Wright objected to the imposition of a 23-hour lock-up policy and requested to be allowed free association with other prisoners within Maghaberry. The prison authorities refused his request and for the rest of his time at the Co. Antrim jail the restrictions on his movements remained in place. However, despite its leader's imprisonment, the Loyalist Volunteer Force continued to grow in and around the Lurgan and Portadown areas of Co. Armagh. Throughout March and April 1997, Billy Wright began negotiations with the authorities about a transfer from Maghaberry Prison to the Maze. This, and other matters relating to his eventual move to the Maze Prison in April 1997 are discussed in detail later in this book.

In the autumn of 1997, the UVF approached Wright and asked him to come back on board with the organisation. Two senior UVF members from Portadown, on a direct order from the UVF's Brigade staff, visited Wright in the Maze Prison and put the offer directly to him. A similar offer was made to another former UVF member from Belfast who had identified himself with Billy Wright, his policies and political thinking. Like Wright, he too had been ostracised from the UVF in recent months. He said: 'Richard Jamison and another Portadown UVF man visited Billy in the Maze and asked him to come back on board with the UVF. The offer came from the Brigade Staff. The idea was that we would both come back on board and the slate would be wiped clear. Now, Billy did not reject the offer out of hand. However, he and I had certain conditions, which we wanted met before we would consider anything. Billy put the proposals to Richard Jamison who took them back to Brigade staff in Belfast.

'What Billy wanted from the UVF leadership would not have been detrimental to the UVF, quite the opposite actually as it would have made the UVF more democratic in the long run. He wanted them to introduce a rulebook, something akin to the IRA's Green Book (the IRA's operational handbook and code of disciplinary conduct). The book would have become the UVF's organisational manual. Its contents would have been used as a basis for future policy and discipline within the organisation. What Billy was putting forward was common sense; it would have removed the decision-making policy from individuals and ensured that in future all decisions were made, not on a personal viewpoint, but based on the rulebook itself. It was democratic not despotic, as was the current practice within the UVF.

'Another thing he wanted was that all areas of Northern Ireland had to be represented on the UVF's Brigade staff. Not just Belfast but all of Northern Ireland. Billy felt that certain individuals in Belfast exerted far too much influence over areas they knew nothing about. These people were making decisions which influenced the lives of volunteers in Derry and Portadown. Billy thought that was wrong. He firmly believed that the rural areas of Northern Ireland must have the same representation as Belfast had on the UVF's Brigade Staff. Finally, he wanted all members of the UVF to have the freedom to vote according to their individual consciences. He objected strongly to members of the UVF being required to vote for the organisation's political wing, the Progressive Unionist Party. For Billy, freedom of expression at the ballot box was essential. He believed the policies being put forward by the PUP were not reflective of the loyalist working classes: that they were far too Marxist in style and outlook for the ordinary loyalist to understand or identify with. Billy knew very few people outside Belfast would ever vote for the policies that the PUP was putting forward. For him, people had to be allowed to vote whatever way they wanted to, it was a simple as that. Those were the three things that Billy wanted the UVF to implement. Nothing more or nothing less. Now, it wasn't a lot to ask, was it?

'Richard Jamison took the message back to the UVF Brigade Staff but they wouldn't accept any of the three things Billy had asked for. They rejected them all out of hand. When they did that Billy knew the score as far as the UVF were concerned.'

Within weeks of the UVF rejecting Billy Wright's three demands for change within the UVF the situation changed dramatically. A UVF hit team attempted to murder the former colleague who had identified himself with Billy Wright. A number of UVF gunmen entered the premises where the man worked and fired a number of shots at him. Although hit several times and seriously wounded, the man survived the attack. Within two years the UVF again shot him as he sat in his car in a Belfast street. Once again he survived the gun attack. However, in 2001, at the height of the loyalist feud, gunmen murdered his brother in the Shankill area of Belfast.

Less than six weeks after the attempted murder of his friend, Billy

Wright was shot dead inside the Maze Prison. Shortly before 10 a.m. on the morning of 27 December 1997, the most vociferous opponent of the British government's political process in Northern Ireland had ceased to exist – murdered by the INLA. However, the failure of the authorities to address the many unanswered issues which still surround the murder of Billy Wright have prompted questions. Had the INLA alone the ability to carry out the murder? If they had not, and many people believe this to be the case, who assisted them to kill Billy Wright?

5. The Aftermath of Murder

The news of Billy Wright's death shocked and stunned his hometown of Portadown. At first it was dismissed as rumour. However, by early afternoon the news was confirmed: Billy Wright was dead – shot by the INLA inside the Maze Prison. Within hours of the killing violence erupted in a number of Portadown's loyalist estates. A number of cars were hijacked and set alight on the Brownstown Road, close to Wright's home at the Manor. By early evening the town had become enveloped in an uneasy silence. There was an air of menace as groups of loyalist youths began gathering on their local estates. Mark 'Swinger' Fulton, propelled into a position of leadership by his friend's murder, instructed close associates to curb the violence in Portadown. LVF members quickly moved into the loyalist areas and stifled any further trouble in the Co. Armagh town.

Elsewhere in the province the anger at Wright's murder spilled over into yet more bloodshed. At 10.55 p.m., LVF gunmen opened fire on the Glengannon Hotel on the outskirts of Dungannon, Co. Tyrone, fatally wounding a doorman, Seamus Dillon. The hotel disco had been packed with teenagers when the gunmen struck. Two other doormen and a waiter were injured in the attack. The shooting of Seamus Dillon was the first act of retaliation carried out by the LVF in relation to the murder of Billy Wright. More attacks and deaths were to follow in the wake of the loyalist leader's death.

Billy Wright's father, David, heard the news of his son's death on a local radio news bulletin. It was several hours, late in the afternoon of 27 December 1997, before the RUC officially contacted him to tell him that his son was dead. Even then it was police officers from Banbridge, Co. Down, and not the local Portadown station, who contacted the

Wright family. The Northern Ireland Prison Service eventually wrote to David Wright on 12 January 1998, 16 days after the murder, informing him of his son's death. It was a display of callous indifference by the Northern Ireland Prison Service and has not been forgotten by the Wright family. In February 2000, Martin Mogg, governor of the Maze Prison, finally personally apologised to David Wright for the action of the Prison Service following the death of his son.

On the evening of Saturday, 27 December 1997, David Wright travelled to the mortuary of Foster Green Hospital, Belfast, to formally identify his son's body. Following the formal identification, the body was released to the family for burial.

The Wright family had no real say in the organisation of Billy Wright's funeral. Effectively, his former colleagues in the Loyalist Volunteer Force carried out all the arrangements. Some of those arrangements did not meet with the full approval of the family. However, they felt it prudent to go along with them at that point in time. One particular issue, which caused the family intense pain, was the publication in a local newspaper of a picture of the dead Billy Wright lying in his coffin surrounded by men in full paramilitary uniform. The picture was especially distressing to Wright's young children, who were finding it difficult to come to terms with the sudden death of their father. The family also felt that they were not given the privacy they required in the days immediately following the murder. They did not resent the presence of, or wish to turn away, the hundreds of people who were arriving by the hour at Billy Wright's home in Portadown. They did, however, require time to grieve as a family and in private – they were not afforded that privilege. During the days leading up to the funeral a number of other issues came to light. Unfortunately, at the time their significance was not recognised.

Shortly after the body of the paramilitary leader had been brought back to his Portadown home, a former associate began asking questions of those present about the existence of audiotapes belonging to Billy Wright. A number of people, including members of the Wright family, were asked if the tapes were in the house. Unable to find out where they were, Wright's former colleague began a discreet but vain search throughout the house, looking for the tapes. It has subsequently been revealed that Billy Wright had made a number of audiotapes during the later years of his life in relation to a series of specific matters and individuals. Among the audiotapes was one of a senior Belfast UVF and political figure who had visited Wright at his home in Portadown. Another senior UVF figure was also present during meeting.

Unknown to both men, Billy Wright secretly taped the complete contents of the meeting. The tape contained some very embarrassing and damaging revelations by one of the senior UVF men in relation to his Belfast colleagues and the political direction being taken by the Progressive Unionist Party. Wright later contacted another UVF member making him aware of the existence of the tape and its contents. It is understood he later placed his personal papers with his legal representative at that time.

The funeral of Billy Wright took place on Tuesday, 30 December 1997, from his home in Portadown to the town's Seagoe cemetery. An estimated 30,000 mourners took part in the funeral as it made its way through the centre of the Co. Armagh town. Among those present were representatives of loyalist groupings in England and Scotland as well as some of Wright's former colleagues in the UVF. There were so many floral tributes that they had to be carried on separate vehicles. Hundreds of people lined the route of the cortege, watching as family members and associates of the murdered LVF leader took turns to act as pallbearers. Members of the LVF kept the press at a distance throughout the duration of the funeral procession. Earlier, on the morning of the funeral, a local Ulster Unionist councillor had accused the LVF of deliberately intimidating Portadown's business community and of forcing them to close as Wright's funeral took place. The LVF rejected the claims and a number of local business owners publicly stated that they had closed their premises as a mark of respect and of their own free will.

As Billy Wright's coffin reached the Edenderry area of the town a number of women began berating a police officer standing opposite. Angered that the officer had failed to acknowledge the passing of Billy Wright's funeral cortege, one woman called out: 'Aye, the RUC can salute the coffins of murdered IRA men, but you can't salute the coffin of a murdered loyalist. Shame on you, Billy Wright did what you couldn't do. He took on the Provos [provisional IRA] and beat them. He brought them to their knees. All youse could do was try and put him away. It's not the RUC Protestants needed, it was a hundred Billy Wrights.'

It was almost dark when the funeral cortege eventually reached Wright's final resting place in Seagoe cemetery. Among those who spoke at the graveside was Pastor Kenny McClinton, a former loyalist prisoner turned Christian minister. Some years earlier, Billy Wright had helped McClinton resettle in Portadown following an attack on his Shankill Road home by the UVF. As darkness fell, Billy Wright's coffin was lowered into the ground. For many, his demise at the hands of the INLA heralded the end of the LVF and loyalist opposition to the political process. For the UVF it was the final chapter in the life of a man who, once their colleague in arms, had ended his life as their most vociferous critic and opponent. For Wright's father David, who already harboured grave suspicions regarding the circumstances of his son's murder, it was not the end; it was the beginning of a battle to obtain truth and justice.

On 11 January 1998, the LVF carried out another reprisal killing for the death of Billy Wright. Catholic Terry Enright was shot dead as he worked as a doorman at the Space nightclub on Talbot Street, Belfast. Enright was hit four times as two gunmen opened fire on him and a colleague. The Space nightclub was owned by the sister-in-law of David Ervine of the PUP, the political wing of the UVF. Seven days later LVF gunmen struck again. This time they killed 28-year-old Fergal McCusker in Maghera, Co. Londonderry. Fergal McCusker was abducted before being shot dead at close range. His body was found the next morning in the grounds of a local youth club. A number of tit-for-tat-style killings followed the murder of Fergal McCusker. However, the killings stopped after an emotional appeal on television by Wright's father, David. The then Secretary of State for Northern Ireland, Dr Mo Mowlam, later acknowledged the part played by David Wright in the cessation of violence at that time.

On 18 January 1998, David Wright paid his first visit to the Maze Prison following his son's murder. During the visit he spoke to Norman Green, the LVF prisoner who had been sitting alongside Billy Wright when the INLA gunmen struck. As Green, still in a state of extreme distress, recalled the events of the murder, David Wright became even more convinced that his son's killing was not simply the unaided work of three INLA gunmen. He now firmly believed that the British State was involved in the murder of the paramilitary leader. The LVF prisoners in H Block 6, HMP Maze, shared those feelings and they provided David Wright with vital information about events within the Maze Prison on Saturday, 27 December 1997. It was during that particular visit to the Maze that the LVF prisoners gave David Wright their copy of the visiting sheets for the morning of the murder. Although the significance of the sheets was not fully recognised at the time, they were to provide David Wright with irrefutable evidence with which to confront auxiliary prison officer, Jacqueline Wisely, during the 1999 inquest into the death of the loyalist leader. The matter of the visiting sheets is discussed in detail in a later chapter.

It was subsequently established that Billy Wright's papers had been handed over to a third party without the family's approval. David Wright then discovered that they had made their way into the hands of Richard Jamison, the senior UVF representative in Portadown. David Wright arranged a meeting with Jamison to discuss the papers he had in his possession. When asked if he realised that the papers he had were stolen property, Jamison conceded he did. However, when David Wright suggested contacting the authorities about the matter, Jamison replied: 'You do and I'll hit the back of the grate [the fire] with them.'

In other words, Jamison was indicating that if the Wright family made any legal attempt to recover the papers and documents, he, Jamison, would burn them. Faced with this dilemma, David Wright kept talking and eventually agreed to speak to his own solicitor about signing an affidavit in relation to specific matters mentioned in the contentious documents. Several days later, David Wright made his way to Richard Jamison's business premises. Although Jamison was out on business, his secretary contacted him on his mobile telephone. When challenged about possible legal action to recover the paperwork and his signing of the affidavit, Jamison (naming his solicitor) said David Wright was free to do as he wanted about the matter. He then put the phone down on Wright's father, leaving him wondering what to do next. LVF sources have indicated that they believe Billy Wright's paperwork eventually made its way into the hands of senior members of the UVF in Belfast.

Another instance, which also requires recording, happened within weeks of the funeral of Billy Wright taking place. One evening as David Wright was sitting in his Portadown home, his son's girlfriend at the time of his death arrived at the door and handed over a box of letters and sympathy cards which had been received at Billy Wright's home at the Manor, Portadown. Every single envelope had been opened. Amazed, David Wright pointed out to the girlfriend that the envelopes all appeared to be addressed to the Wright family and not herself. He asked why they had been opened, but received no real explanation. However, it has subsequently been discovered that, at the time of Billy Wright's death, many friends and associates had sent donations of money to his family and children. None of those donations ever reached Billy Wright's children or any member of his family. Other monies sent to the Wright children had also disappeared. Another financial matter came to light after David Wright telephoned the Maze Prison to enquire about the location of his son's personal effects, which at that stage had not been returned to his next of kin. During the course of his conversation, a member of the prison staff informed David Wright that a cheque in respect of the money which remained in Billy Wright's prison account had been sent to a solicitor as requested in his (David Wright's) letter. A puzzled David Wright immediately advised the Maze representative that he had not sent any such request in a letter to the prison. It subsequently came to light that the prison service had received a letter signed by an individual purporting to be David Wright. Upon receipt of that letter the Prison Service had issued a cheque in respect of the amount of money held in Billy Wright's bank account.

David Wright lodged a formal complaint with the police in relation to the matter. However, although the cheque in question was subsequently returned to the Prison Authorities, it appears as though the police carried out no further investigations into the matter. David Wright said he had been informed that the cheque had been returned because of a dispute within the family over the sum in question.

'There was never any dispute within the family as I did not sign any letter asking for the release of the money in Billy's prison account. Until the prison authorities informed me to the contrary, I knew nothing about the letter or the cheque. I find it strange that the matter appears not to have been fully investigated despite my complaint to the police. If it has been investigated then I am unaware of the outcome of those investigations,' said David Wright.

In the months that followed his death, a number of loyalist outlets began capitalising in memorabilia depicting images of Billy Wright. Key fobs, plates, fridge magnets, T shirts and pictures all went on sale across Northern Ireland. Large sums of money were raised from the sale of these items. Part of the profits from the sale of the memorabilia was supposed to go to help Billy Wright's children. None of it ever did so. Despite many promises of help, not one single penny of any of the money supposedly raised to help Billy Wright's children ever made its way to their home. Where it went or what it was eventually spent on is anyone's guess.

Perhaps the biggest financial myth about the loyalist leader revolves around his funeral. Following his burial in his hometown, street collections were taken up by a number of individuals to pay for the cost of the funeral and to erect a headstone to mark Billy Wright's final earthly resting place. Although a headstone was eventually erected by former associates at his grave on 7 July 1998, none of the money raised in the various street collections was ever used in relation to funeral expenses. Contrary to media and public opinion, loyalist paramilitaries did not pay for the funeral expenses of Billy Wright. Instead it was those nearest and dearest to him – his close family – who did so. Not one penny collected in the aftermath of the loyalist leader's death was ever offered to or accepted by David Wright or his daughters. Had it been offered at any stage there is no doubt whatsoever that it would have been rejected immediately. It is important to the Wright family that this particular misconception be publicly corrected.

In May 1998, the Loyalist Volunteer Force announced a ceasefire. A masked man, flanked by eight armed LVF volunteers, made the ceasefire announcement. The LVF statement said the signing of the Good Friday Agreement in April that year had indicated the desire of the people of Northern Ireland for peace.

The statement went on to say that it had been Billy Wright's wish that a just and lasting peace would come to the province. He had recognised that without the support of the people the LVF did not have a mandate to continue on a military basis. The Good Friday Agreement had indicated that this mandate no longer existed. However, the LVF statement went on to say the loyalist terror group reserved the right to return to action should the situation require it to do so. Seven months later, the LVF became the first paramilitary organisation to decommission any of its terrorist weaponry and to date none of the other loyalist paramilitaries have relinquished any of their terrorist arsenals. From 1999 to 2001 the Loyalist Volunteer Force appeared to lose direction. Without the organisational ability and political thinking of Billy Wright, the dissident loyalist organisation appeared to be rudderless and adrift on a sea of criticism and public scorn. Early in 2002, the group began to evolve in a more political direction, pursuing the policies originally advocated by Billy Wright at the time of his death. Ironically those policies were gathering more and more support from within loyalist circles, even from within rank-and-file membership of the Ulster Volunteer Force. His supporters claim those policies now vindicate the stance taken by Billy Wright in 1997. They also claim those same policies are the reasons why he died. Not simply murdered by the INLA as the British authorities have maintained – but assassinated by republicans with the assistance of the British state. The state to which Billy Wright had always espoused loyalty.

Wright once said: 'What's in war for me? If peace breaks down I'm a dead man. I've done things in my life that I regret. My life's full of contradictions . . . As for what it has cost me, only eternity will tell, only eternity will tell.'

For Billy Wright's children, his father, David, and his family, the cost has been enormous. As his father said: 'What did Billy Wright get out of Northern Ireland politics? His grave, that's all he got, his grave.'

6. Murder in the Maze

Shortly after 9 a.m. on the morning of Saturday, 27 December 1997, LVF prisoner Norman Green sat alone in the dining area of C wing on H Block 6, HMP Maze. Like many of his fellow LVF prisoners, Green, who was serving a 16-year sentence for paramilitary offences, was looking forward to a visit from his family later that morning – the first visits at the Maze following the two-day Christmas-holiday break.

There was little or no activity on C wing that morning. Most of the other prisoners were still asleep. After making himself a cup of coffee, Green walked across to the canteen area of D Wing where he saw Billy Wright and another LVF prisoner, Alfie Phillips. A number of other prisoners were also in the canteen at that time. Green joined Wright and Phillips at their table where they chatted generally, waiting to be 'called' for their visit.

There were no set times for individual prison visits to the H Blocks at HMP Maze. Prisoners could, if they wished, take their visits at any time during the allocated visiting hours, morning or afternoon. The visiting procedure for LVF prisoners was basic and routine. On arrival at the Maze, all visitors reported to the Visits Reception Office located outside the perimeter wall of the prison. A permit detailing the prisoner taking the visit was handed in to staff manning the reception area. Visits were normally arranged one week in advance and permits were posted out to friends or family. All visit details were logged and recorded. Prison staff then contacted the appropriate H Block and the prisoner taking the visit was taken to the designated visits area by prison transport. Each prisoner was 'called' for his visit only when his visitor reported to the Visits Office.

At the same time, the visitor was subjected to a rigorous body search carried out by prison staff before being driven in a prison van into the Maze Prison itself. Search procedures at the Maze are applicable to both male and female visitors and are intended to prevent illegal substances or items being brought into the prison and used by the inmates.

At approximately 9.40 a.m., a prison officer on H Block 6 called out the names of Wright and Green for visits. Former LVF inmates at the Maze have said prison officers routinely shouted out the names of prisoners when the prisoner's visitors had arrived at the prison. According to the former prisoners, shouting out the names of individual prisoners saved prison staff the bother of having to approach the grilles leading to the H Block accommodation wings. They also said the shouts were audible to prisoners housed on the block's other wings.

It was not normal for Billy Wright to take a Saturday-morning visit. Wright's usual visitors each Saturday were his two young daughters and they always came to see him in the afternoon. However, because it was Christmas the two girls wanted to stay at home. The visit was subsequently rearranged for Eleanor Reilly – Wright's girlfriend – early on Saturday, 27 December. The change to Wright's visit was telephoned to the Maze shortly after 8.15 a.m. that morning. Prior to the morning of Saturday, 27 December, Billy Wright had never taken a Saturday-morning visit.

Following the visits call, Green and Wright made their way from the canteen to the first of the three metal grilles providing access to the central area of the H Block; the area is commonly known as 'the Circle'. All prisoners, entering or exiting the Maze H Blocks, must do so via a series of metal grilles, which are manually opened and closed by prison staff. The three grilles are located between the Circle and the respective wings. A further three are located between the Circle and the door, which leads out to the H Block forecourt.

It only took a few minutes for Billy Wright and Norman Green to pass through the three grilles between the wing and the Circle area. Both men then made their way to the first of the two grilles leading to the forecourt area when the transport taking them to the visits area was parked. Neither Green nor Wright noticed the INLA prisoner, John 'Sonny' Glennon, painting the mural on the wall between the grilles on the adjoining A and B wings which housed prisoners from the volatile republican splinter group.

Prior to August 1997, it had been common practice for all prisoners on H Block 6 to walk the entire length of the forecourt and through the steel gates before boarding the transport taking them to the visiting area. However, following an INLA threat against LVF prisoners, this procedure had been changed and prison vans were permitted to enter the forecourt to park close to the entrance of the block accommodation. Each paramilitary faction had separate transport to prevent any form of contact or violence occurring between the rival groups. According to LVF prisoners, both vans would reverse as close as possible to the H Block. The move was designed to eliminate the possibility of any attack being carried out by a rival faction. The INLA van always parked alongside the republican A and B wings, the LVF van alongside the loyalist C and D wings. That was standard procedure. Both vans were clearly identifiable to the rival groups on H Block 6. The INLA van was always red, the LVF van was always white. The move was designed to eliminate the possibility of attack by a rival faction. However, on the morning of Saturday, 27 December that procedure had changed for the first time with the LVF transport alongside the INLA wings and vice versa.

As Green and Wright emerged from the accommodation entrance they noticed immediately that their transport was parked alongside the cell windows of the INLA wing. Both men, accompanied by the escorting prison officer, Stephen Sterritt, made their way across to the van, entering via a side door. Once inside, the three occupants, who chatted about Christmas, had only seconds to wait before the van began to move forward slowly towards the main gates of H Block 6.

The seating inside the LVF transport was arranged in a sideways fashion. Directly behind the driver and facing the sliding door was a row of eight seats. On the other side there were four seats from the rear of the van to the sliding door with a further two seats behind the driver/passenger compartment. Billy Wright sat in the middle of the row directly behind the driver and facing the sliding door of the van. Immediately to his left was Norman Green, on his right was prison officer Stephen Sterritt. It is standard procedure within the Maze that two prisoners or less be accompanied by one escorting officer. Three prisoners and above require two officers. The escorting officers always sat in the rear of the transport along with the prisoners. Despite the vehicle having an internal locking system it was not normal procedure for prison officers to lock the van doors during the journeys to the LVF visits area.

As Billy Wright and Norman Green made their way from the LVF wings and across the Circle area they were watched by INLA prisoner, John 'Sonny' Glennon, who was purporting to be painting a mural in the sterile area between A and B wings. Unknown to prison staff, Glennon was armed with a modified .22 Derringer pistol and was part of the three-man INLA Active Service Unit (ASU) which was about to launch an attack on Billy Wright. Glennon had been in position from well before 9 a.m. Two other INLA prisoners, Christopher 'Crip' McWilliams and John Kennaway, who made up the ASU, were waiting close to the canteen area on A wing. McWilliams had a .38 Markov PA63 semi-automatic pistol concealed inside the waistband of his trousers. Both INLA weapons had been smuggled into the Maze Prison in the weeks immediately prior to the murder of Billy Wright.

On seeing Wright and Green emerge from the LVF wings and enter the Circle area, Glennon gave a prearranged signal to alert McWilliams and Kennaway. He then left the wall mural and made his way to A wing canteen. The INLA subsequently claimed that Glennon then stood on a table situated beneath a window overlooking the forecourt of H Block 6, watching for Wright to emerge. By this stage McWilliams and Kennaway had left the canteen area and moved into position at the turnstile entrance leading to A wing exercise yard. As Wright and Green entered the prison van parked in the forecourt, the three INLA prisoners moved through the turnstile and out towards the exercise yard itself. Kennaway kicked open a pre-cut section of prison fence before clambering through. Once clear of the hole he was quickly followed by McWilliams and Glennon.

Kennaway then stood against the wall of A wing and hoisted McWilliams and Glennon onto the roof before hauling himself up. At this stage the three INLA prisoners ran across the roof and jumped down into the forecourt close to the prison van containing Billy Wright. They were now in the intended killing zone. McWilliams and Glennon, both weapons now drawn and clearly visible to prison staff on duty at the gate, rushed towards the white van driven by auxiliary prison officer John Parks. McWilliams and Kennaway ran to the front of the van, bringing it to a halt. Within seconds Glennon and McWilliams made their way to the side door of the van. Kennaway remained with the driver, preventing the van moving off in the direction of the main gates and safety.

As the van containing Billy Wright and Norman Green edged slowly forward towards the main gates the occupants heard three loud bangs on the side door of the vehicle. As the side and rear windows of the prison van were obscured by an opaque plastic film, it was impossible for those inside to see out. Only individual silhouettes were visible to the occupants. As the vehicle came to a halt, the side door of the van was pulled open and McWilliams shouted, 'Armed INLA volunteers.'

At this stage, according to Norman Green, prison officer Sterritt allegedly cowered back into the corner of vehicle, shielding his head with his arms. Billy Wright then jumped to his feet, striking out at McWilliams, who fired a single shot in Wright's direction. McWilliams stepped back, firing three further shots at Billy Wright, who continued to lash out at his assailant. The three shots from the .38 Markov pistol struck Wright in the upper-body area and he staggered back into the interior of the van. McWilliams then entered the van and fired a further three aimed shots into the body of Billy Wright. The three INLA gunmen then made their way back over the prison roof and returned to the wing by the same route they had taken minutes earlier.

After the seventh shot struck him, Billy Wright fell backwards, his body falling across the legs of fellow prisoner, Norman Green. Green claims that at this stage prison officer Stephen Sterritt got up, climbed over Billy Wright's body and left the immediate area of the shooting. The driver, John Parks, had also walked to safety at the main gate of H Block 6. Now alone, Norman Green, unsure what was happening, comforted the dying Billy Wright. He spoke to him, but there was no movement from the fatally wounded LVF leader. Green, in a state of severe shock, clambered out of the van, shouting in the direction of his colleagues on the LVF wings.

'I was left alone with Billy, I tried to get help but no one came. I got back into the van and tried to help Billy. I wiped the blood from his mouth and gave him the kiss of life. It was no good. Billy gave a long sigh and I knew he was dead. It was at least another 20 minutes before help came,' said Green.

Eventually prison staff came to Green's assistance and he was taken to the prison hospital for treatment. However, he was then placed in a cell within the prison hospital and left alone for a further protracted period. He was eventually returned to the LVF wing later that day after a series of personal requests. At no time that day did he receive any form of medical assistance from the prison authorities.

In the minutes immediately after the shooting of Billy Wright the situation on the LVF wings was extremely dangerous. A number of prisoners tried to force their way out of the wings and into the Circle area. At one stage they nearly succeeded in doing so, as a prison officer prepared to unlock the metal grilles leading to the wing. All attempts to calm the loyalist prisoners proved unsuccessful until a governor grade officer arrived and informed the LVF inmates that Billy Wright had been taken to the prison hospital for treatment. The officer did not, however, inform the LVF prisoners that Wright was already dead, something he already knew to be true.

One LVF prisoner who witnessed the murder from his cell window said: 'We were sitting in the cell for a very short time when one of the lads said, "What's going on out there?" I got off my bed and looked out my window. I saw the white van. I hadn't got a clue what to make of it, but it had a sliding door on the passenger's side door. This door was facing my cell window. It was approximately 15–20 ft away from where I was. There was three boys standing at the sliding door, which I could clearly see was open. I saw Billy Wright standing at the back of the van directly behind the open door, kicking out at a person I know as Christopher McWilliams. I saw that McWilliams had a gun in his right hand. To McWilliams' right was a person I know to be John Kennaway – he also had a handgun. There was another person to McWilliams's right, I don't know this person's name. I saw Billy Wright move towards McWilliams, he was still kicking out at them. McWilliams took a couple of steps back and started firing. I would say he fired four or five times. I don't know if Kennaway fired any shots or not. At this stage I started banging on my cell window. I didn't see Billy fall. As I was banging on the window all three turned and looked in my direction. I immediately identified Christopher McWilliams, who stopped shooting when he heard me banging, then he turned round and continued to fire a few more shots.'

Within minutes of McWilliams, Glennon and Kennaway returning to A and B wings, INLA prisoners gathered at the grilles leading to the Circle area. Here they began to taunt the LVF inmates, shouting, 'We got the Rat' – a direct reference to Wright's nickname of 'King Rat'.

A senior officer went to the INLA grille and was informed by McWilliams that the republican splinter group had carried out an operation against the loyalist leader, Billy Wright. The officer was also informed that the INLA operation was directed solely against Wright and that prison officers' lives were not in danger. McWilliams requested that the Roman Catholic prison chaplain, Father Murphy, be allowed onto H Block 6 to speak with the INLA prisoners. Then and only then would the INLA prisoners involved in the operation against Billy Wright surrender themselves and their weapons.

Following discussions with the chaplain, INLA prisoners surrendered the weapons used to kill Billy Wright. The resulting negotiations saw McWilliams and Glennon hand over a shoebox containing the two firearms, a pair of wire cutters and two pieces of metal tubing. It was later proved by RUC detectives that all the items had been used by the INLA ASU to carry out the murder of Billy Wright. Later McWilliams, Glennon and Kennaway were removed from A and B wings of H Block 6. They were arrested under section 14 of the Prevention of Terrorism (Temporary Provisions) Act 1968. All three were later charged with the murder of Billy Wright. The remaining INLA prisoners in A and B wings were searched and removed to another wing within the Maze Prison itself. However, it was four weeks later before they were questioned about the murder of Billy Wright.

An examination of the murder scene and the INLA wings by RUC detectives subsequently revealed that a section of the fence in the exercise yard had been cut through and pieces of shoelace had been used to secure the cut section in position. A chair had also been placed in front of the cut section to hide it from the view of prison officers and the officer manning the observation tower overlooking the exercise yard and A and B wings. The officer in the observation tower could not have seen the hole in the fencing. However, he could have seen the three INLA prisoners making their way through the cut section of fencing and onto the roof towards the murder scene. The officer in question, Raymond Hill, was not in the tower at the time of the attack. Minutes before the INLA killers struck, Hill had been ordered out of the observation tower by senior prison staff.

The order to stand Hill down from his post in A and B wing observation tower was in direct contravention of a local agreement between prison management at the Maze and the Prison Officers Association. That agreement stated, because of the close proximity of the INLA and LVF prisoners, under no circumstances were the observation towers on H Block 6 to be stood down. At 9.30 a.m. on 27 December 1997 that agreement was breached for the first time ever. Minutes earlier, Eleanor Reilly, Billy Wright's visitor that morning, had reported to the Visits Reception Office.

On the afternoon of Saturday, 27 December 1997, a few hours after the murder of Billy Wright had been made known to the media, the publicity bureau of the Irish Republican Socialist Party, the political wing of the INLA, issued the following statement:

> The Irish National Liberation Army claims responsibility for the execution of 'King Rat', Billy Wright. This action was taken against the backdrop of continuing genocide against the Nationalist Community. These attacks are being mainly conducted by the LVF, until this morning by Billy Wright. The

execution of Wright is in keeping with the Irish National
Liberation Army's position of defence and retaliation – it does
not breach our no first strike policy. In conclusion we warn
Loyalist Paramilitaries against further attacks on the Nationalist
Community. If this warning is not heeded we will have no
hesitation in making sure those who prey on the nationalist
working class will pay the ultimate price.

However, within days of the murder, Wright's father, David, visited the
Maze Prison and spoke to the LVF prisoners who witnessed his son's
killing. He also spoke at length to Norman Green, who was still visibly
traumatised by the events of the previous days.

During the course of that visit, David Wright was given vital
information regarding the circumstances of his son's death. He also
obtained the original visiting list for 27 December 1997, which had
been prepared by a member of the prison staff before being issued to
the prisoners on 26 December 1997. For the first time ever the names
of INLA and LVF visits were included on the list. That list and the
initial information he had been given was sufficient for David Wright
to state publicly for the first time: 'It's my belief that Billy's murder was
state arranged, state sponsored and state sanctioned, in collusion with
some of those in prison management.' He has never moved away from
that position.

On 29 December 1997, two days after the murder of Billy Wright,
the Loyalist Volunteer Force prisoners on H Block 6 issued the
following statement:

> On 27 December 1997 our dear friend and comrade, Billy
> Wright, was mercilessly slain by pseudo Republicans from the
> INLA as he left H Block 6 on his way to a visit.
>
> Christopher McWilliams, John Kennaway and John 'Sonny'
> Glennon using at least two weapons carried out the murder.
> Since news of Billy's murder broke the press and media have
> offered a myriad of conflicting reports as to the nature of the
> cowardly slaying. Today, we the Loyalist Volunteer Force
> prisoners will put the record straight.
>
> In early April of this year two of the above killers,
> McWilliams and Kennaway, were involved in a hostage taking
> incident in HMP Maghaberry. The two pulled guns on a
> member of staff, taking them to the prison hospital and forced
> the officer to take them to Foyle House, where remand

prisoners were held. On entering the House, they demanded to see Kevin McAlorum, a member of an opposing INLA faction. After negotiations the pair surrendered their weapons and were taken to the punishment unit, but not before attempting to fire at least five shots at prison staff. After a few days, McWilliams and Kennaway were moved to the INLA wing in the Maze. The pair later publicly claimed that their intended target was Billy Wright who had been held in the punishment unit since the first day of his incarceration. Even though the authorities were aware of this, the two misfits were placed on a wing facing Billy and three colleagues who had been moved there from Maghaberry a week previously.

As the number of LVF prisoners at the Maze increased we were given two wings on H Block 6. During their time there countless representations were made to various prison governors by the Loyalist Volunteer command to have the INLA moved to another block. These requests were ignored. After the disturbances of H6 in August, the Loyalist Volunteer prisoners were moved to an empty block (H2) where they were held on Rule 32 [23-hour lock-up per day] for two months. On our return to H6 prison staff informed us that the INLA had issued a blanket death threat on all LVF prisoners. However, the prison management refused to take the threats seriously even when the INLA promised to launch a 'spectacular'. These are the events leading up to Billy's death.

In relation to the events surrounding the day of the murder, there are grave irregularities and questions to be answered. Firstly, the day before the shooting, Loyalist Volunteer Force prisoners received a photocopy list with details of LVF and INLA visits for Saturday, 27 December 1997. The INLA were also given a copy of the same list. Therefore the INLA knew Billy was taking a visit the following day. However, they had no idea of what time the visit had been arranged for. That morning was the first time Billy had ever taken a Saturday-morning visit since entering the Maze in April, therefore no fixed pattern of visits time had been set. How then did the INLA know the time of Billy's visit?

On the morning of the shooting the exercise yards linked to the LVF wings remained locked, yet the yard linked to the INLA wings was opened. We consider this to be extremely sinister considering the fact that the INLA needed their yard open to enable them to scale the wall. Also the watchtower overlooking the INLA yard was unoccupied, as the officer was allegedly needed to staff the visits area. This allowed the murderers to cut through the wire fence and scale the wall before going over the roof undetected (if the watchtower had been manned the alarm would have been raised immediately).

Serious questions must also be asked about the treatment of the prisoner who was in the van alongside Billy Wright. In a profound state of shock the man was taken to the prison hospital after trying to resuscitate Billy. The distraught prisoner was then locked in a cell in the prison hospital on his own for four hours instead of being afforded the same care as was given to the prison staff who were on the periphery of the murder.

The Loyalist Volunteer Force prisoners demand that the government answer these questions and that they inform the public as to why no action was taken against McWilliams and Kennaway over the Maghaberry incident by the police or the prison authorities. Why were the requests to have the INLA prisoners moved to another block constantly ignored? We call for the setting up of an immediate inquiry to examine the circumstances of the murder of Billy Wright.

Although the LVF statement came 48 hours after the killing of Billy Wright, it was clear that at that point in time the LVF prisoners had concerns as to how the murder had been allowed to happen and the circumstances surrounding it. Even at that very early stage the LVF prisoners had suspicions that elements of the state had to be involved in the murder of Billy Wright.

7. The Starry Plough

In April 1999 the INLA released a detailed account of what it called the 'sequence of events' leading to and following the operation to execute Billy Wright inside the Maze Prison. The account, which appeared in the republican newspaper *The Starry Plough*, is considered to be significant as it was the first occasion the dissident republican group had publicly detailed any of its military operations in the media. It is worth noting that prior to the murder of Billy Wright the INLA had never before gone into any kind of detail in relation to its military operations. Despite a bloody and violent history of murder and violence, involving some of the most notorious terrorists to emerge throughout the Troubles, prior to the Wright killing the INLA had never felt the need to justify any of its actions. What had prompted it to speak out on this occasion in such graphic detail?

It is clear allegations that the volatile republican splinter grouping had colluded with other elements to kill Wright had touched a raw nerve. Clearly, the INLA had been angered by suggestions that it had acted in conjunction with some elements of the British state to murder Billy Wright or that the organisation lacked the capability of carrying out such a complex operation without the assistance of a third party.

The most strident of the collusion allegations came from Billy Wright's father David who claimed he had been reliably informed that the INLA were incapable of either planning or putting into practice an operation such as the one which had been mounted within the Maze Prison to kill his son. David Wright said his information had come from sources within the IRA itself and had been conveyed to him via a source in Dublin.

There was also an unwritten law within the prison system that rival

85

paramilitary factions would not attack each other within a prison. The INLA had broken that unwritten law and in doing had endangered the privileges and concessions earned over the years by the IRA in respect of their prisoners. By giving David Wright the information the IRA were pointing the figure of suspicion at the British authorities.

A few weeks before the INLA article appeared in *The Starry Plough*, David Wright had said the dissident republican group were 'incapable' of carrying out the murder of his son on their own.

Continuing, David Wright said: 'During a recent visit to Dublin, where I discussed the circumstances of my son's death with officials from the Irish government, I was approached by a third party. I was told that very senior members of the Provisional Republican Movement had information that the INLA had assistance in killing my son. I was also told that those same republicans considered the INLA incapable of putting that operation together on their own and they could not have acted alone. In other words they colluded with others to kill my son.'

He went on to say that it was his belief, and the belief of many others, that the INLA had in fact colluded with the British state in the murder of his son. David Wright had chosen his words carefully in the knowledge that by saying the INLA had colluded with the British state he was accusing them of being in league with their avowed enemy. In other words he was accusing the INLA of working hand in glove with the apparatus of the British state – the self-same state they claimed to be waging a war against in the name of Irish Freedom. Shortly after David Wright had made his views known, the INLA article in *The Starry Plough* was published.

The INLA stated that the main purpose in publishing the newspaper article was to counteract what they called the unfounded allegations that they had colluded with elements of the security services to murder Billy Wright inside the Maze. The dissident republican group described the allegations as 'ludicrous', saying they were promoted from within loyalist circles or ill-informed elements within the wider republican/nationalist community. To refute in total these allegations the INLA said they were providing a detailed account of what led up to the murder of Billy Wright as well as what actually took place inside the Maze Prison on the morning of Saturday, 27 December 1997.

According to the INLA, the arrival of the LVF prisoners on H6 after they had been forced off mainstream loyalist blocks elsewhere caused immediate concern within the leadership of the INLA and their prisoners inside the Maze Prison. Immediately prior to the transfer of the LVF from Maghaberry in 1997, the INLA claimed their prisoners on C and D wings at H6 had been in the final stages of completing plans to allow selected INLA inmates to escape from the Maze. The unexpected arrival of the LVF on H6 with the subsequent moving of the INLA to A and B wings within the block forced these plans to be aborted.

However, before detailing the specifics of its operation to kill Billy Wright, the INLA said it was necessary to highlight the work undertaken by their intelligence section. The INLA said their original plan was to provide the prison officers on duty in H6 with the opportunity to see the INLA Active Service Unit as soon as it went into action. The INLA claimed that its intelligence had shown the ASU would have certainly been noticed as the three men were clambering through the hole which had been cut in the security fence close to the entrance to the A wing exercise yard. The prison officer on duty in the watchtower overlooking the area would have immediately noted movement in this area, the INLA said. In response to seeing the ASU making its way through the security fencing, the INLA claimed the guard in the watchtower would have immediately sounded the alarm. This, according to the INLA, would have resulted in the automatic locking down of all grilles within H6, stopping all movement going in or out of the block itself. Movement would only have recommenced once the prison authorities had investigated the alarm and the central lock-down mechanism had been released by the Maze Emergency Control Room (ECR). Had that been the actual case on the morning of Saturday, 27 December 1997, the INLA claimed Billy Wright would have been immobile inside the prison van in the forecourt of H6 and would have remained so until the alert had been cleared. Such a delay, the INLA claimed, would have given the INLA extra time to successfully complete the operation to kill Wright.

The INLA say they were unaware that the prison officer in the watchtower had been stood down that particular morning. However, the dissident republicans claim the split-second timing of the murder attack ensured that the ASU of McWilliams, Glennon and Kennaway required no extra time to carry out the shooting dead of Billy Wright.

According to the INLA, there was nothing prison authorities could have done which would have deterred or prevented the death of Billy Wright. Once the ASU had successfully breached the security fence close to the entrance to A wing it became irrelevant whether or not an alarm was raised, as by that stage the ASU members would have already reached their objective: the prison van containing Billy Wright.

According to the INLA account, the actual INLA operation to kill Billy Wright got under way around 8 a.m. on Saturday, 27 December 1997, when the three volunteers making up the ASU were put on standby. By that stage all three men were totally familiar with the specific roles to which they had been assigned. Following a morning 'headcount' by prison staff, all three INLA volunteers had breakfast in the canteen of A wing. At this stage they placed a table under the canteen window, which the INLA claimed gave them a clear view into the forecourt area of H6. They also state that by this time the two prison vans used to take the LVF and INLA prisoners to their respective visits area were already in place. However, this account of the operation to kill Billy Wright makes no mention of whether the LVF bus was parked close to the INLA wing.

Immediately after breakfast, McWilliams and Glennon armed themselves with weapons, a .38 calibre Markov PA63 semi-automatic pistol and a modified .22 Derringer pistol. The INLA said that during a test firing of the Derringer pistol within the Maze Prison, one barrel had been found to be defective. The weapons were test fired inside a cell on A wing, H Block 6 – the INLA accommodation. The gun was wrapped in a prison towel to muffle the sound of the gunshot. The RUC investigation team later confirmed this information. As no prison officers patrolled the accommodation area itself prison staff would have been unaware of the test firing.

Both weapons were fully loaded and had been hidden in the washroom area of the wing after they had been brought into the Maze Prison some time earlier. The weapons were then checked and concealed in the waistband of McWilliams and Glennon's clothing before they returned to the canteen area where they were joined by the remaining ASU member, John Kennaway, for a final briefing.

The INLA state that at 9 a.m., Glennon took up a position pretending to be painting a wall mural within the confines of the sterile area separating A and B wings. His position, the INLA claim, gave him a clear and almost unimpaired line of sight directly across the Circle area and into the entrance to the LVF wings directly opposite. In the eventuality of Billy Wright being spotted making his way to a visit, the INLA had arranged for Glennon to give a prearranged coded message to alert the other two members of the ASU. The code was basic and as follows: if Wright came into the Circle area accompanied by one other prisoner Glennon was to call out: 'Pass me the paints out of Cell Two' alerting McWilliams and Kennaway that Wright and another prisoner were on the way out of H6; the call of 'Pass me the paints from Cell

Three', would have denoted the fact that two other LVF prisoners accompanied Wright.

However, the INLA account makes no mention of any code that might have been used had Wright appeared unaccompanied. Did they have prior knowledge that this would not be the case? The INLA said the reason behind the use of codes was to provide the ASU with what they termed 'up-to-the-minute intelligence' on the number of LVF prisoners they would have to confront in order to successfully carry out the murder of Billy Wright.

At 9.40 a.m., as Glennon, armed with the Derringer pistol, was continuing to pretend to work on the wall mural he claims he was alerted by the sound of an intercom buzzing inside the block control room some distance away from his location. It is also worth pointing out that a prison officer on duty in the sterile area between A and B wings from 8 a.m. that morning failed to notice that the INLA mural had already been completed and that Glennon had nothing to paint! Glennon continued to watch as a member of prison staff approached the metal grilles at the entrance to the LVF wings and spoke to an LVF prisoner. A shout of 'C'mon Billy, that's us for a visit' was then heard coming from inside the LVF wings. Glennon continued to work on the wall mural beside the prison officer and seconds later heard the sound of buzzers, which indicated the opening of grilles on the LVF wings. At this stage, Billy Wright and another LVF prisoner, Norman Green, left the wing and walked towards to circle area of H6.

Glennon immediately shouted the prearranged coded message, 'Pass me the paints out of Cell Two'; alerting the remaining ASU members to the fact that Wright, accompanied by one other person, was now on his way to a visit. Glennon then left his position at the mural, went back into the canteen area and climbed onto the table beneath the window looking out into the forecourt area of H6.

This aspect of the INLA version of the murder of Billy is vital as the dissident republicans claim it 'overlooked the forecourt of H Block 6 with the entrance being clearly in view'. However, during two visits to the scene of the murder on H Block 6, HMP Maze, the author and other individuals have compiled evidence that contradicts the statement. That evidence and other material collated during the author's visits to the Maze will be further discussed in a later chapter.

On hearing the coded call, McWilliams and Kennaway took up a position at the turnstile leading to A wing exercise yard awaiting the second signal from Glennon. This second signal was not to be given until the INLA was sure Billy Wright had entered the prison van parked close to the INLA accommodation on H6. Once he had seen Wright and his fellow LVF prisoner enter the van, Glennon shouted, 'Go . . . Go . . . Go . . .' At this second signal McWilliams and Kennaway moved through the turnstile and out into the area leading to A wing exercise yard. Within seconds Glennon, armed with the .22 Derringer pistol, followed them. Kennaway then kicked open the pre-cut section of the security fencing before clambering through the hole and into the sterile area. McWilliams and Glennon closely followed him. Once they had cleared the hole in the security fence the three members of the INLA ASU ran to the outside wall of Cell 26, where Kennaway stood with his back to the wall, and hoisted McWilliams and Glennon up and onto the roof of the block. He then hauled himself onto the roof and followed McWilliams and Glennon, who by this time had crossed the roof and had jumped down into the forecourt of H6.

At this juncture the prison van containing Billy Wright, Norman Green and the two prison officers was slowly edging its way towards the main entrance gates of H6, which the INLA claim were already open. This particular statement contradicts the evidence of a prison officer who stated in a written inquest deposition that the gates were closed at that point in time. McWilliams, on reaching the forecourt area, produced the semi-automatic pistol and ran to the front of the prison van, bringing it to a halt. At this stage it is claimed prison staff in the forecourt area spotted McWilliams and, seeing he was armed, attempted to close the block entrance gates. Within a few seconds, Glennon and Kennaway, who then remained with the driver to prevent the van from moving off, joined McWilliams. At this point McWilliams and Glennon ran around to the side of the prison van and pulled open the sliding door of the vehicle. Incidentally, it should be noted that although the prison van containing the LVF prisoner was fitted with an internal-locking system, it had not been used to secure the vehicle that particular morning. Also, the side door of the van giving access to the passenger compartment could only be opened from the outside.

As they pulled open the sliding doors of the van, McWilliams shouted: 'Armed INLA volunteers.' According to the INLA version of the killing, the two members of the ASU – McWilliams and Glennon – subdued prison officer Stephen Sterritt, shouting at him to get down. The INLA claim Sterritt reacted by dashing to the corner of the van in a state of shock. At this point the LVF prisoners – Wright and Green – attempted to get clear of the van but were thwarted by the INLA volunteers. McWilliams then fired a single shot at Billy Wright, who again attempted to fight off his assailants and escape out of the van.

Forced back, McWilliams then took aim and fired three deliberate shots into the torso of Billy Wright. At the impact of the shots, Wright staggered back into the inside of the prison van before trying once again to fight his way out of the vehicle.

The INLA claim Glennon then provided covering fire from the Derringer pistol. However, this would appear to be questionable as the Derringer pistol had two twin barrels, one of which the INLA had admitted was defective prior to the attack being mounted. Therefore, at the most, Glennon could only have discharged one round from the weapon. As the pathologists report did not indicate the presence of a .22 bullet wound on the body of Billy Wright it can only be assumed that Glennon missed his target with the one shot he fired. After discharging the Derringer pistol, Glennon stepped back, allowing McWilliams to enter the prison van and fire a further three rounds into the upper body of Billy Wright. One of these last three shots was to prove fatal.

The INLA have always stressed that the Maze operation was directed solely against Billy Wright and that at no time was any other prisoner or member of the prison staff under threat of death or injury. This instruction was not to be overruled unless the actions of the other LVF prisoners or prison staff endangered the lives of the members of the INLA ASU.

Following the attack on Wright, the INLA prisoners made their way back over the prison roof and re-entered A wing using the same route they had originally taken to access the forecourt of H6. Once again, this aspect of the INLA version of the killing of Billy Wright will be examined in a later chapter.

The INLA say, from start to finish, that the entire operation to kill Billy Wright took no more than 90 seconds – a figure which would appear to be at variance with the RUC's assessment of some 60 seconds.

Once inside A wing, the three members of the murder team informed the remaining INLA prisoners of what had just taken place. They then entered into negotiations with prison staff and the Roman Catholic chaplain at the Maze before surrendering themselves and the equipment they had used in the attack on Billy Wright. The three members of the ASU were subsequently arrested and taken to the reception area within the Maze Prison. On his arrest, McWilliams issued a short statement, which had been prepared before the murder of Billy Wright had taken place. The statement said: 'Billy Wright was executed for one reason and for one reason only, and that was for directing and waging his campaign of terror against the nationalist people from his prison cell in Long Kesh.'

In April 1999, the INLA claimed allegations that the dissident republican group had colluded with others to murder Billy Wright had been made to forward a narrow political agenda and that such allegations ignore the facts of the killing itself. They also dismissed suggestions that the murder was an attack on the peace process, saying those who promoted that argument suffered from the same political tunnel vision which had led to the claims that the Good Friday Agreement would bring peace to Ireland. On the contrary, *The Starry Plough* article on the murder of Billy Wright concluded by saying: 'The INLA execution of the Loyalist Volunteer Force leader, Billy Wright, a recognised sectarian killer who often worked for MI5, far from being an attack on the peace process was a positive blow for peace in Ireland.'

Wright's killer, Christopher 'Crip' McWilliams, would echo those same sentiments as he spoke to the media following his early release from Magilligan Prison in October 2000. At the time of their release from prison, McWilliams, Glennon and Kennaway had served just two years of the life sentence imposed upon them for the murder of Billy Wright.

8. A Gunman Speaks

A matter of weeks after his release from prison, Christopher 'Crip' McWilliams took part in an interview in which he discussed the operation to kill Billy Wright. In the interview McWilliams practically mirrored the INLA newspaper article in *The Starry Plough*. However, there are a number of points raised by McWilliams that must be noted and addressed.

According to McWilliams, the initial approach in relation to the proposed operation to kill Billy Wright came from the INLA's internal security within the Maze Prison. Some 18 months after the INLA article was published in *The Starry Plough*, McWilliams claims he was asked: 'Would I volunteer to more or less go on the operation and not to be making any quick decisions or anything like that but to think over it.'

This statement would appear to contradict the INLA assertion that none of their prisoners in the Maze, other than the three men involved in the shooting, knew anything about the operation to kill Billy Wright. To quote McWilliams himself: 'Not even the OC [officer commanding] of the wing knew about the operation.' If this was the case, how does McWilliams explain his earlier remark in which he claimed he was approached by the INLA's internal security within the Maze to take part in the operation to kill Wright? Neither McWilliams nor the INLA themselves have ever clarified what they meant by the internal security within the Maze. As all INLA prisoners were housed on H6 at that time, where was this internal security unit housed? Who were they and how did they approach McWilliams and his two comrades to plan the murder itself?

McWilliams also claimed to have known the thinking that lay

behind the operation to kill Wright and that it went back to the height of the Orange Order dispute at Drumcree Church near Portadown, Co. Armagh, in 1995–6. He said the LVF had emerged at that particular time as a result of the ongoing dispute over the Orange Order being prevented from walking back to Portadown town centre via the nationalist Garvaghy Road area. McWilliams described the LVF as 'more or less psychopathic killers' who had defected to that particular organisation from the UDA and UVF. He blamed the LVF for carrying out the murder of Lurgan taxi driver Michael McGoldrick in July 1996 and the shooting dead in July the following year of Bernadette Martin, aged 18, at Aghalee, near Lurgan. Both murders were particularly callous and at the time caused widespread revulsion. The LVF were suspected of having carried out both attacks. The subject of the killing of Michael McGoldrick has been addressed earlier in this book.

In his interview description of the attack that killed Billy Wright, McWilliams reiterated the point that after the loyalist leader moved out of the Circle area and towards the entrance leading onto the forecourt of H6, another member of the ASU, John Glennon, left his position at the wall mural and made his way into the canteen area on A wing. Once in the canteen area McWilliams said Glennon: 'Jumped onto the table and had a clear view out to the forecourt. At that stage you saw Billy Wright coming through the grilles along with another prisoner. The two of them stepped into the van and the minute he stepped into the van comrade Glennon shouted, "Go, Go, Go".'

The reference to the clear view from the canteen window is important in the context of the overall INLA operation in that the killers allege that it allowed them to see Wright enter the prison van. Then and only then did the three members of the INLA ASU swing into action and leave the A wing accommodation area to make their way into the block forecourt via the hole in the security fence and across the prison roof. A visit by David Wright, Jane Winter of British Irish Rights Watch, Mags O'Conner, NIHRC, engineer Laurence McGill, solicitor John McAtamney and this author to the canteen area on A wing, H Block 6, was later to show that it would have been impossible for anyone to have seen out the window, let alone have a clear view of anyone or anything inside the forecourt area. A more detailed explanation of the findings in relation to the canteen window will be discussed later in the book when an independent engineer's report into the murder of Billy Wright is examined in detail. However, it is sufficient to say at this stage that this particular aspect of the INLA version of events is called into doubt. Again the assertion by the INLA that they could see out of the canteen window is called into question by an admission by McWilliams himself to a member of the media crew conducting the interview.

According to the crewmember, McWilliams confirmed the attack had been mounted from the canteen area and not from a cell on A wing as the Northern Ireland Prison Service seemed to think. McWilliams said the reason for selecting the canteen and not a cell was that Billy Wright could have seen the INLA ASU in the cell, but he could not see into the canteen. Is it not therefore logical to conclude that if Billy Wright could not see in through the window, then neither could the INLA see out through the very same window?

The INLA gunman went on to claim that, following the murder of Billy Wright, the ASU re-entered A wing via the turnstile to the exercise yard. Again this particular part of the operation will be discussed in a later chapter. At this stage it is sufficient to say that a visit to A wing by the author and others revealed evidence that disputes this statement.

In April 1997, Christopher 'Crip' McWilliams and John Kennaway were involved in an incident at Maghaberry Prison, Co. Antrim, in which a prison officer was taken hostage at gunpoint. Although the hostage situation ended when the prisoners surrendered their weapons and gave themselves up, it was never explained how the weapons used in the incident had been brought into the prison. When asked to explain how the weapons had entered Maghaberry Prison, in April 1997, McWilliams refused to discuss the incident. He also refused to comment on speculation that the intended target of the April attack was in fact Billy Wright, who was being held in the Co. Antrim jail at the time.

Likewise, when asked how the INLA had managed to smuggle guns and wire cutters into the Maze Prison, McWilliams would not answer the question. He refused to confirm or deny whether the INLA used the same method to get guns into the Maze as had been used in the Maghaberry incident. He also declined to reveal exactly how long the weapons had been inside the Maze before the murder took place. It seems strange, when the INLA and McWilliams himself were taking the unprecedented step of explaining in detail every other aspect of the operation to kill Billy Wright, that they steadfastly refused to provide any detail whatsoever as to how they managed to get guns into a high-security prison. McWilliams also refused to comment on whether or not the murder weapons were smuggled into the prison by visitors attending a Christmas party in mid-December 1997. 'I'm not prepared to disclose how we got the weapons in or whatever,' he said. However, during the course of a conversation with a member of the Irish Republican Socialist Party, the political wing of the INLA, it was stated to the author that one of the weapons used in the murder attack had been brought into the Maze by the wife of a senior IRSP member who had attended the INLA Christmas Party in December 1997.

McWilliams went on to reveal that throughout 1997 the OC of the INLA prisoners at the Maze had campaigned to have the LVF prisoners removed from H6. He said there had been six months of continuous arguments with the prison authorities to have Billy Wright and the other LVF prisoners relocated elsewhere within the confines of the Maze. However, despite the INLA protestations, the prison authorities refused to relocate the LVF prisoners within the Maze. Referring directly to the allegations that prison management had not reacted to warnings from prison officers of the distinct possibility of trouble involving INLA and LVF prisoners, McWilliams said he did not believe the authorities had taken the matter seriously, that they had turned a blind eye to it. He confirmed that prison authorities had been warned on numerous occasions, in particular the three months prior to the murder, that unless Wright and his fellow LVF prisoners were removed from H6 there would be trouble. Despite those warnings having been given, the LVF prisoners were allowed to remain on H6.

McWilliams then discussed the cutting of the security fence close to the A wing exercise yard area. According to McWilliams the wire had been breached on Christmas night and that he himself had been the person who had cut the hole in the prison fence. He revealed that over the years it had become a tradition amongst the prisoners in the Maze to make homemade alcohol to celebrate the Christmas and New Year festivities. He claimed the relaxed prison regime over the holiday period, combined with the intoxicated state of the INLA prisoners, allowed the three INLA prisoners to slip out into the exercise yard and cut the security fence unnoticed. McWilliams said he was aware that the observation post overlooking the exercise yard was unmanned between the hours of 9 p.m. and 11 p.m., when the yard was secured for the night. It was during this two-hour period that the security fence was breached. Once the hole had been cut, the severed section was replaced and tied with shoelaces and disguised to prevent detection by prison staff. Three chairs were then placed in front of the fence before McWilliams and his two companions simply walked back into A wing.

Christopher McWilliams said the INLA were confident that the hole would remain undetected for a day and a half because of the relaxed Christmas-period atmosphere. He went on to say the absence of spot

The last photograph of LVF leader Billy Wright, taken inside
the Maze prison a few weeks before his death.

Billy Wright's father, David.

A loyalist mural on the Shankill Road, Belfast.
The mural describes Billy Wright as a 'loyalist martyr'.

Armed LVF volunteers announce their ceasefire to the media in May 1998.

LVF gunmen fire a volley of shots in Portadown's Corcrain estate during the height of the Drumcree protests in 2000. In the background is the Belfast loyalist, Johnny Adair and supporters of the UFF.

Billy Wright pictured with his pet dog at his Portadown home in 1996.

David Wright delivering a copy of the British Irish Rights Watch report into his son's murder to Number 10 Downing Street, October 2000.

LVF prisoners in paramilitary uniform on H Block 6, HM Prison Maze.

Armed LVF volunteers on patrol in the IRA heartland of East Tyrone.

Billy Wright pictured
beside a Drumcree mural
in Portadown, Co.
Armagh, in August 1996.

Billy Wright adresses a crowd of 15,000 at Brownstown Park, Portadown, immediately after his expulsion from the UVF in August 1996. Alongside Wright is the Democratic Unionist Party Assembly Member, the Reverend William McCrea.

Billy Wright in Brownstown Park, Portadown, shortly before he was sentenced to death by the UVF in August 1996.

Billy Wright pictured at the site of the Orange Order protest at Drumcree Church in August 1996.

Billy Wright shortly before his arrest and imprisonment in 1997.

Billy Wright in the canteen area of the LVF accommodation on H Block 6, HM Prison Maze, shortly before his murder on 27 December 1997.

27 December 1998 LVF prisoners on H Block 6 mark the first anniversary of the murder of Billy Wright inside the Maze prison.

checks or searches by prison staff of the INLA wings also enabled the breach in the security fence to remain undetected. According to McWilliams, prison staff had no control on the INLA wings. He said: 'Whenever prison staff come onto the wings they haven't any control on our wings. The INLA are in full control of the wings.'

McWilliams even went as far as to say: 'It couldn't be discovered because of the fact that there was no fabric check and there was no . . . you know what I mean . . . there was no searches over Christmas and actually, I would even go to the extent of saying [that] during the Christmas period there the prison officers are sitting in the Circle or whatever and usually come in half drunk.'

If McWilliam's comments are accurate, and the Northern Ireland Prison Service has never denied them, then they paint a picture of a prison where the prisoners dictated the terms and where nothing was right.

The INLA also dismissed the possibility that a security camera covering the area could have detected the breach in the exercise yard fencing. According to McWilliams, the area where the hole was cut was a blind spot. He said the security camera, positioned at the far end of the exercise yard, took in an aerial view of the area. However, he said the camera's view had been obscured by two large metal gates, which opened into the A wing exercise yard. McWilliams told how on the night the fence was cut, Glennon and Kennaway stood in the darkness beside the sterile area, pretending to have a conversation. As they did so, McWilliams said he crawled out and cut the fence. However, why, if as McWilliams states, the area where the hole was cut was a blind spot and free from detection by the security camera, with no guards on duty at the time, did the two INLA volunteers need to stand pretending to have a conversation? Nobody was going to see them. The observation tower was unmanned and the camera unable to cover that particular area of the fence, therefore there was no cause for alarm at the possibility of detection. More importantly, how did the INLA prisoners know the area where the fence was breached was a blind spot? It beggars belief that any INLA prisoner had been given access to the control room area of H6 and allowed to view the monitors screening pictures from the security cameras in the exercise yards. The same can be said about the observation post overlooking the A wing exercise yard. The INLA did not have access to the post to see at first hand an elevated view of A and B wings.

How then did they know the area they had selected to cut the security fence was a blind spot? How did they become knowledgeable of that vital piece of information? Did someone convey that information to them? If so, who was that individual and who ordered that person to act in that manner?

When asked about the absence of the prison guard from the observation tower overlooking the exercise yard, McWilliams said that had been part of the overall operation to murder Billy Wright. He said that in any prison situation when there was a breach of security or any incident occurred, an alarm was activated. According to McWilliams part of the INLA plan included the prison guard seeing the three attackers breach the security fence and clamber up onto the prison roof. At that stage the guard would have activated the alarm system, which in turn would have led to the lock down of the entrance and exit points on H6. With all possible avenues of escape closed off to him, Billy Wright would have been trapped in the prison van within the confines of the forecourt of H6. McWilliams argued that such a scenario suited the INLA as it provided them with an easy target for their ASU.

When asked how they knew Billy Wright was taking a visit on the morning of Saturday, 27 December 1997, Christopher McWilliams said, 'Our intelligence told us.' He said the INLA had been observing Wright's movements within H6 for several months before launching its murder attack. McWilliams acknowledged the fact that the INLA had received a copy of the LVF visits sheets for 27 December 1997. However, he rejected suggestions that the information contained in the visits sheets had significantly assisted the INLA in the murder of Billy Wright. The INLA claimed they had noted what days Wright had his visits and the times they had taken place.

McWilliams acknowledged that Wright's visits had varied and had taken place mainly on a Tuesday or Wednesday but that there was no set time for the visits. There was also what McWilliams described as the odd Saturday visit. However, whilst acknowledging the accuracy of the INLA information in relation to the weekday visits, the assessment of the odd Saturday visit is extremely questionable. Former close associates of Wright maintained he always took a visit from his two young daughters on Saturday afternoons. They explained that as the children were at school during the week the only available time for them to visit their father was Saturday – not the morning but the afternoon. The first time ever that Billy Wright took a Saturday-morning visit was on 27 December 1997. What is even more significant is that that particular visit had been due to take place on the Saturday afternoon. However, with it being Christmas, Billy Wright's two daughters preferred to remain at home with their mother. The visit was changed at short notice and rearranged for the morning of the 27 December 1997. Instead of his two daughters, Billy Wright was due to receive a visit from a female friend.

The timing of the change of visit is significant, as Wright was not informed of the alteration in plans until 8.30 a.m. on the morning of the visit when a phone call was made to the Maze informing him of the changes. According to Christopher McWilliams, the three INLA volunteers were armed and on stand-by to carry out the operation from that time the same morning. If that is the case, and there is nothing to contradict McWilliams' statement, how exactly did the INLA know Billy Wright was taking a morning visit that day? John Glennon was also standing in position within the sterile area between A and B wings, pretending to be painting an already-completed wall mural. Was it his intention to stand there indefinitely waiting for Billy Wright to appear sometime between the hours of 9.30 a.m. and 4.30 p.m. that day? Would a member of the prison staff not eventually have questioned his presence at an already-completed wall mural?

Billy Wright's father maintains that only his son and certain prison staff knew the information relating to the change in the visiting arrangements. He argues that someone must have given the information to the INLA. Had this not been the case, David Wright maintains the INLA ASU would have had to wait in a state of indefinite armed readiness throughout the course of the morning and early afternoon, increasing the risk of detection by prison staff. That, says David Wright, was a risk they could not and did not have to take.

The INLA said their intelligence analysis also showed that prisoners involved in a relationship or who had children would most probably take the first visit available after Christmas to find out how they had spent the holiday period. The INLA were therefore anticipating that Wright, in common with many other prisoners, would take the first available visit after Christmas: Saturday, 27 December. McWilliams said the INLA were extremely confident that Wright would have a visit that particular Saturday. If that failed to happen then the murder attack would have been postponed and rescheduled for the first visits of the New Year.

While confirming that they had been watching and planning to kill Billy Wright for a period of months, McWilliams revealed that the 27 December operation was not the original plan chosen by the INLA. Instead, the INLA said it had considered at least two other alternatives. The first was to launch a night-time attack on the LVF accommodation on H6. The plan involved three armed INLA volunteers breaking through the turnstiles on their wings in the early hours of the morning, crossing over the LVF exercise yards and forcing the turnstile to gain access to the accommodation area. Once inside the LVF wing it was the INLA's intention to eliminate Billy Wright inside his prison cell.

McWilliams said the INLA had been working on this type of plan for at least two months. They had been observing LVF prisoners going to and from their visits. Watching across the forecourt area, the INLA said it was possible to see the LVF prisoners entering their cells. However, although the INLA were fairly confident they knew the cells of a number of other senior LVF prisoners, they could not determine which cell belonged to Billy Wright. The plan, which, had it gone ahead would have involved an attack with handguns and grenades, was then abandoned.

Another possible attack which the INLA had considered at that time was just as audacious. According to McWilliams, shortly after his transfer to the Maze from Maghaberry, the LVF had asked for a meeting with the OC of the INLA prisoners held on H6. McWilliams said they had discussed arranging a meeting with the LVF in an office within the Circle area of H6. Once inside the Circle area the INLA's intention was to take control of the area and shoot Billy Wright dead. He did not give a reason why this particular plan had been abandoned in favour of the one to kill Wright as he sat in a prison van.

McWilliams said the INLA was confident that once they had managed to breach the security fence inside H6 nothing would have prevented them from killing Billy Wright. However, he admitted that the prison authorities had suspicions that an attack on Wright was being planned. Referring to prison officers' warnings of a possible attack taking place, McWilliams said: 'I don't believe that the administration took it as serious . . . obviously they did turn a blind eye on it. They were warned on numerous occasions, right, that there's a possibility that there's going to be trouble on the outside and inside; and at the end of the day they were warned on many, many times there throughout the last three or four months beforehand . . . that if Billy Wright and the LVF weren't removed from the republican block there would be trouble, so obviously they did turn a blind eye to it.'

McWilliams also maintained the INLA volunteers took advantage of what he described as 'security lapses' within the Maze and other weaknesses within the prison system. However he did not elaborate on what precisely he meant by 'security lapses'.

Surprisingly, McWilliams said he would be prepared to cooperate with any public inquiry into the murder of Billy Wright. He said the allegations that the INLA had colluded in the murder were completely untrue. The INLA had nothing to fear from any form of inquiry, he said.

'As I have said before . . . Billy Wright . . . at the end of the day, we knew what we were doing when we executed Billy Wright. It was through no help of any outsiders, only the INLA in conjunction with the leadership on the outside, that we carried it out, that we were able to carry out our operation.

'As I was saying, we have absolutely nothing . . . no fears of any inquiry and if they do want an independent inquiry we have absolutely no problems with it and would fully support the British government and we'd fully support any inquiry, right, calls for any inquiry, for the British government to instigate any inquiry, but at the same time what you've got to understand is here . . . yes we do support calls for an inquiry into Billy Wright but we also support calls for inquiries into the murders of other people, for instance you've got the like of Ronnie Bunting, Noel Lyttle and Miriam Daly who were murdered in controversial circumstances.'

Daly, an INLA member, was shot dead in the hallway of her home in Andersonstown Road, Belfast, in June 1980. Bunting and Lyttle, also members of the INLA, were shot dead in west Belfast in October 1980. The Ulster Defence Association/Ulster Freedom Fighters (UDA/UFF) were blamed for all three killings. However, republicans have always maintained Crown forces colluded with loyalist paramilitaries in all three killings.

At the conclusion of the interview McWilliams described the killing of Billy Wright as a positive blow for the peace process.

All three members of the INLA ASU responsible for the murder of Billy Wright were released from prison in October 2000 – after having served just two years of a life sentence for the murder. The three INLA killers were given early release from prison under the terms of the Belfast Agreement.

9. The Questions Begin

The trial of Christopher 'Crip' McWilliams, John Glennon and John Kennaway for the murder of Loyalist Volunteer Force leader Billy Wright opened at Downpatrick Crown Court on Monday, 19 October 1998. Mr Justice Kerr, sitting without a jury under the Diplock court system, conducted the trial.

The Diplock Court system has operated within Northern Ireland for a number of years. In the normal course of events a defendant will not be returned for trial to the Crown Court until about six or seven months after he has been charged with a scheduled offence. Technically, the defendant will appear at a Magistrate's court for a series of remands before his return for trial.

At the Preliminary Examination [PE] stage the defendant receives a copy of the statements of evidence of prosecution witnesses and is brought to court for a preliminary inquiry. During this particular hearing the defendant does not have to enter a plea of guilty or not guilty to the charge or charges but accepts whether or not there is a prima facie case to answer.

Once a prima facie case has been established (as it usually is) the person is returned for trial to the Crown Court and always receives an arraignment date once he or she is returned to the trial court. It is at the arraignment stage that a plea of guilty or not guilty is entered. The arraignment usually takes place within six weeks of the preliminary inquiry. In reality the whole court process usually lasts eighteen months to two years from when the person was first charged in the Magistrates Court before they were referred to the Crown Court, and indeed a longer time in more serious cases.

However, the murder trial of the three INLA volunteers lasted a little

over a day and a half. In normal circumstances a trial of this type
would have been expected to take up a reasonable amount of court
time, considering the nature of the offence. There was more than a
degree of surprise when, after the charges were put to them, the three
accused pleaded not guilty, but offered no evidence in their defence.
The decision by the three accused to offer no evidence in their defence
had the effect of ensuring that the majority of evidence gathered by the
police in relation to the case would not be required to secure a
conviction. However, it would also not be heard in open court where
it could be reported by the media.

As a result of the decision not to offer any form of defence nothing
of any substance came to light, which would have further fuelled the
embryonic suspicions that the Wright killing might not be as
straightforward as it first appeared. However, the trial, short as it was,
did throw up some interesting points.

First, the decision not to call certain witnesses was not solely
confined to the inquest into Billy Wright's death. The same scenario
arose during the course of the murder trial. An LVF prisoner, who at
that time was temporarily being held at Maghaberry Prison, had been
given a witness summons to attend the trial. The night before the trial
opened, the LVF prisoner asked prison staff at Maghaberry what time
he would be leaving the prison to go to Downpatrick Court. The
prisoner was told he would not be attending court. No reason was
given why the prisoner, an eyewitness to the murder, was not required
to attend or to give his evidence in open court. Another LVF prisoner,
who had witnessed the murder and had also received a summons to
attend court, was not required to do so. Again, no reason was given for
his non-attendance. Most surprisingly, Norman Green, the prisoner
who had been with Billy Wright when the INLA killers struck and who
had witnessed the actual shooting itself, was not even named in the list
of witnesses selected to give evidence at the trial. This appears to be an
unusual practice considering the nature of the evidence the three
prisoners could provide to the trial judge. It is even more puzzling
when none of the witnesses who did give their evidence to Judge Kerr
had actually witnessed the killing itself.

One member of prison staff who did give evidence at the murder
trial was Acting Governor John Brian Barlow, who was on duty in the
Maze security office on the morning of the killing. Although at this
time Barlow's evidence was considered of sufficient importance to
warrant his inclusion in the list of trial witnesses, some four months
later the Coroner, John Leckey, did not consider the same evidence

relevant during the course of the inquest touching on the death of Billy Wright.

A number of prison officers were also listed as witnesses; they included the H6 watchtower guard, Raymond Hill, and the officer on duty at the main gate air lock, John Seaward. The list of witnesses did not, however, include the name of prison officer Brian Thompson, who had been on duty in the entrance hall of H6 and who had witnessed the actions of the three INLA volunteers in the forecourt area.

It is hard to understand why the Director of Public Prosecutions considered eyewitness evidence unnecessary in this particular case. Indeed the DPP was so confident of their ground that their senior counsel called David Wright into an anteroom in Downpatrick Courthouse at lunchtime on the opening day of the murder trial and informed him that a conviction was beyond doubt. However, David Wright was far from impressed and retorted by telling the DPP counsel in plain language that he 'didn't need a wig and gown to see that'. David Wright also told the DPP that he could drive a 'coach and horses' through the evidence the Crown had presented to the Court that morning. He then left the room having made the DPP and RUC fully aware of his feelings.

Following the incident with the DPP, David Wright made his way into the entrance hall of Downpatrick Courthouse where his two daughters were already waiting. As they were standing, chatting about what had taken place, a group of men made their way in through the main door and past the Wright family. As the men, all members of the Northern Ireland Prison Service, were making their way across the hallway one of them turned around and walked back to where David Wright was standing. As he came face to face with David Wright he slipped a small piece of green paper into his hand. The man then turned and walked back to rejoin his companions at the other end of the hallway. It was an incident that had passed almost unnoticed. Certainly the security staff and police officers on duty at the courthouse failed to spot what had happened. David Wright then made his way to the cloakroom area where he examined the small piece of green paper. On it were written the words:

> Mr Wright, please ask *your lawyers* to contact solicitors [in Co. Antrim]. Ref the suppression of statements by the D.P.P. Don't use your own telephone.

The man who had handed over the piece of paper was Brian

Thompson, the prison officer who had been on duty in the entrance hall of H6 on the morning of the murder. Thompson, although present in court that particular morning, had not been included in the list of witnesses drawn up by the Director of Public Prosecutions.

At the conclusion of the murder trial, O'Rourke, McDonald and Tweed, based in the Co. Antrim town of Larne, were contacted. It was subsequently confirmed that statements made by members of the prison service were lodged with the practice. It was clear to David Wright, even at that early stage of his investigation, that there was a deliberate policy within certain sections of the State to prevent the circumstances of his son's murder becoming public knowledge. However, despite their initial attempts to assist David Wright with his investigations in the murder, members of the prison staff later pulled back, despite numerous promises to the contrary, and have remained tight-lipped ever since.

The incident involving Brian Thompson served to confirm, as far as David Wright was concerned, that the trial of the three INLA volunteers would serve no purpose other than to show that as far as the authorities were concerned justice had been done and had been seen to be done. The absence of the LVF witnesses ensured that the court and the media covering the trial remained oblivious to the many irregularities which had taken place within the Maze Prison and which culminated in the death of Billy Wright on 27 December 1997.

The failure to call Norman Green and two other LVF prisoners, who have stated they were prepared to voice their concerns in open court, ensured they were unable to raise such issues as:

- Why did prison staff refuse to unlock the entrance to the LVF exercise yards on the morning of the murder? Staff were asked on three occasions to do so but refused to carry out the request.
- The LVF exercise yards remained closed until well after the murder of Billy Wright had taken place. In contrast to the LVF wings, prison staff on the INLA wings opened the exercise yards there as normal that Saturday morning.
- Why, on the night before the murder, had the prison authorities given the INLA a copy of the LVF visits lists for Saturday, 27 December 1997? This was the first and only recorded instance of this happening. The LVF visits lists also included details of the INLA visits.
- Why was the LVF prison van parked alongside the INLA accommodation that particular morning instead of taking up its

normal position beside the LVF wing?

● Why had the prison officer manning the exercise yard watchtower been removed from his post twice on the morning of the killing?

● Why had prison management ignored warnings from staff and prisoners concerning the threat posed by the INLA?

However, the prisoners never got an opportunity to raise their concerns and it was not until the inquest into Billy Wright's death some four months later that the general public became aware of these issues and the questions they posed in relation the murder itself.

On the second morning of the trial it became apparent that it would soon conclude. With the conclusion of the prosecution case and the defence offering no evidence in support of the not guilty pleas by the three accused, the verdict was something of a formality.

Shortly after the luncheon adjournment, the judge found the three accused guilty of murder. All three – Christopher McWilliams, John Kennaway and John Glennon – were sentenced to life imprisonment for the murder of Billy Wright. However, unknown to the Wright family, all three INLA volunteers appeared at Downpatrick Court the following day charged with possessing firearms and ammunition with intent to endanger life. Once again all three were convicted and sentenced to 20 years' imprisonment. McWilliams' Certificate of Conviction reads as follows:

Christopher Michael Patrick McWilliams (DOB 14.2.62) was indicted, tried and convicted for that the said Christopher Michael Patrick McWilliams with others, on the 27th December 1997, in the County Court Division of Craigavon, murdered William Stephen Wright, contrary to Common Law.

That he, along with others, on 27th day of December 1997, in the County Court Division of Craigavon, had in their possession firearms and ammunition, namely a 9 mm Markov self-loading pistol and a .22-inch-long rifle, double-barrel superposed Derringer together with ammunition suitable for use in same, with intent by means thereof to endanger life or cause serious injury to property or to enable some other person by means to endanger life or cause serious injury to property, contrary to Article 17 of the Firearms (Northern Ireland) Order 1981.

And on the 20th day of October 1998 it was ordered that he
be sentenced as follows:
Count 1 – Life imprisonment.
Count 2 – Twenty years' imprisonment.
Total: Life imprisonment.

The inability of the murder trial to address the concerns he believed to
be relevant to his son's murder only served to compound David
Wright's belief that the truth had not yet been revealed.

David Wright also questioned the ability of the three INLA
volunteers to carry out his son's murder unaided. He believes the
INLA's publication of a full account in April 1999 of the operation
inside the Maze Prison was a clear indication of the concern that
existed within the splinter republican organisation over allegations that
they had colluded with the British state in carrying out the Wright
murder.

'They didn't like it when I accused them of collusion,' David Wright
said. 'But, before I made that comment I had been informed by very
reliable sources that the INLA was incapable of mounting such an
operation unaided. I have heard or seen nothing that would change
that opinion.'

David Wright specifically questions the ability of the three INLA
volunteers to put together the operation which resulted in his son's
death. However, it is only their ability to plan the operation and not
their ability to kill that he questions.

At this stage it is worth looking at the INLA's principal player in the
Wright murder, Christopher 'Crip' McWilliams, and the organisation
to which he belonged.

The Irish National Liberation Army is an extreme republican
paramilitary group established in 1974 as a breakaway from the Official
IRA. Most of the INLA's original membership was drawn from the Official
IRA and Official Sinn Fein. Initially the INLA used the name People's
Liberation Army (PLA). It has also used a number of cover-names, such
as the People's Republican Army (PRA) and the Catholic Reaction Force
(CRF). The INLA is a radical terrorist group dedicated to the removal of
British Forces from Northern Ireland and the eventual unification of
Ireland. The organisation remains dedicated to its objective of a 32-
county Irish socialist republic wherein the Irish working class will control
all means of production, distribution and exchange, administered by the
proletariat through worker's democracy. While acknowledging that
national liberation and socialism cannot be achieved through a military

victory by guerrilla forces in a national liberation campaign, the Irish Republican Socialist Party (IRSP) defend the right of a revolutionary force to employ this type of tactic wherever possible and useful in order to achieve its aims. The IRSP also understands that no parliamentary road to socialism currently exists. As a result it does not feel compelled to participate in all electoral campaigns. However, it is prepared to use parliamentary politics and hold elective office as a means to carrying out its propaganda and when possible to assist the self-organising of the working class towards attaining its immediate objectives.

Throughout Northern Ireland's Troubles, the INLA's actions have included bombings, killings, assassinations, extortion, robbery and kidnapping. During the 1980s the republican splinter group carried out a military campaign against what it termed 'the occupation forces of the Six Counties'. It also successfully carried out a number of high-profile assassinations, including those of Conservative MP Airey Neave within the Palace of Westminster, London, and the killing of loyalists such as Red Hand Commando member John McKeague. The INLA also bombed the Mount Gabriel radar station near Cork City in the Irish Republic. Members of the organisation have also been involved in a series of feuds after splinter groups have developed and a number of previous members have died as a result of the actions of former associates. During the ceasefires of 1994, the INLA did not declare a formal ceasefire. Instead it adopted a policy of no first strike.

In August 1977, Christopher McWilliams' 16-year-old brother Paul was shot dead in controversial circumstances by the British Army. Paul McWilliams, a member of the IRA's Fianna, was shot in the back as he tried to climb through a hole in a fence close to some shops in west Belfast. However, the British Army claimed he had been shot while throwing petrol bombs at the security forces. The army claimed it had only fired on McWilliams after he had ignored warnings to stop. At the inquest into Paul McWilliams' death, an army sergeant said the teenager and two other individuals had been throwing petrol bombs and continued to do so despite a number of warnings. At the time of his death Paul McWilliams had absconded from a training school where he had been detained after being convicted of riotous behaviour. Paul McWilliams' name appears on an IRA roll of honour. After his brother died, 13-year-old Christopher McWilliams placed a death notice in a local paper which read: 'Shot in the back by a coward and died a hero.'

Christopher McWilliams himself first came to the attention of the security forces in June 1984 when he was charged with possession of a weapon with intent and was jailed for 14 years. The charges related to an incident at a flat in the Lenadoon area of Belfast. Four armed INLA volunteers, along with a female colleague, were in the flat when it was raided by police officers. A number of shots were fired during the incident, one of which fatally wounded Constable Michael William Todd, aged 22, from the village of Lamberg near Lisburn, Co. Antrim. McWilliams was one of those arrested when police forced their way into the flat. Also arrested was Belfast man Gino Gallagher, who was later shot dead as part of a feud that split the INLA in the mid-1990s. Gallagher was shot dead as he attended a local Social Security Office on the Lower Falls Road, Belfast.

Within a few months of his release from prison after serving seven years of his fourteen-year sentence, McWilliams was back behind bars charged with the murder of Colin Mahon, a doorman at a Belfast snooker club. Colin Mahon was shot after a row broke out between McWilliams and a group of other patrons. Following the disturbance, McWilliams and some of his companions were ejected from the snooker club. Angry at what had happened, McWilliams collected a handgun and returned to the club, where he shot Colin Mahon dead. However, unknown to McWilliams, the killing had been recorded on a security camera at the snooker club and this evidence was later used to convict him of the Mahon murder.

Following his conviction and life sentence for the Mahon murder, McWilliams was imprisoned in Belfast's Crumlin Road Jail. A condition of McWilliams' conviction ensured that his life sentence for the Mahon killing did not begin until after he had served out the remaining seven-year licence which remained from his previous fourteen-year prison sentence.

Following his committal to Crumlin Road Prison, mainstream republican prisoners rejected McWilliams. This resulted in him being housed in the jail's C wing among the criminal fraternity and some other Irish People's Liberation Organisation (IPLO) members. One prisoner, who was on C wing at that time, said McWilliams quickly sought to establish himself as a 'hard-liner' amongst his fellow prisoners. At that time the IPLO prisoners in the Crumlin Road Prison were leaderless and it did not take McWilliams long to assert himself as a self-styled leader. He did so by attacking or initiating attacks on loyalist inmates who had dissociated themselves from their respective organisations. The attacks mainly involved the scalding of specific prisoners who McWilliams considered to be loyalists. There were also group attacks on lone Protestant inmates within the Crumlin Road Prison. However, during the time McWilliams was trying to assert himself within the prison, the IPLO was losing out in its feud with the INLA. Among those who died in the feud was McWilliams' former associate, Jimmy Brown, shot dead outside Clonard Monastery in August 1992. Security sources believed Brown, a former member of the INLA who had switched to the IPLO, had been involved in the smuggling of drugs into Ireland. They said Brown justified the IPLO involvement in drugs by claiming arms and equipment could be funded by the profits from drugs. The person believed to have been responsible for Brown's murder was later remanded in custody in the same wing where McWilliams was housed. As a result, tensions on the wing increased considerably and quickly spilled over into open violence in which McWilliams and his associates came out second best.

Following the confrontation the prison authorities moved to eliminate the possibility of any future internal violence by transferring McWilliams and his associates to other areas of the jail. As a result, McWilliams found himself among mainstream IRA prisoners who once again rejected him. A former republican prisoner said mainstream IRA prisoners consider McWilliams a common criminal and not a political prisoner. As a result of the mainstream republicans' refusal to accept McWilliams into their wings, he was locked in his cell for 23 hours per day. McWilliams was permitted a one-hour association per day in a small yard isolated from all the other prisoners. McWilliams and his associates were also not allowed to use the main canteen facilities or to attend mass with the other republican prisoners being held at Crumlin Road. The IRA never altered its stance on Christopher McWilliams during his time in the Belfast jail.

Following the closure of the Crumlin Road Prison, IRA prisoners in the Maze refused to accept McWilliams onto any of their H Blocks. As a result, McWilliams was transferred to Maghaberry Prison, Co. Antrim, where for the first few months of his incarceration he kept a low-key profile. However, according to republican sources it was not long before he once again involved himself in illicit activities inside the Co. Antrim Prison. However, the continuing internal friction and feuding inside the INLA itself resulted in spill-over effects within the Maze Prison. Each time there was *coup d'etat* within the INLA, prisoners on the losing side were expelled from the INLA wing at the Maze and transferred to Maghaberry to serve out the remainder of their sentences.

John Kennaway, one of McWilliams' associates in the Wright

killing, was one such prisoner. In all, Kennaway was expelled from the INLA wings twice and it was after he was transferred to Maghaberry that he became friendly with Christopher McWilliams. Former republican prisoners at Maghaberry alleged McWilliams and Kennaway had been making considerable profits by selling cannabis and other recreational drugs to prisoners. It was claimed that both men began to establish contacts with the INLA/IRSP outside the jail. Republican prisoners said McWilliams and Kennaway saw the murder of Gino Gallagher as an 'opportunity' to get back on side with their former comrades in the INLA/IRSP. A number of senior IRSP members were noted visiting both men at Maghaberry. Republican prisoners in Maghaberry at the time said they understood the visits involved the Gallagher faction (which had triumphed in the internal INLA feud) and were a bid to bring McWilliams and Kennaway back into the main INLA fold.

Meanwhile, at the same time as the INLA were negotiating with McWilliams and Kennaway about coming in from the cold, Billy Wright had been sentenced to eight years' imprisonment and had been placed in the Punishment and Segregation Unit (PSU) at Maghaberry Prison. In November 2001, the former governor of Maghaberry, Duncan McLaughlin, told David Wright he had taken the decision to place Billy Wright in the PSU under 23-hour lock-up amid fears for his safety. At that time the LVF leader was still under threat from some of his former associates in the Belfast Brigade of the UVF. He was also under threat of death from all sections of the republican movement.

Shortly after his arrival at Maghaberry, Billy Wright was approached by a member of the Northern Ireland Office who offered the LVF leader a move to a spare wing on H Block 6 at the Maze Prison outside Lisburn. According to one of Wright's associates in Maghaberry (the same prisoner also transferred to the Maze at the same time as Wright), the NIO official, whom he named as McNeill, wanted Billy Wright to take as many loyalists as possible with him to the Maze. At that time Maghaberry, which had a policy of complete integration, was home to a number of opposing loyalist factions and the prison authorities wanted to see as many as possible transferred out and into the segregated blocks at the Maze. Maghaberry had not been designed and purpose built to house paramilitary prisoners and the prison authorities were anxious not to allow the same culture that had evolved within the Maze to develop within the Co. Antrim prison.

Following his discussions at Maghaberry with the NIO official in April 1997, Billy Wright and three associates agreed to a transfer to a wing on H Block 6, HMP Maze. All four men entered the Maze Prison on 26 April 1997. However, just precisely whose idea it was to transfer the LVF prisoners to the Maze is debatable and requires some examination.

10. Contradiction and Conspiracy

According to Billy Wright's close associates the offer of a transfer to the Maze came directly from the Northern Ireland Office via its representative, Seamus McNeill. Prisoners who took part in the April 1997 discussions remain adamant that the transfer to H Block 6 was an NIO idea. That most certainly appears to be the case as Wright wrote in his petition requesting a transfer to the Maze that he had had his safety there assured. Clearly, Billy Wright knew the dangers of such a transfer and it was a decision he would not have taken without considerable thought and discussion with his fellow LVF prisoners. Indeed, those same LVF prisoners have confirmed that the NIO did in fact provide Billy Wright with specific assurances as to his physical safety within the Maze Prison. However, it is unclear just precisely what those assurances were.

David Wright has stated that during a visit to Maghaberry Prison his son told him he was happy to remain there if he could be afforded normal prison conditions and freedom to associate openly with his fellow prisoners. Such a remark indicates that Billy Wright himself did not feel unduly threatened by other loyalist prisoners or paramilitary groups within Maghaberry Prison. David Wright says the LVF prisoners themselves did not initiate the transfer to the Maze Prison.

However, during his meeting with Martin Mogg, Ken Crompton and Brian Barlow at the Maze Prison on 1 February 2000, David Wright was given a different version of the events surrounding his son's transfer to the Maze. According to Martin Mogg, shortly after he had arrived at Maghaberry Prison in March 1997, Billy Wright began a campaign to be transferred to the Maze Prison. Mogg said that on 11 March 1997 the LVF had threatened violence unless Wright's transfer was approved. Mogg said he spoke to Billy Wright who told him that, unless his transfer went ahead, it was his intention to go on a hunger strike. The hunger strike would be timed to culminate in or around the date of the annual Orange Order Drumcree Parade in Portadown in July.

Following this alleged threat, Mogg said he spoke with NIO security minister, Adam Ingram, and the decision was then taken to transfer Billy Wright to the Maze Prison. Mogg said Billy Wright had been advised by the NIO of the decision to transfer him to the Maze. Mogg said that at the same time Billy Wright was also advised that the LVF prisoners were to be accommodated on H Block 6 at the Maze in conjunction with members of the splinter republican group, the INLA. However, in November 2000 former Maghaberry Governor, Duncan McLaughlin, gave yet another version of the transfer procedure to David Wright.

The meeting between David Wright and Duncan McLaughlin took place at 17 University Avenue, Belfast, on the afternoon of 29 November 2000. The meeting, which took place at the request of Mr McLaughlin, came a matter of weeks after the publication of the British Irish Rights Watch report into the murder of Billy Wright. During the course of the meeting, Duncan McLaughlin confirmed 'categorically' that the request to transfer to the Maze had been initiated by Billy Wright himself. He also admitted that he personally took the decision to impose a 23-hour daily lock-up regime upon the LVF leader. However, McLaughlin said he had taken this particular decision after considering the threat to Billy Wright's life posed by other loyalist paramilitary groups held within Maghaberry Prison. Interestingly enough, Duncan McLaughlin substantiated David Wright's remarks that his son's preference was to remain in Maghaberry Prison. However, when pressed on the issues by David Wright, the former Maghaberry governor admitted that he had created the conditions that prevented Billy Wright remaining at Maghaberry Prison. The 23-hour lock-up and the absence of freedom of association left the LVF leader with no other alternative but to agree to the NIO offer of a transfer to the Maze Prison.

Duncan McLaughlin then told David Wright that he had requested the transfer of Billy Wright from Maghaberry to the Maze and that the Northern Ireland Prison Service headquarters in turn ratified the request. If this is the case then Duncan McLaughin's version of Billy Wright's transfer to the Maze contradicts Martin Mogg's claims that Wright himself had requested a transfer. It also questions Mogg's claims that the LVF had threatened violence and that Billy Wright was considering embarking on a hunger strike to achieve his object of a move to the Maze. McLaughlin made no mention of any threats whatsoever from any direction. It seems very strange that there should be such diversity between two senior members of the Northern Ireland Prison Service in relation to the transfer of a prisoner from one prison to another. In an effort to obtain clarity on this particular issue, David Wright wrote to the Northern Ireland Prison Service seeking access to the documentation they held in relation to his son's term of imprisonment between March 1997 and his death on 27 December 1997. The Northern Ireland Prison Service refused to allow David Wright access to any of its documentation in relation to his son. The Prison Service did say it had retained all paperwork relating to Billy Wright and the material would be available to any future inquiry into his death. Earlier, David Wright's solicitors had written to Prison Service headquarters warning them not to destroy any documentation relating to the loyalist leader.

Further anomalies also came to light when David Wright sought clarification on the transfer to the Maze of INLA volunteers, Christopher McWilliams and John Kennaway. According to Duncan McLaughlin, he had applied to have both McWilliams and Kennaway transferred out of Maghaberry following an incident at the prison in April 1997. That incident involved the INLA volunteers taking two prison officers hostage in what was claimed to be an abortive attempt to kill another republican prisoner. In the incident, both prisoners had used guns that had earlier been smuggled into the prison. However, the attempt failed and the INLA volunteers surrendered and handed over their weapons. As with the weapons used in the murder of Billy Wright, it was never discovered how the weapons used in the Maghaberry incident were brought into the prison. Later, both McWilliams and Kennaway boasted to other republican prisoners that their real target that day had been Billy Wright.

Following that incident, Duncan McLaughlin said he had wanted both McWilliams and Kennaway out of Maghaberry. McLaughlin claimed that following the hostage-taking incident both prisoners had become 'acceptable' to the INLA prisoners held in the Maze. In light of this, McLaughlin said he took the decision to recommend the transfer of McWilliams and Kennaway to the Maze. The request was subsequently ratified by Northern Ireland Prison Service headquarters. Duncan McLaughlin rejected a claim by David Wright that his decision to transfer the two INLA prisoners to the Maze had been a 'whim'. He said the primary reason behind the transfer of the two men was concern for the overall security situation within Maghaberry Prison.

However, during the meeting with Martin Mogg and other officials at the Maze, David Wright and Jeffrey Donaldson were told that McWilliams and Kennaway had been transferred to the Maze after threats had been made to their lives. Prison officials rejected suggestions that the transfer of the INLA volunteers had been as a result of the decision to move Billy Wright out of Maghaberry.

Christopher McWilliams' description of his transfer to the Maze is quite straightforward. 'Well I applied, myself and John Kennaway, to be transferred into Long Kesh (the Maze) at that particular time; it was just after the hostage situation in Maghaberry Prison when we took two prison officers hostage with pistols and actually, our request was granted for [us] to be moved into Long Kesh (the Maze).'

When asked if he had been surprised that, after he had been involved in the smuggling of guns into a prison, he had been placed in the same block as Billy Wright, McWilliams responded by saying: 'No I wasn't surprised because anyone there who requests to get off Maghaberry or any other prison, requests to get into republican wings are automatically granted because whenever it's cleared from the INLA prisoners then there's no stopping that, you're automatically transferred into the prison.'

McWilliams' version of the Northern Ireland Prison Service transfer procedures is amazing. However, it is not beyond the bounds of possibility that what he said actually did take place. What is certain, however, is that there is a considerable lack of clarity surrounding the truth behind the transfer of Billy Wright to the Maze Prison in April 1997. Three conflicting versions of the transfer exist. Which is correct; that of Martin Mogg, Duncan McLaughlin or Billy Wright himself? In all probability, the answers lie in the Prison Service papers themselves. However, it is hard to understand why Billy Wright, in light of the obvious danger to his life posed by both loyalist and republican paramilitaries, would agree to a transfer to the Maze, unless, as he himself had written in his application, he had had his safety assured. Once again the question has to asked and answered: who gave Wright those assurances and what precisely did they entail? Either way, they had their desired effect in securing Billy Wright's transfer to H Block 6 HMP Maze.

Not long after Billy Wright's move had taken place, he was joined by a number of other disaffected loyalist prisoners on the LVF wing in H6. As a result of the increased numbers, the prison authorities decided to move the LVF prisoners from their single-wing accommodation to C and D wings on H6. The INLA prisoners, who were currently occupying those two wings at that time, were simply transferred across the block to A and B wings. It appears to be a strange decision to move both sets of paramilitary prisoners onto each other's accommodation. H Block 6 had four wings. The INLA occupied C and D wings, the LVF were accommodated on A wing leaving B wing empty and available for use. Would it not have been simpler for the prison authorities to give the additional LVF prisoners in the Maze the use of B wing therefore eliminating the logistical problems involved in moving both sets of prisoners to new accommodation? Clearly B wing was in a state of readiness as the INLA prisoners on their move immediately occupied it. Why then did the prison authorities consider it necessary to place the LVF prisoners on C and D wings? No explanation has been given for the move.

Following their move across to C and D wings, LVF prisoners claimed their movements to and from H Block 6 were constantly being monitored by the INLA. The LVF claimed they had noticed one particular prisoner, Rory McCallan, a close associate of Christopher McWilliams, observing them from his cell window on A wing. McCallan was a former member of the IPLO and was serving a lengthy term of imprisonment for the attempted murder of a Protestant man in Belfast. Although the LVF prisoners made their concerns known, they said the prison authorities did nothing to address the matter.

However, a former LVF prisoner on H6 at the same time as Billy Wright said Maze Governor Martin Mogg approached the LVF leader with a view to the prisoners and management meeting on a regular basis. Mogg's suggestion was that he and his fellow governors would meet a delegation of the LVF prisoners at a monthly meeting and any areas of concern could be raised and discussed. The offer was accepted and the LVF members who made up the delegation nominated to attend the meetings with the prison management were: Billy Wright, Billy King, Gary Blair and Jeff Deeney. Initially the main area of concern raised by the LVF delegation centred on them having to share a block with the INLA. One of the LVF prisoners present said they had made it clear to the prison governors that as neither the LVF nor the INLA were on ceasefire, the continued housing of both groups within the same H Block was a 'recipe for disaster'. However, despite the issue being raised by the LVF the situation on H6 remained the same.

Matters came to a head in August 1997, when LVF prisoners, angry by the prison authorities' failure to provide them with proper education, facilities, Saturday visits and a designated visiting area, began a series of disturbances within their wings. As a result of the disturbances extensive damage was caused to the LVF accommodation. The prison authorities reacted by moving the LVF prisoners out of H6 and into a wing on H2 where they were held under Rule 32 – 23-hour lock-up. The LVF prisoners remained on H2 in the Maze until their accommodation area on H6 had been repaired and refurbished. The LVF prisoners returned to their original accommodation on H6 in October 1997. Upon their return to H6, prison management advised the LVF prisoners that an INLA blanket death threat had been issued against them. Again it must be asked, if the prison authorities at the Maze were aware of the death threats issued against the LVF by the INLA in October 1997, why did they allow them to return to H6? Surely, in light of the imminent danger to the lives of the LVF inmates it would have been safer to let them remain in H2. Once again the prison authorities and the Northern Ireland Office have failed to provide an acceptable answer to this question. Obviously such an important decision could only have been made at a senior level within the prison service. Who took that decision and why were the LVF prisoners returned to the volatile situation that existed within H Block 6 at the Maze?

It must also be pointed out that only upon their return to H6 in October 1997, two months before the murder of Billy Wright, did the LVF prisoners begin receiving regular Saturday-morning visits. However, it is essential to note that at no time during the period from October to December 1997 did Billy Wright ever take a Saturday-morning visit at the Maze. How, then, can the INLA's claim that they monitored the pattern of Wright's visits before selecting a Saturday morning to launch their murder operation against him stand up to scrutiny?

Within days of their return to C and D wings on H6, prison staff told LVF prisoners how Christopher McWilliams had boasted of the INLA's intention to 'launch a spectacular' within the Maze Prison. Prison staff also said they had noticed suspicious activity within the INLA wing itself. In particular, INLA prisoners had been noticed at the grilles leading to the airlock observing the movements of prisoners entering and leaving the LVF wings via their own air-lock system. As well as reporting their concerns to the LVF prisoners, prison staff also made their concerns known to prison management on at least three occasions. These included written submissions to Maze Governor Martin Mogg, warning of the increasing threat posed to the LVF by the INLA.

Normally, it would be expected that senior prison management would have reacted in some manner to these warnings, especially as prison staff were voicing them. Prison staff at the Maze had been at the cutting edge and interface of prison life since the prison first opened in March 1976. It has been officially stated that prison officers were thoroughly trained and professional individuals competent in every aspect of their job. Surely such professionalism would have included the ability to instinctively tell when prisoners were acting in an unusual and suspicious manner? Prison staff have said, following years of working with some of the most hardened terrorist prisoners, that they could recognise and decode behavioural patterns and detect whether or not there was a sinister inference attached to what initially appeared to be an off-the-cuff remark. If this was so, why did the prison management at the Maze fail to respond to the warnings and concerns raised by prison officers in respect of the suspicions they had about the possibility of an INLA attack on the LVF?

The LVF prisoners have said that when they also raised the possibility of an INLA strike against them with Maze Governor Martin Mogg, and asked him what he intended to do about the matter, his response astounded them. According to the LVF prisoners Martin Mogg informed them that he had spoken to the INLA command structure within the Maze Prison and they had assured him that they would not move against the LVF prisoners. As a result of these assurances from the INLA, the LVF said the governor had chosen to disregard the warning and written submissions made by members of the prison staff on H6. One of the LVF delegation members said he had been amazed that the governor of what was claimed to be the most secure jail in Western Europe was prepared to take the word of a 'maverick' and unpredictable republican organisation instead of the openly expressed concerns of prison staff. The former prisoner said the LVF delegation had left the meeting with Martin Mogg in the knowledge that, 'we were now sitting ducks for an INLA sniper attack at the very least'. The former prisoner described the governor's acceptance of the INLA assurance of no violence towards the LVF as 'the personification of gullibility and naivety'. At that stage the former LVF prisoner said they realised that they could no longer rely upon the prison management at the Maze for protection.

In light of this alarming development, the former prisoner said, under the guidance and direction of Billy Wright the LVF prisoners decided to take their own precautions in order to minimise the possibility of INLA attack. For example, Wright insisted that all the prison vans taking the LVF prisoners to their visiting area should enter the forecourt area of H6 and reverse up to the entrance door to the accommodation area itself. This, Wright believed, would make it more difficult for the INLA to attack the loyalist prisoners as they were leaving the block on their way to a visit. The LVF also insisted that when the prison van reversed up to the entrance door it parked on the side closest to their accommodation. This remained the practice until the morning of the murder, when the white van allocated to the LVF visits had been parked alongside the INLA wings. The LVF prisoners in H6 also refused to share the use of the electronic floor cleaner or episcope with their INLA counterparts, the LVF arguing that there was a real possibility that the INLA prisoners could conceal a booby-trap bomb device within the cleaner itself. The former prisoner accepted that these actions might now appear to have been fruitless and borne little success, as later events proved. However, in November and December 1997, with the LVF prisoners living under what to them was a very real and constant threat, he said the actions had meaning and purpose.

The former loyalist prisoner recalled how in early December 1997, the INLA began work on a republican mural on a wall between A and B wings close to the sterile area leading into the Circle. The location of the mural inside the two metal grilles afforded anyone working on the mural a direct line of sight across the Circle area and into the LVF wings opposite. The prisoner said the LVF found it strange because when they had first moved onto the vacated INLA accommodation on H6 some months earlier there were no murals of any description on any of the walls. They said they had questioned why the INLA had decided to begin work on a wall mural at that point in time. The LVF also questioned the location of the mural itself. They were puzzled as to why the INLA wanted to paint a mural on a wall leading out of their accommodation rather than choose a location central to the wing itself. The LVF prisoner said hindsight had told them precisely why the INLA had selected a wall directly opposite the LVF wing.

Billy Wright's father, David, had been made aware of the LVF prisoners' concerns in relation to the possibility of attack by the INLA in the months preceding December 1997. During his meeting with the management of the Maze Prison in February 2000, David Wright sought to clarify a number of the outstanding issues surrounding his son's death. When he asked why, in light of the concerns of prison staff, the LVF prisoners had continued to be housed on H6, David Wright was told no other accommodation had been available within the Maze at that time. However, it was clear that alternative accommodation had been available as the LVF were being housed in an area of H2 during the time their own accommodation on H6 was being repaired following the disturbances of August 1997. In relation to claims that the INLA prisoners, McWilliams and Kennaway had said they were 'out to get Billy Wright', prison management confirmed that they had not received any intelligence to confirm this statement. However, Prison Governor Ken Crompton did admit to David Wright and Jeffrey Donaldson MP that there had been a reasonable amount of tension between the LVF and INLA in the few months preceding the shooting of Billy Wright. During the course of the meeting it became known that the Board of Visitors at the Maze had also mentioned the concerns of prison officers at the Maze in relation to the potential threat to the LVF posed by the INLA. Crompton said these concerns related to the Circle area of H6 and the agreement which allowed the prison visits van to enter the forecourt area on H6.

When asked about evidence given by prison officer Brian Thompson during the inquest into Billy Wright's death, that he and another prison officer called Gillam had met with Crompton, a Governor Eagleston and an Acting Governor Ramsden on 24 October 1997 and had voiced concerns about the security of the roof area and the possibility of a shooting on H6, Crompton said he had no recollection of such a meeting ever having taken place. Furthermore, Crompton confirmed that there was no record of any meeting between prison staff and prison management for 24 October 1997. Clearly one of the two parties is incorrect in relation to this particular meeting. Either it took place or it did not. If it did, as officer Thompson testified under oath, then what have the prison authorities got to hide by denying it ever took place? Clearly quite a lot because Thompson has said he and his colleague made the prison management aware of the dangers posed by the INLA and the lack of security concerning the roof area of H6. If, as Thompson says, management were alerted to these concerns, why did they not take action of some form or another? If management failed to act then a denial that the meeting had ever taken place would seem plausible and a means of avoiding responsibility for subsequent events within the Maze. If such a meeting did not take place then why did prison staff say it did? Was it an attempt to place responsibility for Wright's death onto the prison management and thereby absolve them of blame? Or were in fact the prison officers accurate in their recollection of the events of 24 October 1997? Prison officer Brian Thompson is adamant that he is correct. Thompson has said that he and his colleagues had made the prison management aware of the threat posed by the INLA and the lack of security concerning H6. If, as Thompson says, Management were alerted to these concerns, why did they not take some form of action?

When asked about a security camera at the Maze which had been defective on the morning of the Wright murder, management confirmed that the pan tilt zoom camera overlooking the roofs of H6 had been reported defective by prison staff in the prison's Emergency Control Room at 11:45 a.m. on 22 December 1997 – five days prior to the murder of Billy Wright. It was also confirmed that the camera still remained inoperative on the morning of the murder itself despite the role it played in the overall security of the Maze. The explanation given was quite astonishing. David Wright was told that responsibility for the repair of the Maze security cameras lay with an outside contractor. In this particular instance there was no record of when the contractor had been notified of the defect or indeed when the camera itself had actually been repaired. What is certain, however, is that the security camera covering the roof accessed by the INLA prisoners on their way to murder Billy Wright was not operating at the time of the murder. Therefore the perpetrators could not be detected crossing the roof area. Prison management admitted that the situation which existed in relation to the security camera was 'not acceptable'.

When asked how the INLA prisoners had managed to smuggle weapons into a high-security prison, a member of prison staff said they had been unable to determine exactly how this had taken place. However, he said it was important to remember the size of the weapons themselves, pointing out that a police search of the INLA wings after the murder of Billy Wright had missed an item of equipment which was later uncovered by prison staff. This failure by the RUC to uncover the item of equipment tends to question the thoroughness of their initial search of the INLA wings in the aftermath of the murder.

However the possibility that the murder weapons were brought into the Maze by members of staff has not been dismissed. It is noted that the Narey Report observed that there were only very cursory searches of prison staff by other colleagues when they reported for duty at the Maze Prison and indeed sometimes the searches appeared not to have taken place at all. Another member of the management team said he believed it possible that the component parts of the weapons could have been smuggled into the prison concealed in the body orifices of visitors. However, while this theory would seem feasible in relation to the Derringer pistol, the same could not apply to all the parts of the Markov semi-automatic pistol. Any person, male or female, attempting to conceal the 'L'-shaped pistol grip section of this type of pistol inside a body orifice would have experienced remarkable discomfort in an upright position, to say the least. What an individual would have experienced whilst attempting to walk is another thing altogether. Certainly, at the very least, the individual would have aroused the interest if not the suspicions of even the most unalert prison officer.

The prison management proved to be somewhat vague over the issue of when the INLA volunteers had managed to cut the hole in the prison fence leading to A wing exercise yard. Acting Governor Barlow was of the opinion that the hole had been cut the night before the murder itself. It was confirmed that the exercise yard security cameras had been fully operational throughout the whole Christmas period but that they had failed to detect the INLA prisoners cutting the wire. However, if the INLA are correct, then they already knew cameras could not detect them or for that matter anyone else as the area they had chosen was a blind spot. Once again it must be asked: how did the INLA know the precise spot they had selected to breach the wire was a blind spot? Were they personally made aware of this or had they had access to information to tell them precisely where to cut the fence? Once again, this aspect of the murder has never been satisfactorily resolved by any of the investigations, which the government say have been both thorough and rigorous.

11. 'Stand Down the Guard!'

When David Wright raised the matter of the removal of the prison officer from his post in the observation tower overlooking the INLA exercise yard on the morning of Saturday, 27 December 1997, senior governors at the Maze admitted that the tower 'should not have been dropped'. However, when asked who would have issued the order to stand down the guard in the observation post, David Wright was told: 'Security would have ordered dropping H6 tower.'

By security, prison management were referring directly to the internal system within the Maze operated by members of prison staff. Clearly, both Mogg and Crompton were admitting, in the presence of Jeffrey Donaldson MP, that the order to remove the guard from his post that particular morning had been issued by a member of staff from the internal security section of the Maze Prison. It had already been established at the inquest into Billy Wright's death that the Security Governor of the Maze Prison, Stephen Davis, had not been on duty in the Maze when Billy Wright was shot dead. Martin Mogg and Kenneth Crompton were also absent from the Maze on the morning of the murder. It had also already been established that three governor grades were on duty that particular morning: Governor Maguire, Governor McKee and Acting Governor Barlow. Despite extensive enquiries and repeated requests to the NIO for clarity, it has not been possible to publicly identify the person who was in overall control of the Maze Prison on Saturday, 27 December 1997. Although David Wright has been made aware of the officer's identity by prison staff within the Maze, he has chosen not to make that information public.

As a result of a judicial review application in February 2001 at the Belfast High Court, David Wright was given access to the depositions of two potential inquest witnesses who had not been called to give evidence during the inquest. Initially, the Coroner for Greater Belfast had denied David Wright access to the documents. However, following the hearing of the judicial review application before Mr Justice Kerr in February 2001, the Coroner's office handed over the relevant depositions, accepting that David Wright had been entitled to have access to them under the current human rights legislation. One of the withheld depositions/statements was that of Acting Governor John Brian Barlow – one of the three governor grades on duty at the Maze on the day of the murder. Barlow's statement reads: 'At around 10:00 a.m. I was in the security department when I received a telephone call from the Emergency Control Room stating that an alarm had been received from H Block 6. I did not know the caller.'

It is unclear from his statement whether or not Barlow was the person in charge of Maze security on 27 December 1997. If he was then it is logical to conclude that he would have been aware of the order to stand down the guard from the observation post overlooking the INLA exercise yards on H6. He would also have known the origin of the order and who had issued it in the first place. If it came from a higher authority within the Maze, where did it come from? If it was the Maze security department who issued the order, why was it given and who gave it? After all, there was an internal agreement in place that this particular post should not be stood down under any circumstances. Why was that agreement broken for the first time just minutes before Billy Wright was shot dead? Acting Governor Barlow may not have been able to provide the answers to all those questions, but he could have at least confirmed whether or not he was the officer in charge of the Maze security on 27 December 1997. However, none of these questions could be put to Acting Governor Barlow, as he was one of the two inquest witnesses not required to give evidence during the course of the inquest into the death of Billy Wright.

Having established that the Maze security section would have issued the order standing down the observation tower on H6, Martin Mogg proceeded to contradict the evidence of Raymond Hill, the officer who had been on duty in the post at the time of the murder. In his evidence to Mr Justice Kerr during the October 1998 trial of the three INLA volunteers, Raymond Hill stated under oath that he had been ordered from his post twice on the morning of the murder. During the February 1999 inquest into Billy Wright's death he again stated he had twice been ordered to leave his post in the observation tower on the morning of 27 December 1997. In a meeting with David Wright, Hill again was adamant that he had been ordered to quit his post on two occasions shortly before the murder of Billy Wright took place. However, in February 2000, Maze Governor Martin Mogg told David Wright that Hill had been mistaken and he had only been stood down from the observation post once on the morning of the killing. What evidence the Maze Governor had to support that claim has never been made public. Does he base his claim on information recorded in the H6 Control Room Journal on the day of the murder? If so, why was the journal not used to contradict Hill's evidence at the inquest and murder trial? Had the information been supplied to Martin Mogg via a third party? If so what was the source of the information and why has it not been made public? Again, as neither Martin Mogg nor Kenneth Crompton were listed as witnesses at any of the public investigations into the murder of Billy Wright it has not been possible to put any of these questions directly to them. It is worth noting that David Wright made two requests, one written and one verbal, to the Coroner to have Martin Mogg, Kenneth Crompton and another senior member of the Prison Service, Alan Shannon, added to the list of inquest witnesses. On both occasions David Wright's requests were refused.

It is also worth noting that the senior governors at the Maze confirmed that there was no entry of the phone call ordering the standing down of the observation tower recorded in the H6 principal officer's journal for 27 December 1997. Considering the significance of such a phone call and the local agreement which existed in relation to the H6 watchtowers, it is difficult to understand why this fact was not recorded in the journal. There can be no disputing the fact that the call was made to H6. Senior officer Arthur Gallagher, who was on duty alongside senior officer Brian Patrick Molloy in H Block 6 prior to the shooting, confirms this in his inquest deposition. However, the section of Gallagher's deposition containing this piece of information had been redacted before it was handed out at the inquest. The redacted portion of Gallagher's deposition, though, proved possible to read and it states:

> Prior to this incident taking place, I had been in the PO's bunk with PO Molloy when we received a telephone call from the AIMS office directing us to remove the men from the two observation towers and send them to work in the visits area. The caller was informed that we were already understaffed and that the officer in the observation tower overlooking C and D wings had already been removed to work on the block. We were instructed to have the officer in the tower overlooking A

and B wings sent to visits. The officer was called from the tower and informed of this direction, but he objected and telephoned a member of the Prison Officer's Association, expressing his opinion that he should not be stood down from the tower. A short time later we received a call from a member of the POA, who I believe was John Blundell, who informed us that the tower should not be left unmanned. I informed the officer of this and he returned to the observation tower.

As only Gallagher and Molloy were present when the call was received, only one of them could have taken the call. It has never been established which officer it was. In his statement to the RUC, Molloy makes no mention whatsoever of any telephone call ordering the standing down of the observation tower. It appears strange that he would fail to mention such a significant occurrence or to realise its relevance in relation to the events that subsequently unfolded that morning. It is also possible that the RUC detectives investigating the murder did not question him about the telephone call. If that is the case, further questions are raised in relation to the thoroughness of the overall police investigation into Billy Wright's murder. However, it is the redaction of the section of Gallagher's deposition referring to the telephone call that causes most concern. Why was it redacted in the first place considering its relevance to the chain of events within the Maze on 27 December 1997? David Wright wrote to the Coroner, John Leckey, on 21 September 2000 seeking clarification on the Gallagher statement. In a reply dated 22 September 2000, Siobhan Broderick, solicitor to the Coroner stated:

> You ask about the alteration of the deposition of senior officer Arthur Gallagher. In advance of the inquest the statement that senior officer Arthur Gallagher had made to the police who were conducting the criminal investigation into the death of your son was typed into the form of a draft deposition. On reading that draft, HM Coroner concluded that the final paragraphs of the witness statement of Mr Gallagher were not relevant to the purpose of the inquest and for that reason he caused those paragraphs to be deleted.

David Wright and others find the comments that the Coroner concluded a section of a deposition, which clearly proved a telephone call ordering the standing down of a vital observation post had been received by a senior prison officer on duty in H6 on the morning Billy Wright was shot dead was not relevant to the inquest, surprising. The Coroner also decided to stand down one of the individuals mentioned in the redacted section of the Gallagher deposition. When asked why he had done so the Coroner's solicitor's letter of the 22 September said:

> You ask why HM Coroner decided not to call Mr Barlow and Mr Molloy to give evidence at the inquest and whether HM Coroner recorded the reasons for such a decision. Having considered all the evidence available to the inquest HM Coroner concluded that it was not necessary for Mr Barlow and Mr Molloy to give evidence as to how your son came by his death on 27 December 1997. HM Coroner did not record the reasons for his decision.

David Wright disagrees with the Coroner's decision not to call both Barlow and Molloy to give evidence at the inquest. Both were on duty in the Maze at the time of the murder. Molloy is alleged to have been the officer in charge of H Block 6 that particular morning. Surely his evidence would have been extremely relevant especially in the light of the redacted section of senior officer Gallagher's deposition? Barlow was one of the three governor grades on duty within the prison and by his own admission was in the security department when he received notification of a shooting incident on H6. From shortly after that point in time, Barlow was present on H6 speaking to both INLA and LVF prisoners. In fact it can be said that he oversaw events on H6 following the murder of Billy Wright. It should be noted that Barlow and Molloy were named on the witness list, summonsed and present at Downpatrick Courthouse during the inquest and ready to give evidence if called, but it was at lunchtime on the third day of the inquest that the counsel for the Coroner advised both men that they were not required to give evidence.

However, the failure to call Barlow and Molloy prevented David Wright from receiving the opportunity to cross-examine them as to the chain of events, that culminated in the death of his son and would possibly have shed some light on the circumstances leading up to the murder.

Neither Martin Mogg nor Kenneth Crompton were able to throw any light whatsoever on the irregularities surrounding the INLA and LVF visiting lists for Saturday, 27 December 1997. They could not explain the discrepancies between the two sheets, nor could they explain why two different sheets had been presented at the inquest. Despite the fact that the handwriting was identical on all the visiting sheets, prison management could offer no explanation as to why there were so many obvious irregularities. However, it was accepted that the visiting sheet given to David Wright by the LVF prisoners within days of the murder and submitted to the inquest was the sheet given to the LVF prisoners by prison staff on the evening of 26 December 1997. In light of this they could not explain the origins of the document submitted to the inquest by the prison authorities, which purported to be the original visits list drawn up by auxiliary prison officer Jacqueline Wisely. No explanation was ever offered as why the LVF visiting list had been given to the INLA the night before the murder.

Among those present at the February 2000 meeting in the Maze was Acting Governor John Brian Barlow – one of the three governor grades on duty at the Maze Prison on 27 December 1997. As a Grade V officer, Barlow would have held a junior status within the governor grades in the Northern Ireland prison system. However, one particular comment he made during the course of that visit to the Maze is interesting to note.

Following their discussions with the prison management, David Wright, Jeffrey Donaldson and the author were taken on a tour of the murder scene on H Block 6. At that time the Maze was still an operational prison and two wings, A and B, on H6 were still occupied by a number of LVF prisoners. Some of these prisoners had been on H6 when Billy Wright was shot dead. However, there was no contact between the prisoners and David Wright on that particular occasion. The presence of the LVF prisoners on A and B wings also prevented a visit to the accommodation area taking place. Nevertheless, the visit proved both informative and enlightening. It also helped to provide a greater understanding of the logistics involved in the INLA murder operation. As well as being allowed into the forecourt and exercise yards of H6, the prison authorities also agreed to allow all three visitors to view and enter the observation tower overlooking A and B wing exercise yard.

The first thing that became apparent on entering the observation tower was the clarity of vision and the area visible to the occupant. As well as having a clear and unobstructed view of the exercise yards, it was also possible to see across and into a section of the forecourt area itself. While it was accepted that it would have proved extremely difficult, if not almost impossible, to spot where the hole had been cut in the security fence, it was obvious to anyone standing in the tower that the area would have been clearly visible to the officer on duty – a fact confirmed by all three visitors and supported by the photographic evidence taken by an official photographer supplied by the Northern Ireland Prison Service. When this was pointed out to members of prison management present in the watchtower it produced a surprising response from Acting Governor Brian Barlow in relation to the events of Saturday, 27 December 1997.

Following David Wright's comments that had a prison officer been present in the watchtower when the three INLA volunteers entered the exercise-yard area he would have become suspicious when they began to remove the cut section of fencing, Barlow said: 'Mr Wright, it didn't make any difference what time of the day it was. Eight o'clock, nine o'clock, ten o'clock, eleven o'clock or twelve o'clock, they were going ahead that day.'

Although the Maze management stated that they did not know how the weapons used by the INLA to kill Billy Wright had been smuggled into the Maze Prison, they did confirm that certain improved security measures had been in place within the Maze since May 1997. These measures had been outlined by the then Northern Ireland Minister of State Adam Ingram to the House of Commons on 21 January 1998 – a matter of weeks after the murder of Billy Wright had taken place.

Pages 978–84 of *Hansard* record in detail the parliamentary exchanges between the minister and the Lagan Valley Ulster Unionist MP, Jeffrey Donaldson.

However, it is important to detail what the minister told the House in response to Jeffrey Donaldson's remarks in relation to the concerns expressed by the people of Northern Ireland about the prison service, the competence of those who ran the service and those in ministerial positions who had the ultimate responsibility for prisons in Northern Ireland.

Pages 984–7 of *Hansard*, dated 21 January 1998, read:

> 1.19 p.m.
> The Minister of State, Northern Ireland Office [Mr Adam Ingram]: I congratulate the hon. Member for Lagan Valley [Mr Donaldson] on having obtained this Adjournment debate. In the time available after all the interventions from Opposition Members, I might not be able to deal with all his points, but I shall do my best.
>
> The hon. Gentleman mentioned the Steele Report[1] and it should be put on record that the decision not to publish that report was taken by the previous Government. The incoming Government took on board the range of measures set out in

that report, which specifically dealt with a tunnel escape attempt and set out various means of avoiding such escape attempts in the future. I shall comment on those measures later.

The hon. Gentleman made several strong criticisms of the operational regime at the Maze and in respect of recent incidents, including the escape of Liam Averill and the murder of Billy Wright. Unfortunately, many of his accusations and the conclusions he draws from them are based on, as yet, unsubstantiated allegations made by a number of sources, some of them anonymous. That is not to say that I am dismissing them out of hand – far from it. There can be no question that the escape of Liam Averill and the murder of Billy Wright were extremely serious breaches of security. Those incidents have cast considerable doubt on the effectiveness of the security arrangements that were in operation at the prison at the time and, as the hon. Gentleman said, they have seriously damaged public confidence in the management and control of the prison.

Let me assure the hon. Gentleman that I share each and every one of the concerns that he raises. I can equally assure him that all the points he makes are taken very seriously indeed. Later in my speech, I shall return to the way in which the Government are dealing with them. However, before I do so, it is important to place the Maze Prison and those who are held there, in proper context.

I have said this before, both in the house and elsewhere, but it is worth repeating: the Maze is unique. There is no prison anywhere in the democratic world that has such a concentration of terrorist murderers or those convicted of terrorist-related crimes – more than 500 dedicated terrorists who consider themselves not to be criminals, but prisoners of war. It should also be remembered that 29 prison officers have been killed and innumerable numbers threatened, along with their families, over the past 25 years or so. That is the reality not mentioned by the hon. Gentleman.

Mr Donaldson: As many of the murdered prison officers were constituents of mine, let me make it absolutely clear that we deplore those murders. We have nothing but the utmost admiration for the prison officers of Northern Ireland and nothing in what I have said is intended as a criticism of them. My remarks are a criticism of management and of those in principal control in the Northern Ireland Office; in no way are they a criticism of the prison officers who serve in the Maze Prison.

Mr Ingram: Of course I fully understand the hon. Gentleman's point, but he did not mention the Maze Prison's uniqueness, nor did he try to place what happens in that prison in context or acknowledge the pressures on serving officers resulting from having to deal with those difficult prisoners. That creates unique and difficult conditions, which run throughout the management of the prison, from bottom to top and from top to bottom. That reality should never be ignored by those who comment on events and the regime at the Maze.

Given those conditions, the attendant security and control problems are understandably and uniquely complex and difficult when balanced against the need to maintain a humanitarian regime. Those who are charged with the management responsibility of undertaking such a challenging role are regularly faced with the need to make difficult and sensitive decisions about security at the prison. That is an unenviable task, which they have to perform on our behalf.

That situation is what the Government have faced since taking office last May and what previous Governments have faced in the years before that. It is why the Government have put in place a progressive programme of tightened security measures, including twice daily head counts; cell fabric checks; a comprehensive search of cells and the blocks; control of materials available to prisoners; the installation of enhanced closed-circuit television in the blocks; and the scanning of all visitors along with other measures, with more to come.

It is not the case, as the hon. Gentleman maintains, that security has been relaxed since May. The opposite is true, as the measures I have described prove. Of course, the matter does not rest there. In light of the most recent, extremely serious breaches of security, my right hon. friend the Secretary of State has commissioned a full, rigorous independent inquiry into events at the Maze. She has also asked Her Majesty's Chief Inspector of Prisons to carry out a full inspection at the Maze Prison when the inquiry team has completed its work and reported its findings. Both those reports will be published and copies placed in the Library of the House.

The inquiry is well under way and its report is expected soon, I understand that the hon. Member for Lagan Valley has taken the opportunity to put his views directly to the inquiry team and I have no doubt that what he has already submitted and what he said in the House today, if that differs from his submission, will be fully considered by the inquiry team. However, as the inquiry is not yet complete, I am sure that the hon. Gentleman will understand why it would be inappropriate for me to respond today to his detailed points.

I am, of course, only too well aware of the considerable speculation about what actually happened before, during and after the circumstances that led to the murder of Billy Wright. However, as the hon. Gentleman knows, that murder is the subject of a Royal Ulster Constabulary investigation and any criminal charges, which may flow from it. The hon. Gentleman clearly has his own views on what went wrong, or what seemed to go wrong, on that occasion and in relation to the escape of Liam Averill.

The hon. Gentleman may well have obtained his information from sources inside the prison – sources who may have identified or commented on real or perceived shortcomings in security procedures generally within the H Blocks. I hope that, if he has not done so already, he will encourage those who gave that information to speak frankly to and cooperate fully with the inquiry team.

It is interesting to note the minister's remarks in relation to the 'progressive programme of security measures', which had been introduced at the Maze since the Labour government under Prime Minister Tony Blair took office in May 1997. However, in view of the circumstances of the murder of Billy Wright, these measures have proven to have been inadequate as they failed to detect the smuggling of guns into the Maze Prison or to prevent the murder itself. If, as the minister informed the House of Commons in January 1998, these security measures had been in place at the time of Billy Wright's death, how did the murder occur? It is clear from the minister's remarks that the implementation of all the security measures required the involvement of prison staff at one level or another. It would seem improbable that, with such a level of security in place within the Maze, the INLA could succeed in killing a fellow inmate – yet they did succeed, despite the enhanced security measures. The failure to operate any one of these security measures, deliberately or otherwise, could have assisted the INLA in their ultimate objective: the death of Billy Wright. Collusion, after all, can be both active and passive.

STAND DOWN THE GUARD!'

NOTE:

[1] The Steele Report was commissioned by the then Conservative government under Prime Minister John Major, following the discovery of an IRA escape tunnel at the Maze in March 1997. John Steele, a senior civil servant in the Northern Ireland Office, was tasked to conduct an internal inquiry into the IRA escape tunnel incident. Although Steele completed his report, it was never published or its contents made known. The decision not to publish the Steele Report was taken by the Major administration before it left office in May 1997.

12. The Official Stonewall

During his remarks to the House of Commons in January 1998, Northern Ireland Office Minister of State Adam Ingram listed a series of security measures that he said had been put in place within the Maze Prison since May 1997. Included in the measures outlined by the minister were: twice daily head counts of the prisoners; comprehensive cell and block searches; and cell fabric checks. It would appear that such measures, correctly and regularly operated, would have been sufficient to deter the INLA from retaining the weapons used to murder Billy Wright on their accommodation block. However, the enhanced security measures failed to detect the weapons entering the Maze Prison or where they were being hidden in readiness for the murder itself. During the 1999 inquest into the murder of Billy Wright, the Maze Security Governor, Stephen Davis, testified that prison staff did not enter the INLA wings on H6 because they feared for their safety. He further admitted that the area of the INLA exercise yards had not been checked since July 1997, a full five months before the INLA murdered Billy Wright. Governor Davis also told the inquest that prisoners were free to move up and down the wing on a 24-hour basis. He also said it would have been dangerous for a member of the prison staff to have entered the exercise yard areas. In light of Governor Davis' remarks it is clear that the measures described by the minister were not in fact being operated within the INLA Blocks on H6. If they were not operational and prisoners were free to move as they pleased on a 24-hour daily basis, the INLA would have had no major concerns that once they had succeeded in getting the guns into the prison they would remain undiscovered until required for use.

However, the issue of how the weapons entered the Maze remains unresolved. IRSP sources maintain one of the weapons used to kill Billy Wright was brought into the Maze by the wife of one of their members in mid-December 1997. The minister told the House all visitors were scanned before entering the prison. Anyone who has ever visited the Maze Prison will have experienced at first hand the search procedures used there. All visitors, male and female, are physically searched before being allowed to proceed into the main prison area. The search takes place inside a 'search box' between the visits arrival area and the waiting room for the visits transport. As well as being physically searched by prison staff, all monies, car keys, and other personal items must be handed over to prison staff. These items are then placed in a container and held at the visits area for collection on the completion of the visit. In light of these physical search procedures, it is difficult to imagine how a semi-automatic pistol could have been brought into the Maze Prison undetected. However, the RUC have never been able to establish precisely how and when the weapons used in the murder entered the Maze Prison.

In November 2000, the Minister of State, Adam Ingram, took part in an interview on national television. The interview formed part of a television report into the circumstances of the murder of Billy Wright. It was put to the minister that it was incredible that two terrorist groups, the LVF and the INLA, neither of which were on ceasefire, had been housed in the same H Block at the Maze Prison. In response, Adam Ingram conceded that the arrangement for the INLA and LVF prisoners on H6 was imperfect. However, he pointed out that at that time the Maze Prison was full to capacity. The minister also pointed out that it was Billy Wright who had requested a transfer to the Maze from Maghaberry and in doing so he was fully aware of what to expect within the Maze. The events leading up to Wright's transfer to the Maze Prison have already been covered elsewhere in this book. At this stage it is sufficient to say that Billy Wright had been given specific assurances from either the NIO or the Northern Ireland Prison Services with regard to his personal safety at the Maze. Former LVF prisoners have confirmed this to be the case and it also can be verified by reading Wright's transfer petition. It is Wright's former associates' belief that the safety assurances were simply nothing more than an inducement designed to persuade the loyalist leader to move to the Maze.

When asked why nobody in prison management at the Maze had taken seriously warnings by prison officers of the likelihood of an attack over the roof of H6, Adam Ingram said it had always been recognised that the roof area was suspect. He said this had been identified in the Narey Report published in April 1998. The minister said the design of the Maze Prison was not perfect and the Narey Report had identified lapses in security arrangements within the prison. The minister did not answer the question of why warnings by prison officers had not been taken seriously prior to the murder of Billy Wright. During the course of the television interview, Adam Ingram went on to say some weaknesses in the security profile of the Maze were a direct result of threats to the lives of prison staff – that they effectively could not go into certain areas of the prison because of the threats to their personal safety. The minister's remark must be put in context against his comments in the House of Commons on 21 January 1998 when he outlined a progressive programme of tightened security measures which had been put in place in the Maze since May 1997. It must also be viewed in light of the admission by Maze Security Governor Stephen Davis in relation to prison staff entering the INLA wings and exercise yards. Christopher McWilliams also made it clear that prison staff were under control of the INLA if and when they did enter the wings. McWilliams said: 'The INLA are in control of the wings.'

As mentioned earlier, it would be impossible for prison staff to have carried out the progressive series of security measures outlined by the minister if they did not have access to the wings of H Block 6.

Adam Ingram said a culture of fear existed within the Maze when Billy Wright was murdered. That same culture of fear, he said, led to practices that were not desirable – although the minister did not elaborate on exactly what these undesirable practices were. In relation to the INLA receiving details of the LVF visits for Saturday, 27 December 1997, Adam Ingram said there appeared to be some confusion on the matter. He said the Narey Report had never fully identified what had happened although he had said it was likely that the INLA had received details of the LVF visits. The minister said there was no justification for this happening and it shouldn't have happened.

When he was asked about the absence of the prison officer from his post in the observation tower, Adam Ingram once again referred to the Narey Report, saying the report had confirmed what had happened. The minister said there had been a misunderstanding between the governor and the staff. The minute it was identified that the observation post was empty, after a complaint from the officer who had been stood down, he was returned to his post. That is not the case, as has already been discussed and established in an earlier chapter. However, the minister did confirm one important fact: that a governor grade was involved in the standing down of the watchtower. Adam Ingram again used the Narey Report to support his argument that the manning of the watchtower and the raising of the alarm would not have saved Billy Wright from INLA attack. The minister said the Narey Report had made it clear that it had taken the INLA gunmen just 30 seconds to get through the fence, over the prison roof and into the killing area. He went on to claim that had a guard in the watchtower set off the alarm, it would have put Billy Wright at risk by preventing him from returning to his cell. The independent engineer's report estimates the time taken by the three INLA volunteers to get through the hole in the fence, over the wall, across the roof and reach the prison van and Billy Wright as approximately 83 seconds, some 53 seconds more than Narey's estimate. It also has to be pointed out that the sounding of the alarm would not have prevented Billy Wright re-entering the accommodation area of H6 as only the four inner grilles leading to the Circle area were automatically locked down in the event of an alarm being raised by prison staff. All the other grilles and doors were manually operated by prison staff on duty. When asked if he thought a public inquiry should be held into the circumstances of the death of Billy Wright, Adam Ingram said he did not.

More than a year earlier, in September 1999, Adam Ingram met David Wright at Castle Buildings, Stormont. The meeting was also attended by Ulster Unionist Party leader David Trimble MP. During the course of the meeting David Wright spent a considerable time detailing his family's concerns in relation to the murder of his son. However, the minister, after listening intently to David Wright, failed to provide him with any satisfactory answers to the issues that had been raised. Neither did Adam Ingram provide any further information in relation to the loyalist leader's death throughout the remainder of his time at the Northern Ireland Office. It should be noted that during the meeting, David Trimble MP described the concerns surrounding the murder of Billy Wright as a boil, which had to be lanced. It is also worth noting that Trimble, who was David Wright's Westminster representative, entered the meeting well after it had started and left before it had concluded. The significance of his action was not lost on David Wright who, as Trimble was leaving, dismissed him with a contemptuous wave of his hand, saying: 'Don't let me detain you, Mr Trimble.' Following the meeting David Wright remarked that by leaving the meeting with Adam Ingram early, the Ulster Unionist Party leader displayed: 'Utter contempt for my family's concerns. It is clear he has no time for the Billy Wright issue or what it might uncover.'

The British administration has always proved reluctant either to meet with David Wright or to address his concerns. The government has always maintained that it was the INLA who were responsible for the death of the LVF leader. They argue the circumstances of the murder have been adequately investigated on a number of separate occasions. The RUC investigation, the murder trial, the inquest and the Narey Report, the government claim, have been sufficient to establish the truth about what happened inside the Maze Prison on 27 December 1997. The defects in all four of these 'investigations' have already been pointed out in this book. It is sufficient to say that none of the above have managed to allay the intense suspicion that Billy Wright's death was not indeed the opportune killing of a loyalist by republicans. Far too many questions concerning the killing remain unanswered. It is as though the authorities believe that if they ignore the problem it will eventually go away.

The British government's approach to the Wright family is in marked contrast to its approach to other families with concerns about the death of loved ones. The families of murder victims Pat Finucane, a lawyer, and Rosemary Nelson, a solicitor, have met with the British Prime Minister Tony Blair and Irish Taoiseach Bertie Ahern, on several occasions to highlight their concerns. On the other hand, British Prime Minister Tony Blair has consistently refused to meet with any member of the Wright family despite numerous requests for him to do so. In a letter dated 5 May 1999, Tony Blair informed David Wright that his son's murder had been thoroughly and rigorously investigated. Mr Blair politely, but firmly, declined to meet with the Wright family. The British Prime Minister has never moved from this position. The closest David Wright has ever come to meeting the British Prime Minister was in October 2000 when members of the Wright family delivered a copy of the British Irish Rights Watch Report into Billy Wright's murder to 10 Downing Street. Accompanied by the Ulster Unionist MP for Lagan Valley, Jeffrey Donaldson, David Wright handed over a copy of the report to staff in Number 10. As David Wright was giving a series of media interviews, the Prime Minister's official car pulled up outside the front door of 10 Downing Street. Unfazed by the imminent appearance of Blair, David Wright continued with his interview as anxious security staff looked on. At one point, the curtains on a window of 10 Downing Street were pulled to the side and someone looked out to see if the interviews had finished. As they did so the figure of the British Prime Minister could be seen waiting inside. It appeared as though Tony Blair was reluctant to venture outside alone, as long as members of the Wright family were present. However, within seconds of the family walking out through the security gates of Downing Street, the Prime Minister's car, with Blair inside, swept past. As it did so David Wright remarked: 'My, my, the most powerful man in Great Britain had to hide behind his front curtains, too frightened to meet a 69-year-old grandfather from Portadown.'

Likewise, Irish Taoiseach Bertie Ahern has avoided any face-to-face meeting with David Wright. Although Ahern has never openly refused a meeting, it is clear he has difficulty with the public perception of Billy Wright. It has become clear that Ahern, although he has not hesitated to meet with the nationalist victims of violence, does not consider the time politically correct to meet with the loyalist victims of violence. In adopting such a stance both prime ministers are guilty of discrimination and selectivity. The concerns and grief of Billy Wright's family are no more or no less than the concerns and grief of the families of Pat Finucane and Rosemary Nelson. All three deserve equal treatment irrespective of the public perception of what the victim was alleged to be.

However, it was not only prime ministers who refused to meet with David Wright. Throughout her tenure as Secretary of State for Northern Ireland, Dr Mo Mowlam also refused to consider any form of meeting with the Wright family, despite continued requests and political pressure. The Secretary of State did, however, meet with the relatives of nationalist victims of violence to listen to their concerns. Mowlam also paid a much-publicised visit to the Maze Prison shortly after the murder of Billy Wright. During her visit to the top security prison she met senior loyalist and republican paramilitary prisoners. Media crews were also allowed inside the prison to cover the visit. At the time of Mowlam's visit to the Maze, David Wright commented: 'I wonder who guaranteed her safety inside the Maze?'

Mowlam's successor, Peter Mandelson, adopted the same 'no meeting' policy in relation to the Wright family. Although he responded to all correspondence in relation to the murder of the loyalist leader, he would never agree to a face-to-face meeting with the family. Indeed, Mandelson's attitude to the Wright murder gave the impression of complete indifference. In February 2000, David Wright learnt from the BBC *Spotlight* programme that traces of cannabis had been found in his son's blood. Shortly afterwards he discovered that photographs from his son's postmortem were being circulated in areas of north Belfast and offered to the media for sale. He wrote to Mandelson concerning the sources of the material. Despite the fact that such material could only have originated from within a small circle of individuals with access to the postmortem results and photographs, Peter Mandelson upheld the integrity of all those concerned. In a letter to David Wright dated 8 May 2000, Mandelson wrote:

> I am assured that neither the Forensic Science Agency, the State
> Pathology Department nor the RUC made the information
> (concerning the traces of cannabis) available to the Press. Nor
> were they the source of the photographs. I am satisfied they are
> highly scrupulous in their responsibilities.

After the circulation of the postmortem photographs had been
reported in the media, the human-rights organisation, British Irish
Rights Watch, wrote to Peter Mandelson demanding an immediate and
thorough investigation.

In a reply the Mandelson said: ' . . . this matter is not new and has
been thoroughly investigated and I am satisfied that the material did
not enter the public domain via any official source.'

It is unlikely that the material in question would have been leaked
to the media deliberately. However, it is the fact that the material has
reached the public domain at all – by whatever unofficial source – that
raises immediate cause for concern. Clearly Peter Mandelson was
totally indifferent to this particular aspect of the Wright case.

In the early part of 2001, Dr John Reid took over the post of
Secretary of State for Northern Ireland, following the resignation of
Peter Mandelson. In due course David Wright wrote to Dr Reid seeking
a meeting with him. Surprisingly, Dr Reid agreed to the meeting, which
took place at Castle Buildings, Stormont, on Tuesday, 13 March 2001.
Although he listened intently to what David Wright had to say it was
clear that the government's position in relation to the murder of Billy
Wright had not altered, despite changes at the Northern Ireland Office.
Dr Reid made it clear that if new evidence came to light in relation to
the killing then the government would look at it with an open mind.
However, he went on to say that the position of the government had
been made clear and it was not persuaded of the need for a public
inquiry into the circumstances of the murder of Billy Wright.

During the course of his meeting with the Secretary of State, David
Wright handed over a written submission outlining his family's
concerns in relation to the murder. The dossier also contained a list of
questions, which had yet to be answered regarding the circumstances
surrounding the loyalist leader's death. The Secretary of State told
David Wright that he would respond in person to the issues raised in
the submission. That response never came and the Secretary of State
never addressed the areas of concern. However, it has to be said that
almost 18 months after the meeting with Dr Reid, the Northern Ireland
Office wrote to David Wright advising him that the submission was to

be passed to the international judge who would be appointed to carry out the independent inquiry into the murder of the loyalist leader.

After he had returned home following the Reid meeting, David Wright was contacted by a member of the Committee on the Administration for Justice who informed him that the Northern Ireland Office had issued a press release, via e-mail, stating that the British government's position on the murder of Billy Wright remained unchanged. However, it was the time of the e-mail press release that proved to be interesting. It had been released at 3.15 p.m. on 13 March 2001 – a full 15 minutes before David Wright's meeting with Dr Reid had ended. Clearly the NIO had already prepared a press release before the meeting between David Wright and the Secretary of State had actually taken place. Obviously, the British authorities had no intention of altering their position on the Wright issue, irrespective of whatever his father had to say to Dr John Reid. When challenged over the matter of the early issue of the press release, the NIO put it down to an administrative error.

If, as the British government would insist, the murder of Billy Wright involved no one other than members of the Irish National Liberation Army, it is difficult to understand the official reluctance to make information available. The authorities' failure to provide answers to the outstanding questions which still surround the circumstances of the loyalist leader's death only serve to fuel suspicions of the existence of some form of outside involvement and an official cover-up. The government's continued reluctance to provide answers is aided and abetted by an obvious lack of pressure from Unionist politicians, 99 per cent of whom have done absolutely nothing in the way of helping the Wright family to obtain the answers they seek. With the exception of the Ulster Unionist MP for Lagan Valley, Jeffrey Donaldson, who has continued to support the Wright family in their quest for justice and the truth, not one prominent Unionist politician has put his or her head above the parapet for a protracted period of time.

Other members of the Ulster Unionist Party, although having initially paid lip service to the Wright case, now appear to be suffering from severe laryngitis and selective amnesia. Particularly at local level, support from political figures has been distinctly lacking since Wright was killed. Although many local politicians, including those from Sinn Fein, have endorsed the calls for a public inquiry to be set up into the loyalist leader's death, none of them have gone any further than timid vocal support. It is ironic that many of those self-same politicians who privately welcomed Billy Wright's involvement in the Orange Order's Drumcree dispute in 1995–6, lacked the moral courage to align themselves alongside his family in the quest for justice. The Orange Order in Portadown is particularly deserving of criticism for failing to publicly support the Wright family. Portadown Orangeman Harold Gracey shared a platform with Wright in 1996 following a death threat on the loyalist leader from the UVF. Rank-and-file members of the Orange Order will admit that Billy Wright's presence at Drumcree was instrumental in the Orange Parade getting down the Garvaghy Road in 1996. In 2001, those very same Portadown Orangemen passed a resolution to issue a press statement in support of a public inquiry into Wright's murder. However, they failed to make that release public, giving no reasons for their action.

It appears the majority of Unionist politicians and senior Orangemen have been influenced by the media perception of what Wright was supposed to be. Unlike the nationalist/republican community, who stick to a cause, seeing it through to its final objective no matter what criticism is levelled at them, unionists are influenced by public opinion. When it comes to loyalist paramilitaries, the self-righteous, so-called God-fearing unionist, who privately approved of Billy Wright but who would never admit so in public, will shy away from supporting anything to do with such a 'notorious figure of the Troubles'. Such a stance is nothing less than sheer hypocrisy, but nothing less than can be expected as recent history has proved.

It is not only the Ulster Unionist Party that has failed to support the Wright family campaign for the truth. The hard-line Democratic Unionist Party has also been conspicuous by its absence from the front line of the campaign. Once again, the DUP, after an initial flurry of activity following the Wright murder, has faded well into the background. Despite its promises to do plenty, the DUP did practically nothing. One party official could not even take the time to raise the matter of the publication of the postmortem photographs with the RUC. Even those party members who had held private meetings with Billy Wright in Portadown or who had appeared in public with the loyalist leader, had their hard-line enthusiasm effectively neutered by Wright's brutal murder. Was that part of the chilling overall signal to be sent out to hard-line unionists/loyalists by the death of the loyalist leader? If you oppose the political process this is what can happen. If it was then it clearly had the desired effect within unionism and loyalism and it left David Wright and his family almost unaided in their search for the truth and justice.

The lack of support for the Wright family, within all shades of unionism, is a damning indictment of the two-faced nature of unionist politics. In political terms, public opinion and image is in most cases always more important that the truth itself. Truth is always a major casualty when it comes to politics. Likewise perception is not always the truth, but in the case of Billy Wright it has been accepted as the truth. As far as Billy Wright's murder is concerned, perception has played a major part in preventing the truth being made known.

In August 2001, following all-party discussions at Weston Park, Shropshire, the British and Irish governments agreed on a series of proposals aimed at building support for the 1998 Belfast Agreement. The Weston Park proposals included the appointment of an independent international judge to carry out investigations into allegations of collusion in a number of murders in Northern Ireland. The murders to be investigated were:

- RUC officers, Chief Superintendent Harry Breen and Superintendent Bob Buchanan, who were shot dead by the IRA near Jonesborough, south Armagh in March 1989.
- Belfast solicitor, Pat Finucane, shot dead by loyalists in his north Belfast home in February 1989.
- Lord Justice and Lady Gibson, blown up in a 500 lb IRA landmine attack on their car near Killeen, south Armagh in 1987.
- Robert Hamill, who died as a result of injuries he received when he was attacked by a crowd of loyalists in Portadown, Co. Armagh, in May 1997.
- Solicitor, Rosemary Nelson, killed in a loyalist booby-trap car bomb just yards from her home in Lurgan, Co. Armagh, in March 1999.
- LVF leader, Billy Wright, shot dead by the INLA at the Maze Prison in December 1997.

In July 2002, 11 months after the Weston Park talks, the British and Irish governments announced that retired Canadian judge, Mr Justice Cory, had been appointed to oversee the inquiries into the collusion allegations. Judge Cory began his investigations into the six cases on 1 August 2002. It is unclear when the judge will complete his investigations.

Judge Cory has the power to recommend the setting up of a public inquiry into any of the six murders should he consider it necessary. Both the British and Irish governments have given an undertaking to implement Judge Cory's recommendations.

13. Establishing the Facts

In order to have an understanding of the events surrounding the murder of Billy Wright it is necessary to create a picture of H Block 6 itself. The H Blocks derived their name from the actual shape of the buildings themselves. They simply form the shape of the letter 'H'. The two legs of the 'H' are occupied by cells and the cross bar, known as 'the Circle', contains the block administration, control room, prison officers' tea room and the principal officer's office. In H6 the 'Circle' area also formed a sort of 'no man's land' between the rival paramilitary prisoners belonging to the INLA and the LVF. The main entrance to the block accommodation area is via a door located at the top end of the forecourt area and directly opposite the vehicular air lock at the main gate. Close to the entrance door is a small window, which looks out onto the forecourt area of the block. On entering this doorway there is another airlock formed by two steel grilles. Prison officers control both grilles. However, only one of these grilles, the one leading immediately into the Circle area, is electronically controlled in the event of an alarm or an emergency occurring. On most occasions they are opened and closed manually by prison staff using a key. One prison officer operates the main door of the block and the first of the metal grilles. This position is known as the 'hall guard'. On the morning of Saturday, 27 December 1997, prison officer Brian Thompson was on duty at this location. The second of the two metal grilles leads into the cross bar of the H Block – the Circle. Once inside the Circle there are two arms of the cross bar, the left leading to the INLA accommodation areas on A and B wings; the right to the LVF on C and D wings. Once again, entrance to either side of the accommodation wings is through another airlock consisting of two metal grilles. Both grilles are opened and closed manually by prison staff. However, the inner grille leading directly to the Circle area can be electronically locked in the event of an emergency. A member of prison staff is located in the sterile area between each wing and operates the grille leading directly onto the accommodation areas. Another prison officer, known as the 'Circle guard' control all the metal grilles leading directly into the Circle area itself. The other principal features of the Circle are the control room and the location of the principal officer and his second in command.

Two members of prison staff man the control room – the nerve centre of the block itself. One officer is responsible for manning the telephones and entries in the control room journal. The other officer operates the electronic locking system and the internal intercom system. There are also CCTV monitors located inside the control room area. On the morning Wright was murdered, prison officer Alan Danks was responsible for the telephones and journal while prison officer Aidan Joseph Flannigan operated the intercom and the locking system. The office of the principal officer – the man in charge of the block – is located close to the control room. Evidence presented during the inquest into Billy Wright's death indicates that two members of staff were using this office: senior officers Arthur Gallagher and Brian Patrick Molloy. It is understood that senior officer Molloy was the officer in charge of H6 on the morning of the Wright murder. However, the Northern Ireland Prison Service has never confirmed who was in charge of H6 that particular day.

Entrance to the forecourt area of the H Block is via two large metal gates, which form a vehicular airlock. The forecourt area of H6, where Billy Wright was murdered, measures 28.9 m wide (95 ft) and 45 m long (150 ft). On the morning of 27 December 1997, two prison visits vans were parked in the forecourt area. A red van to be used by INLA prisoners was parked adjacent to the LVF accommodation. A white van, to be used by the LVF prisoners was parked close to the INLA canteen area near a lamp standard. It is understood that prior to the morning of the Wright murder the INLA had arrived at H6 first and had parked in the position normally occupied by the LVF transport. LVF prisoners in the Maze at that time state that this was the first time the INLA van had occupied the position normally taken by their transport. The prisoners noted that this forced Billy Wright to walk closer to the INLA accommodation and therefore exposed him to risk of attack.

The accommodation areas on H6 were allocated to the rival paramilitary groupings, the INLA and the LVF. The right-hand leg of the block, A and B wings, contained INLA prisoners, while the left-hand leg, C and D wings, housed the LVF prisoners, including Billy Wright. Each wing contained 26 cells, a canteen/recreation area and washing and toilet facilities. Each wing measures 31 m (102 ft) long and 9.1 m (30 ft) wide externally. Entrance to the exercise yard was via a turnstile located opposite the canteen area. There was also another door located at the end of the wing accommodation besides cells 12 and 13. It is understood this door is normally kept secured and is under the control of prison staff at all times.

On the morning of the murder, the three INLA prisoners made their way out of A wing via the turnstile and into a small external corridor area leading to the exercise yard. They gained access to a further fenced-in external corridor running down the side of A wing via a hole, measuring 27 in. by 24 in., which had previously been cut in a 3 in. by 5 in. weld mesh fence. They then made their way down the external corridor a distance of some 23 ft and scaled the side of the building. At that particular point the height of the building is 9 ft 7in. They then crossed the 30 ft flat roof of A wing before jumping down into the forecourt area of H6. Once inside the forecourt area the three INLA prisoners made their way another 30 to 40 ft to the prison van containing Billy Wright, Norman Green and the two prison officers. Their next action was to shoot Wright dead before returning to A wing via the same route they had used seconds earlier.

The nearest observation post to the murder was a watchtower located at a point almost mid-way in the external fencing of A and B wing exercise yards. The watchtower is 25 ft above ground level and is 90 ft horizontally away from the position where the hole had been cut in the security fence.

On the afternoon of Friday, 9 March 2001, David Wright paid his second visit to the Maze Prison. On this occasion he was accompanied by Jane Winter of the human-rights organisation, British Irish Rights Watch; Mags O'Connor, Northern Ireland Human Rights Commission; Laurence McGill, chartered consultant engineer; Dick Mullan, caretaker governor HMP Maze; and Steven Murphy, solicitor for the Northern Ireland Prison Service. The author and David Wright's legal representative were also present during the visit to the prison. The purpose of the visit was to allow the human rights and legal representatives to see at first hand the scene of the murder. The prison authorities had also given permission for the consultant engineer to carry out an extensive examination of H6 itself.

The visit proved to be a harrowing experience for David Wright.

However, he later remarked it had been essential for him to make the visit as it gave him an unexpected second opportunity to check at first hand the scene of the murder. Clarity of fact was vital, he remarked, and his intense questioning of senior prison staff provided further information, which confirmed his belief that the circumstances of his son's murder were not as portrayed by the British authorities.

The initial examination of the forecourt area showed the final resting position of the prison van after the shooting was 100 ft from the centre of the main gate airlock. Based on a calculation using a reasonable acceleration of 10 ft per second, which would have been well within the capability of the van, it would have taken just 4.5 seconds for it to reach the airlock. The watchtower, the prison officer's post at the main gate and the main doorway airlock are all fitted with intercom systems. Had a warning been passed to the prison officer on duty at the main gate would he not have had sufficient time to fully open the main gates to allow the van containing Billy Wright and the others to enter the main airlock area before securing the gates again? This could have been completed in a matter of some 10–15 seconds and would have removed Wright, Green and the prison staff accompanying them to a place of safety. This would also have extended dramatically the distance between the three INLA attackers and the prison van itself.

Whether or not the main gates were actually secured at the time of the shooting is questionable. In his evidence at the inquest, the officer on duty at the main gate airlock, John Seaward, said when the prison van with Wright inside began to move towards him, he started to open the first of the two half gates which make up the overall inner gates of the airlock itself. At this stage Seaward noticed two other prison officers pushing meal trolleys towards his location. As he started to open the second half of the gate Seaward said he noticed someone on the roof of A wing. At this stage one half of the inner gate must have been fully opened and the other partly so. Seaward also recalled that by the time the first INLA gunman stopped the van he was about 10 ft away from him. Therefore the prison van itself must have been very close to the airlock. As the other two members of the INLA ASU jumped down into the forecourt area, the other two prison officers – who by this time had reached the airlock – assisted Seaward in closing the inner gates, effectively preventing the only means of escape available to the van and its occupants. Once they had secured the inner gate, Seaward then opened the pedestrian gate, which allowed the three officers to get outside the perimeter fence of H6. Only after they had exited the main gates did one of the prison officers activate the alarm.

The depositions of the two other prison officers, Ian Cardwell and Brian Richardson, confirm that as they approached the inner gate of H6 it was partially open. The INLA prisoner, Christopher McWilliams, said that when he jumped down into the forecourt area and ran to the front of the prison van the inner gates of the airlock were 'lying open'. It is clear from the inquest depositions of prison officers Cardwell, Richardson and Seaward that they still had time to secure the inner gates before Wright's assassins discharged any shots. It is also clear from the consultant engineer's report that there would have been sufficient time for the driver of the prison van to get his vehicle inside the airlock.

During the course of the inquest it was suggested that the time taken by the INLA to carry out the murder of Billy Wight ranged from between a conservative 30 seconds to a maximum of 60 seconds. This is a crucial issue and requires careful examination. It would appear that the INLA had prior warning, in some form, that Billy Wright was due to take a visit on the morning of Saturday, 27 December 1997. By their own admissions, they were armed and on standby ready to carry out the murder attack. However, despite their admitted state of readiness, the three INLA volunteers could not afford to launch the attack too early, otherwise there was a real possibility they would have arrived in the forecourt area before Billy Wright and Norman Green had left the security of the main building itself. On the other hand, if they had left it too late to stage the attack then the prison van and its intended target would have simply driven out of H6 and on to the LVF visits area.

If it is accepted that the INLA weapons were in a position of relative accessibility it can be assumed that the ASU members were in fact in position, awaiting a signal confirming that Billy Wright was either out of or about to leave the security of the block building itself. The easiest and earliest point where Wright could have been seen leaving the LVF wing was from where the INLA wing joins the sterile area leading to the Circle area. From that position there is a clear line of sight across to where the LVF prisoners were located. During the March 2001 visit to the Maze and following its closure as an operational prison, David Wright and his companions were allowed to enter the H6 accommodation area. The visit confirmed that there was a clear line of vision from one leg of the H Block to the other and into the respective airlocks leading into the Circle area. However, the INLA claimed that their ASU did not launch their attack until they saw Billy Wright exit the block accommodation area and physically enter the prison van itself. The INLA claimed prisoner John Glennon had stood on a table in the canteen area and looked out of a window and watched Wright and his companion enter the prison van. The INLA also pointed out that Glennon had a clear view of the forecourt area from his position at the canteen window. However, during the March 2001 visit to the prison and the A wing canteen, the INLA theory was tested and proven to be incorrect.

After a detailed examination of the canteen area it was found that it would have not been possible for anyone to have seen out of the windows let alone recognise any individual in the forecourt area. The visit showed that the glass in the windows of the A wing canteen was of the frosted-wire type. They had also been externally covered with an opaque plastic self-adhesive material making it impossible for anyone inside to see out. Likewise, it would also have been impossible for anyone on the outside to have seen into the canteen area. The centre of one of the windows was also partially obscured by the presence of a large extractor fan. An examination of the forecourt area also showed there was no direct line of sight from the canteen windows to the entrance door of H6. The INLA prisoner, John Glennon, could therefore not have seen Billy Wright leave the security of H6, nor could he have seen him enter the prison van in preparation for the journey to the visits area. How then did the INLA ASU know precisely when to launch their murder attack?

Without doubt the INLA had to estimate with as much accuracy as was possible the time it would take them to make their way out of the A wing accommodation area and into the forecourt area. It can only be assumed that the three INLA volunteers who formed the ASU that carried out the murder did not have an opportunity to practise their plan. However, given the obviously lax regime that appeared to exist within the Maze Prison in December 1997, it is clear that they certainly would have had ample opportunity and time to inspect their route and any potential obstacles that they might incur.

Without doubt the speed of the INLA operation would have depended upon the ability and levels of fitness of the individuals involved. Assuming that the three participants had both ability and fitness, the consultant engineer has indicated the timings would be as follows:

● To remove the wire grill from the section of the security fence outside the turnstile leading to A wing exercise yard and expose the hole – 10 seconds.

- Crawl through the hole, measuring 24 in. by 27 in., at a rate of 4 seconds per person with a single-second interval between them – 14 seconds.
- Run to the widow inside the external corridor alongside A wing – 3 seconds.
- Scale the wall onto the flat roof of the prison – 20–30 seconds.
- Traverse the flat roof of A wing – 4 seconds.
- Jump down from the roof and into the courtyard – 7 seconds.
- Cross the yard to the prison van – 5 seconds.

Of the above timings the one most likely to vary is the actual scaling of the outer wall of the accommodation block. An examination of the actual area itself revealed a 1.25 in. window ledge 5 ft above ground level. At a height of 7 ft above ground level there is a window opening light, which could have afforded a handhold for anyone clambering up the wall. At this point an individual standing on the ledge would be able to reach the top of the roof with ease. It is extremely unlikely that a person would have been able to hoist himself up on his own, but he could by manoeuvring to the edge of the actual window opening, have been able to place his foot in the opening light and gain access in that manner.

However, it would appear to be much more likely that the three individuals helped each other onto the prison roof, with the smallest of the three INLA volunteers holding onto the opening light and being boosted up onto the roof by the two others. Once on the roof itself he would then have received the weapons before the second person would have begun the climb, being boosted from below and hauled up from above. The third individual would in turn mount the window ledge and be pulled onto the roof by the other two. It would appear a rather risky, if not extremely dangerous, venture, for any individual to climb onto the prison roof carrying a loaded semi-automatic pistol in the waistband of his clothing. To do so could result in the weapon falling to the ground with any resulting damage rendering it unworkable. There would also be an even greater danger of the weapon being accidentally discharged, causing injury to the individual himself and alerting prison staff to the operation. Excluding any mishaps, the consultant engineer was of the opinion that three agile and fit individuals could have concluded this particular section of the operation in 20–30 seconds, giving the time taken to travel the overall distance from A wing to the prison van at 61–71 seconds. This figure is a minimum of 30 seconds more than the time estimated by the RUC murder-investigation team. Furthermore, following the attack the INLA ASU have admitted that they returned to their accommodation in A wing via the same route. This in turn adds at least a minimum of another 60 seconds to the overall time the INLA volunteers would have taken to carry out the complete operation. The total overall time taken by the INLA ASU is therefore believed to have been around two minutes.

However, the claim by Christopher McWilliams and the INLA that they had re-entered A wing via the exercise yard turnstile must be questioned. During the March 2001 visit to the Maze, David Wright and the author examined the exit and turnstile on A wing. The entrance to the yard itself consisted of a series of heavy plastic strips suspended from the doorframe. Once through the plastic strips, entrance to the exercise yard is via an upright metal turnstile mechanism. After passing through the turnstile it is only a distance of a few feet to where the INLA prisoners breached the fencing. However, as the author tried to exit A wing via the turnstile mechanism he was stopped by a senior member of the Northern Ireland Prison Service who informed him that the system only operated on a one-way basis, allowing persons to exit from the wing only. Beyond the turnstile it was impossible for anyone to return to the wing using the same method. In light of this discovery, how did the three INLA prisoners re-enter A wing after they had killed Billy Wright? Just as importantly, how did they manage to re-enter the wing on Christmas night after they had cut the hole in the security fence? Had the turnstile itself been 'doctored' to allow them to exit and enter the block on both occasions, or were they facilitated in their work by another means, as yet unrevealed and undetected?

The observation tower situated at a point approximately mid-way along the perimeter fencing of A and B wings gives a clear view of both the exercise yards. It also provides a clear line of sight onto the flat roof of the H Block building and a partial line of vision onto a section of the forecourt area. The glass in the observation tower is darkened and allows the prison officer manning the post to observe the complete area without being observed himself. The type of glass fitted to the observation post prevents any individual from knowing whether the position is manned or not. However, it is clear that anyone inside the observation tower would not have been able to clearly see the area where the hole had been cut. The individual's vision is impaired by two sections of weld mesh fence, with the result that the making out of precise detail would have proved extremely difficult. As the hole in the fence had been cut prior to the murder attack itself and the dislodged section replaced and tied in place with shoelaces, it would have not have been possible for an officer to detect this from his post in the observation tower. Movement in the area of the hole on the other hand would have been clearly visible to him.

During his first visit to the Maze Prison in February 2000, David Wright, accompanied by Jeffrey Donaldson MP and the author, stood inside the A and B wing observation post. It was clear that a guard on duty in that location could see anyone standing at the position where the hole had been cut. To prove the point, David Wright asked a member of prison staff to stand where the hole had been cut whilst he himself made his way up and into the observation tower. Once inside the observation post the figure of the prison officer was clearly discernible alongside the security fence. Although Mr Wright was not permitted to take pictures from the observation post itself, an official prison authority photographer did so on his behalf. Those pictures clearly show that any prison officer in the observation post would have seen the three INLA gunmen exit A wing and begin to remove the cut section of fencing. The fact was that the prison officer had been removed from the observation tower for A and B wings twice on the morning of the murder to enable the INLA ASU to carry out that particular section of their operation free from the threat of possible detection. Despite repeated requests for them to do so, neither the Northern Ireland Office nor the Prison Service have satisfactorily explained why the guard was removed from the observation post overlooking A and B wings on H Block 6. The continued refusal of both parties to do so has compounded the suspicion that the prison officer had been deliberately removed.

Prison officer Raymond Hill, the officer removed from the observation post, publicly stated during the inquest into the death of Billy Wright that had he been in post when the killers emerged and began to remove the cut section of fencing he would have sounded the alarm. Hill stated that, in all probability, as a result of such an action, Billy Wright would still have been alive.

14. Investigation or Whitewash?

Referring to the murder of Billy Wright, the Narey Report said his life could not have been saved even if the prison officer had been on duty inside the observation post. In Section 3, Paragraph 19 Narey states:

> In our view, whether or not the tower was manned, Mr Wright would still have been shot. Even if the tower officer had raised the alarm immediately, only one member of staff could have gained access to the forecourt, and had he intervened to protect Mr Wright, it is likely that he too would have been shot. Moreover, the fact that the alleged perpetrators made no attempt to disguise themselves indicates that potential detection or identification was of little concern to them.

Narey's comments are not correct, as it is clear that once the INLA prisoners had emerged from the H Block they would have been clearly visible to the guard in the watchtower. There would have been considerable activity from the moment they began to remove the cut section of the security fence. Does Narey believe that such activity in a sterile area by three paramilitary prisoners would not have attracted the attention of an observer in the watchtower and immediately alerted him to the fact that such behaviour was far from normal?

As previously stated, the entrance to H6, the block control room, the main gate airlock and the watchtower were all fitted with an intercom system. The passing of a simple fact that three INLA prisoners were breaking through a security fence should have made even the most unalert prison officer realise who exactly the potential target was, especially as Billy Wright had just made his way out of the block accommodation area and was on his way through one of the airlocks.

What Narey fails to recognise is that from that precise point in time there would have been over one full minute before the three INLA attackers arrived at the prison van. That is assuming the INLA operation continued without incident. It can be argued that it might not have been possible to spot the three men at this point but surely it must be conceded that the unusual activity in the area of the security fencing would have drawn the attention of an observer. Even had the officer in the watchtower failed to see the three INLA prisoners at that point, he would undoubtedly have seen the first man attempt to scale the wall and gain access to the prison-roof area. From that point there was still an estimated time of 45 seconds before the INLA ASU reached the prison van and carried out the murder.

The standard operational procedure within HMP Maze is that in such emergencies the normal drill is to set off the alarm system after which the officer turns his attention to securing all possible exit points. The sounding of the alarm, combined with the information that INLA prisoners were attempting to scale the wall of the accommodation area would not only have alerted prison staff, it would also have alerted Billy Wright to the fact that something was wrong. It can also be argued that Wright, in anticipation, might well have made his way back to the block entrance or to the main gate airlock, which was already partially open, rather than remaining in a position where he was trapped. Prison staff at the main door and the airlock are certainly trained to stop prisoners escaping. They are not trained to prevent prisoners entering the jail's accommodation.

Had a prison officer been on duty in the observation tower as the INLA prisoners began to breach the security fence, he would most certainly have been alerted to the fact that something unusual was happening and raised the alarm. The INLA recorded that the ASU did not move until Billy Wright had entered the prison van. At that point the INLA ASU was approximately some 60–70 seconds from its intended target. Even when they had breached the wire and were attempting to scale the wall of the accommodation area they were still approximately 45 seconds from Billy Wright inside the prison van. Had the alarm been sounded at that particular point in the INLA operation there would still have been sufficient time for Billy Wright to walk back to the safety of the accommodation area or the main gate airlock. Narey's statement that the manning of the watchtower would not have prevented the murder taking place is, to say the least, most surprising.

In a memorandum to the Select Committee on Northern Ireland affairs, the Prison Officers Association said: 'In fact the murder of Billy Wright could have been avoided had the H6 observation tower not been stood down to allow staff to go on visits.'

However, former Secretary of State for Northern Ireland, Peter Mandelson, disagrees with the POA view. In a letter to David Wright dated 8 May 2000, Mandelson wrote:

> Depositions made available to the Court state that the INLA prisoners positioned themselves in such a way as to observe your son's departure from the block. The INLA prisoners did not move out of their wing until they were sure that your son had already emerged from the block.

However, David Wright's visit to the Maze in March 2001 established that the INLA would have been unable to observe Billy Wright emerge from the block or indeed, for that matter, enter the prison van. That evidence contradicts the INLA's version of events and immediately raises the question: how exactly were the INLA made aware that Billy Wright had emerged from H6 and entered the prison van? It is vital that the truth about this aspect is established.

The INLA say the three volunteers were unaware that the watchtower was unmanned at the time of the attack. On the contrary, the INLA claim that the overall murder plan took account of the fact that a prison officer would be on duty in the watchtower. In *The Starry Plough* article of March/April 1999, the INLA stated:

> The plan was to provide the prison officers on duty in H Block 6 the opportunity to spot the INLA Active Service Unit as soon as the operation was underway.
>
> Intelligence has shown that the ASU would have been likely to be spotted as they were attempting to pass through the hole in the fence in A wing exercise yard, as this movement would have served immediately to attract the attention of the prison officer occupying the observation post overlooking the immediate area.
>
> On response to seeing the INLA ASU breaching the fence the prison officer would have automatically activated the alarm. Once the alarm had been activated normal procedure would

have been to stop all movement in the block, all gates would have been locked down automatically and therefore movement could not recommence until the prison authorities had investigated the alarm alert.

Had this been the case on the morning of 27 December 1997, the van containing Billy Wright would have had to remain immobilised inside the block forecourt until the alarm had been cleared.

The delay would have presented the ASU with added time to successfully complete the operation.

The INLA also claimed their operation to kill Billy Wright 'took less than 90 seconds from start to finish'. As Section 3, Paragraph 17 of the Narey Report says, 'Our best estimate [is that] it would take little more that 30 seconds for the INLA prisoners to climb and cross the roof.' However, it is worth noting that in his report Narey records that the Emergency Control Room at the Maze was first informed of the attack on Billy Wright at 9.59 a.m. and that the INLA ASU had returned to their wing over the roof by 10.07 a.m. – a gap of some eight minutes. A further one or two minutes should be added to that time to cover the period before the shooting. As neither Neary nor the RUC murder investigation has established an accurate minute-by-minute account of events, it is impossible for them to arrive at the conclusion that no difference would have been made had the watchtower been manned that morning. The engineer's report and the timings of the murder certainly indicate that had the observation post been manned then the outcome of the events of Saturday, 27 December 1997 might well have been very different indeed.

It is also interesting to note Section 3, Paragraph 20 of the Narey Report, which states:

> Indeed, if proper CCTV coverage of the exercise yards (with adequate monitoring arrangements) were introduced we consider that the manning of the watchtowers might be dispensed with. As things are the watchtowers provide a very expensive way of monitoring the yards. Incidents would be managed at a lesser expense and with greater effectiveness if yards were comprehensively covered by CCTV and monitored for the control room.

Considering a Pan Tilt Zoom (PTZ) camera overlooking the roof area of H6 had been reported inoperative five days before the Wright murder and remained inoperative on the morning of the murder, it is difficult to see how the introduction of CCTV would have increased the effectiveness of the Maze security. CCTV cameras were already in place within the area of H6 on the morning Billy Wright was shot dead yet the cameras and the prison staff monitoring them in the block control room failed to detect the INLA operation taking place.

In his report, the engineer stated that the section of fence, which had been breached, was made up of 3 mm stands set vertically at 12 mm spaces and horizontally at 72 mm spaces. The fence itself was constructed from high-grade steel. To cut a hole of the dimensions such as the INLA had, 24 in. by 27 in. would require in the region of 120 cuts. The INLA ASU cut the hole in the fence using a set of wire cutters, which had been strengthened by the addition of two sections of hollow metal chair legs to provide additional leverage when attempting to cut through the fence. It is estimated that each strand of steel could be cut in a minimum of three seconds in daylight. However, in the hours of darkness, when the INLA ASU said they had cut the hole, the operation would have been much slower. The engineer's report estimated that in the dark and in order to minimise the noise, it would have taken some ten seconds to cut through each metal strand. The time required to cut through the fence in darkness would therefore be in the region of some 20 minutes in total.

In his report the engineer stated the calculations were based on the wire having been cut using a thin-nosed scissor-action wire cutter. However, the INLA did not use a thin-nosed scissor-action wire cutter. Instead they used a standard round-nosed set of wire cutters to cut the hole in the security fence. After he received a copy of the engineer's report, David Wright managed to obtain a section of fencing identical to that used in the construction of the Maze Prison. By careful study of photographs it proved possible to identify and obtain a set of wire cutters identical to those used by the INLA ASU in December 1997. It was the intention to carry out a reconstruction of the cutting of the hole. However, it was discovered that the set of wire cutters proved to be too large to fit through the spaces of the high-grade steel fencing, let alone cut through the individual metal strands. This in turn raises yet more questions: how exactly did the INLA cut through the prison fencing? Was it done for them by others?

The October 2000 British Irish Rights Watch Report into the murder of Billy Wright mentions that while on night duty patrol in the area of H6, a member of the prison staff heard a rasping sound coming from the area of the INLA accommodation. This refers to an incident that occurred in early December 1997 when, one evening at 8.57 p.m., a dog handler, prison officer McCarthy, reported hearing what was described as a rasping sound coming from the vicinity of the INLA wings. This incident was reported to H6 and subsequently recorded in the night guard journal. It was also reported to the Emergency Control Room in the Maze. However, it seems puzzling, after admissions by both staff and prisoners that prison officers did not venture onto the wings amid concerns for their personal safety, how the senior officer was able to attribute the rasping sound to INLA prisoner's handicrafts. During the inquest, Maze Security Governor Stephen Davis stated that the exercise yards on H6 had not been inspected since July 1997. From that statement it must be concluded that the senior officer did not physically check the exercise-yard area in relation to the rasping sound. How then were prison staff able to state that the rasping noise was simply the work of handicraft activity?

It is possible that what officer McCarthy heard was the fence being cut. On the other hand he may have heard the chair legs being cut in preparation for the adaptation of the wire cutters. It is known that the murderers had sawn the metal legs off a chair using hacksaw blades taken from a prison workshop. If this did happen some time before the murder attack, no member of prison staff appears to have noticed the damaged chair.

There are too many unanswered questions surrounding the circumstances of the death of Billy Wright. Despite numerous requests for clarification, the Northern Ireland Office has yet to provide satisfactory answers to any of these questions. The Northern Ireland Prison Service and the Police Service of Northern Ireland have also been less than forthcoming in relation to the provision of specific and detailed information. Indeed, it can be said that all three parties have sheltered behind claims that the murder has been thoroughly investigated on three occasions. However, it is clear that none of these so-called investigations have managed to get to the heart of the crime.

One prime example of the failure to address an issue of importance is the matter of the defective security camera. As stated earlier, on 22 December 1997, a full five days before the murder of Billy Wright, the Pan Tilt Zoom overhead security camera No 3 which overlooked the rooftops of H6, had been reported defective by the senior officer on duty in the Emergency Control Room of the Maze. The camera, a vital piece of surveillance equipment at the Maze, remained inoperative with the consequence that the three INLA prisoners were able to cross the prison roof undetected by any security camera. Once the staff in the Emergency Control Room had been alerted to the shooting incident they trained another camera, No 4, onto the roof of H6, but by the time they had managed to do so the murder had taken place and the killers had returned to the safety of their accommodation on A wing. There is no mention of this particular aspect of the murder in the Narey Report. Therefore, there is a significant ommision in Narey's report. This raises the question: why did the Northern Ireland Prison Service fail to take prompt action to have the camera repaired? After all, the camera played a vital role in the security operation of the Maze Prison and was not simply there for ornamental purposes.

Another issue is the failure by the British government to identify and name the duty officer in charge of the Maze Prison on 27 December 1997. No one described as having fulfilled that function has ever appeared at the murder trial or the inquest. Witness depositions have identified a number of governor-grade officers as having been present inside the Maze Prison at the time Billy Wright was shot dead. According to prison officer Hill, Governor John Brian Barlow was on duty and present at H6 following the shooting. However, in December 1997, Barlow was an 'acting governor grade' and held the substantive rank of principal officer within the Northern Ireland Prison Service. As an acting governor, Barlow would not have been of sufficient seniority to have overall control of the prison.

The withheld deposition of senior officer Brian Patrick Molloy identifies a Governor William McKee as also having been on duty that particular morning. It is clear that McKee held a superior rank to that of Barlow as Molloy said he contacted McKee by telephone following the shooting incident to 'inform him of the seriousness of the incident'.

Another withheld deposition, that of John Brian Barlow, also shows that Governor William McKee was on duty on 27 December 1997. Barlow, who was in the security department of the Maze when he learnt of the shooting incident in H6, spoke to McKee to advise him of a conversation he had had with one of the INLA gunmen, Christopher McWilliams. Barlow's deposition identifies McKee as having been in the command post when he spoke with him. Barlow's deposition also identifies another governor-grade officer as having been present at that time. Towards the end of his deposition Barlow says a Governor Maguire contacted him regarding the evacuation of H6 A wing. At the beginning of his statement Barlow states: 'During the weekends three governors are always on duty between the hours of 7.30 a.m. and 5 p.m. Outside these hours one governor of the three will be on duty and call.'

It would appear from the witness depositions that the three governor grades on duty on Saturday, 27 December 1997 were Governor Barlow, Governor Maguire and Governor McKee. Having already discounted Barlow on seniority grounds, either Maguire or McKee must have been the person in overall charge of the Maze on the morning Billy Wright was shot dead. However, neither the Northern Ireland Prison Service nor the Northern Ireland Office has ever confirmed or denied this.

It is hard to understand the official reluctance to identify the prison official in charge of the Maze on the morning of the murder. The refusal by HM government to identify the Maze Governor on security grounds is strange considering it had already allowed a number of senior prison staff to be publicly identified. For example, Governor Stephen Davis had been clearly identified as the Maze Security Governor during the course of the inquest proceedings in February 1999. Other members of prison staff had also been identified in television and media reports at that time. The protecting of one member of the Northern Ireland Prison Service, whilst at the same time having an apparent disregard for the security of other staff members, is grossly unfair. Are all members of the Northern Ireland Prison Service not deserving of the same degree of personal security as has been afforded to the duty governor of the Maze on 27 December 1997? Is the security of one particular prison officer more important that that of his colleagues? In this instance this is clearly the case. However, the authorities have never given any reason for this act of inequality and disparity of treatment.

When an individual is committed to prison by the State, he or she has the right to expect to be held in conditions of safety. It is the responsibility of the prison authorities to do everything in their power to ensure the safety of all prisoners. This is especially important when prisoners from opposing political factions are housed on the same accommodation block. Quite clearly, as can be seen from the catalogue of concerns that have arisen from this particular murder, the Northern Ireland Prison Service failed to protect Billy Wright's right to life as enshrined in Article 3 of the Universal Declaration of Human Rights.

In its October 2000 report, 'A Recipe for Disaster – the Murder of Billy Wright in the Maze Prison', British Irish Rights Watch states:

Many of the factors which contributed to the murder of Billy Wright stemmed from policy decisions concerning the running of prisons in Northern Ireland which cannot be said to have a direct impact on those particular events. However, two management decisions did have a direct impact, i.e. the decision to house LVF and INLA prisoners in the same block and the decision to transfer Christopher McWilliams and John Kennaway from Maghaberry to the Maze despite their past record of hostage taking and gun smuggling. If those decisions were made after all due consideration, then the authorities should have been doubly alive to the risks they posed, and should have been highly alert to the possibility of an attack on such an obvious target as Billy Wright. In such circumstances, it is deplorable that warnings by prison officers should have gone unheeded: that a security camera should have been left un-repaired; that prisoners should have been able to smuggle guns and wire cutters into the jail, and to cut through the wire undetected; that a crucial watchtower should have been left unmanned; and that prisoners should have had access to the visiting schedule of an opposing faction.

Primary responsibility for Billy Wright's murder obviously lies with the three INLA men who killed him in cold blood. However, that such a notorious figure could have been so easily murdered within the confines of a prison places a very high responsibility on the state, both in relation to Billy Wright himself and in relation to the terrible aftermath unleashed by his death, which led to a series of further murders. It may be that the state's responsibility lies in nothing more-or-less than mismanagement and incompetence. Even so, when the list of poor decisions and mistakes is as long as it is in this case, rigorous scrutiny is required to ensure no further repetition.

When someone with a profile as high as Billy Wright is murdered by a group like the INLA inside a jail, the question must arise as to whether or not there was any collusion in the murder.

Important issues surrounding the murder of Billy Wright remain unresolved despite two internal prison investigations, a police investigation, a murder trial and an inquest. The British government argues that these investigations were rigorous and thorough. However, the Prison Authorities did not physically check the exercise yard in relation to the rasping sound. Therefore the claim that this was simply the work of handicraft activity was no more than their assessment, which was not based upon any hard evidence. The government has argued that the Narey Report has fulfilled the role of a public inquiry into the killing. That is not the case as the Narey inquiry was carried out within days of the murder itself. Narey's original terms of reference, which were to investigate the escape of a prisoner from the Maze, did not include an investigation into the Wright murder. Narey acknowledges this in the introduction to his report:

> On 11 December 1997 I was asked by the Secretary of State for Northern Ireland to conduct an inquiry into the circumstances surrounding the escape of a prisoner from the Maze on 10 December.
>
> During the course of our inquiry a prisoner was shot dead on 27 December. The inquiry was subsequently extended with the following terms of reference:
> 1. To enquire into the circumstances surrounding the escape of a prisoner from HMP Maze on 10 December 1997 and the murder of a prisoner on 27 December 1997.

However in Section 3, Paragraph 2 of his report Narey, referring to the Wright murder states:

> We are conscious that the incident is the subject of an ongoing police investigation and it would be inappropriate for us to comment in detail on the precise circumstances or persons involved. We have therefore confined our inquiry to the background of the shooting and the general issues it raises, particularly the scope for illicit items to be smuggled into the prison.

It is worth noting the findings of the Narey Report in relation to the smuggling of weapons into the Maze Prison. Section 3, Paragraph 6 of the Narey Report states: 'It has been impossible to establish how the firearms used in the shooting of Billy Wright entered the prison.'

The section of the Narey Report dealing with the murder of Billy Wright consists of 6 pages out of a 58-page document. Clearly this particular investigation of the murder of the LVF leader was neither as thorough or as rigorous, nor what would have been demanded by the general public.

15. The Inquest

The inquest into the death of Billy Wright took place in February 1999, 14 months after his death. Ironically, the venue chosen for the inquest, Downpatrick Courthouse, was the same location where Wright's killers, McWilliams, Glennon and Kennaway, had been tried and convicted of his murder four months earlier. The coroner in charge of the inquest proceedings was John Leckey, LLM, and Coroner for Greater Belfast.

Prior to the inquest, the Coroner had written to Wright's father, David, on 22 January 1999 confirming that he was allowing a period of two weeks for the hearing. The Coroner also asked David Wright to supply him with a statement containing his late son's full name, date of birth, address, occupation, marital status and last gainful employment. At this stage the Coroner also advised David Wright that he was free to raise any concerns about the circumstances in which his son met his death. In response to the request, on the 29 January 1999 David Wright supplied the Coroner with a dossier containing the results of his own investigations into the circumstances of his son's death. The dossier was hand delivered to the Coroner's officer in Newtownabbey, just outside Belfast, by an associate of David Wright.

Some two weeks later, David Wright received a copy of the list of witnesses to be called to give evidence at the inquest. To his amazement, none of the three senior governors of the Maze Prison were listed to attend the inquest or to give evidence. After discussions with his legal advisors, David Wright contacted the Coroner's office, requesting that the names of the Maze Prison's senior management team, Martin Mogg, Ken Crompton and Alan Shannon be added to the list of inquest witnesses. However, the Coroner declined to make any changes to his original list of inquest witnesses.

The inquest itself opened at 10.50 a.m. on Monday, 22 February 1999, under the direction of the Coroner, John Leckey. Before swearing in a jury, the Coroner informed the court that he had acceded to David Wright's request that he be allowed to represent himself at the inquest. There was an immediate objection from legal counsel representing the Northern Ireland Prison Service who argued that David Wright, as father of the deceased, had no real right to take part in the inquest proceedings or to question witnesses. However, the Coroner said in his opinion David Wright was a 'properly interested party' in relation to the inquest proceedings. Accordingly, he overruled the Northern Ireland Prison Service's objections. David Wright subsequently took his place in the well of the court alongside counsel for his grandchildren, the Prison Officers Association and the Northern Ireland Prison Service. At this stage David Wright again requested that the Coroner add the names of the members of the Maze Prison's senior management team, Martin Mogg, Ken Crompton and Alan Shannon, to the list of inquest witnesses. Once again the Coroner refused the request, apparently because Mogg, Crompton and Shannon were not on duty at the Maze on the morning of the murder. Following this ruling, the Coroner proceeded to swear in the jury of six men and two women. In his opening remarks, John Leckey outlined the facts relevant to the case. He also instructed the jury members that their function was limited in that they were to determine only who the deceased was and how and where he or she died.

The first person called to give evidence at the inquest was the Security Governor at the Maze, Stephen Davis. Although not included in the original list of witnesses drawn up by the Coroner, Davis, who took up his position as Security Governor in August 1997, had been called to provide background information on the Maze at the time of the Wright killing. Like Mogg, Shannon and Compton, Davis was not on duty on the morning of the murder but he was called as a witness. To enable Davis to explain the layout of an H Block, a model was sited in the well of the court in full view of the Coroner, the jury and the legal representatives. Using the model to point out the various locations, Governor Davis told the inquest that the same routine and pattern of operation applied to all the Maze H Blocks. He explained the layout of an H Block and the four wings that housed the cellular accommodation. During the course of his evidence Davis emphasised that because of the threat posed to each other by the LVF and INLA, prison vans were permitted to enter the forecourt of H Block 6. This provision, he said, did not apply to any of the other H Blocks at the Maze.

Surprisingly, Davis also revealed that the LVF and INLA prisoners on H6 were not locked in their cells, and that they had unsupervised access to the wings and exercise yards after 10 p.m. each night. He also revealed that prison staff did not check the INLA exercise yard during the hours of darkness. These were remarkable admissions indeed for a top security prison housing some of Northern Ireland's most notorious and infamous prisoners. However, these were only the first in a series of startling revelations by Governor Davis during his return to the witness box at the conclusion of the inquest.

Medical evidence on the cause of death was provided by Dr John Press, consultant pathologist, who carried out the postmortem on the body of Billy Wright. Dr Press said Wright had died due to a bullet wound to the chest. He said the paramilitary leader had been hit a number of times and these wounds would have caused rapid death within three to four minutes. He said there had been no evidence of alcohol in the body. Dr Press made no mention of, nor was the court informed of, any blood test having been carried out to determine the presence of illegal substances in Billy Wright's body.

The next witness to give evidence to the inquest was Billy Wright's father, David Wright, who said he wished to place before the court a series of matters or irregularities that gave cause for concern. Mr Wright told the court that on Friday, 26 December 1997 (the day prior to the murder), LVF prisoners had been given a photocopy of a sheet detailing the following day's visit. This was normal practice, however on this occasion, for the first time ever, the sheet contained details of the visits being taken by INLA prisoners. Normally LVF prisoners received a visit sheet which detailed only their own visits. The INLA prisoners received a different sheet with only their own visit details. David Wright told the court that considering the LVF sheet was a photocopy; it was logical to conclude that INLA prisoners received a similar copy. Therefore the INLA prisoners had prior knowledge (a day's notice) that Billy Wright was taking a visit the following day.

Another factor which in a way serves to corroborate David Wright's point is that this would have been his son's first ever Saturday-morning visit since arriving at the Maze some nine months earlier. In 1997, LVF prisoners housed in H Block 6 at the Maze had been denied Saturday-morning visits from April until the end of August.

For a further two months, following rioting by the LVF at the Maze on 13 August, the prisoners were held on a 23-hour lock-up policy at a different location within the Maze Prison. During his nine months at the Maze Billy Wright never took a Saturday-morning visit – a fact substantiated by visiting records. In other words Billy Wright had set no pattern of regular Saturday-morning visits, which would have allowed the INLA to monitor his movements. David Wright also raised the question of why the turnstile leading to the LVF exercise yard had remained locked on the morning of the murder. The INLA turnstile, however, had been unlocked in accordance with normal prison routine. This gave the INLA access to the exercise yard – a vital factor in the murder plan as they could only gain access to the roof via the yard itself.

Turning to the matter of the hole in the security fencing, David Wright questioned how this could have been cut without detection. He said to cut through a 20 ft hardened steel fence was a time-consuming task. This in turn prompted the question: how and when was the wire cut and by whom? It must have been cut well in advance so why had the breach in the security fencing not been detected by staff or the security cameras which were strategically placed within the exercise yard itself? David Wright also referred to the absence of the prison officer from the watchtower overlooking the INLA exercise yard close to A and B wings on H Block 6. He said the removal of the guard had been the result of a direct order from a governor-grade officer. Had the watchtower been manned the prison officer on duty would have seen the murderers, raised the alarm and in all probability prevented the murder taking place. David Wright went on to question how, despite the presence of high-security surveillance cameras and an army watchtower in close proximity to the murder scene, the INLA killers had moved unnoticed and undetected until after the murder had taken place.

David Wright informed the inquest jury that since the LVF prisoners had been transferred onto H Block 6 at the Maze their command structure had made numerous representations to senior prison management to have the INLA prisoners removed to another location within the confines of the jail. There were a number of reasons behind the request. Firstly, neither the LVF nor the INLA were part of the so-called ceasefire strategy, which existed in 1997 and found living in close proximity with one another antagonistic and intolerable. In other words both paramilitary groups considered the prison authorities' policy of forced coexistence a recipe for disaster. Secondly, when LVF prisoners returned to H Block 6 following the restricted 23-hour lock-up regime prison staff notified them that the INLA had issued a blanket death threat against all of them. Once again prison authorities did not consider the threat serious enough to justify the removal of either the LVF or INLA from H Block 6. On another occasion a prison officer told senior LVF prisoners that the INLA had promised to launch a 'spectacular' against them. Even this information failed to convince the prison authorities or the Northern Ireland Office to move one group of prisoners elsewhere.

David Wright said he questioned why, in light of evidence that showed officers on H Block 6 had sent three separate reports to prison management warning of a planned attack naming three INLA prisoners as the probable assailants, no action was taken. These same reports had expressed fears over the INLA prisoners' ability to gain access to the roof of H Block 6 (indeed as subsequent events later proved, this was the manner of attack adopted by the gunmen). In concluding his evidence to the inquest, David Wright said the points he had raised caused him great concern and they had led him to believe that his son's murder had been 'state orchestrated, state sponsored and state sanctioned, in collusion with some of those in prison management'.

At this point, Mr Nicholas Hanna, counsel for the Northern Ireland Prison Service expressed concern at David Wright's remarks, claiming he had provided the court with a list of questions and not relevant evidence.

After directing the jury to retire from the court, the Coroner, John Lackey, said David Wright's deposition had raised relevant issues of concern to the next of kin. The Coroner said he was satisfied that the questions posed would receive answers. However, in responding to the Coroner, Hanna said he objected to the Northern Ireland Prison Service being placed on trial at the inquest. However, the evidence of the next witness, auxiliary prison officer Jacqueline Wisely, raised further contentious issues and resulted in yet another a clash between David Wright and the Prison Service.

Jacqueline Wisely told the inquest that she had been employed at the Maze Prison since February 1997. She said that on 23 December that year she had been detailed by a principal officer to arrange the visiting permits for prisoners on the following Saturday, 27 December. Wisely said she filled out all the passes she had before phoning each of the Maze H Blocks to see if there were additional passes for any prisoners. She did not recall which blocks had extra requests but she did recall there were very few to be added on. Wisely then collated all the visitors' permits and sent a visits sheet to each individual block by internal mail. As there were no visits at the Maze on Christmas Eve, Christmas Day or Boxing Day, the visits for Saturday, 27 December were prepared four days in advance. Due to Christmas parole, a significant number of the prison population were away from the prison and, therefore, there would not have been the same volume of visits. Wisely told the court she performed the visits duty on an almost daily basis and considered herself to be au fait with the running of the system.

She went on to say that it was normal prison practice to send two separate visiting sheets to H Block 6 as it was the only block housing two opposing factions with INLA prisoners occupying A and B wings and the LVF prisoners in C and D wings. Jacqueline Wisely said she sent two separate visits sheets to H6 on Tuesday, 23 December. She sent one visit sheet to each of the prison's other H Blocks. She said she could not account for what happened to the individual visits sheets once they arrive at the designated blocks.

Jacqueline Wisely said she had been shown the two visiting sheets relating to H6 dated 27 December 1997. She said one sheet corresponded with the LVF visits while the other corresponded with the INLA visits. She confirmed that it was her handwriting that appeared – except for one or two entries, which she maintained would have been made by other members of staff during her absence at meal periods etc. Wisely went on to say that she accepted there were a few INLA prisoner names appended to the LVF visit-sheet. However, she said there were no LVF names on the visit-sheet which went to the INLA prisoners on A and B wings. She acknowledged a mistake had been made on the C and D wings visit-sheet in that the names of both LVF and INLA prisoners had been included.

However, she remained adamant that she had put copies of the LVF and INLA visits sheets into separate envelopes before sending them to the principal officer at H Block 6. The original document was retained in the prison visits office, she said.

However, the whole credibility of Jacqueline Wisely's evidence was called into question when David Wright produced a document, which he said had been given to him by LVF prisoners during a visit to the Maze a few days after the murder of his son. The document was the LVF visit-sheet for Saturday, 27 December 1997 and it differed from the one Wisely claimed she had sent to H6 on Tuesday, 23 December 1997. The production of yet another visits sheet at the inquest caused consternation in the court. It also came as a major shock to prison officer Jacqueline Wisely.

The authenticity of the document produced by David Wright was immediately questioned. David Wright was challenged on how he had obtained the visiting sheet and asked if he had made it available to the RUC murder investigation team. Despite the protestations, David Wright remained adamant that what he had handed to the court was the real LVF visits sheet and it was up to the Coroner to determine otherwise. However, following an adjournment to enable scrutiny of the David Wright document, it was accepted that it was the LVF visiting sheet for Saturday, 27 December 1997.

In all, four visit-sheets were submitted to the inquest as originals prepared by prison staff. Two of the sheets detailed the LVF visits on the day of the murder. The other two sheets related to the INLA visits. However, the fifth sheet, produced by David Wright at the inquest, also showed LVF visits. This sheet, the LVF prisoners said, was the one given to them on Friday, 26 December, the day before the murder. This particular list contains a total of 22 names, 17 of which were LVF prisoners, including Billy Wright. There were, however, the names of five INLA prisoners on the same list. The LVF list submitted to the inquest and compiled by Jacqueline Wisely contains a total of 25 names. It includes the five INLA prisoners and the names of three other LVF prisoners, McClean, McCready and Robley, who were not included on the list given to the LVF on 26 December. The INLA lists submitted to the inquest as originals contain only the names of nine INLA prisoners. Only one of the five INLA prisoners included on the list given to the LVF prisoners was included in the list given to the inquest.

The handwriting on all the sheets submitted to the inquest is identical and was accepted by prison officer Jacqueline Wisely as being her own. The discrepancies outlined in the visit sheets give rise to considerable concern. They also cast a considerable doubt on the provenance of the 'original' sheets submitted to the inquest. Furthermore, Wisely's argument that, although she made a mistake by including INLA names on the LVF visits sheet, she did not include LVF names on the INLA visits, fails to stand up to scrutiny once the provenance of the lists submitted to the inquest is called into question.

The issue surrounding the visit-sheets and the evidence given to the inquest by auxiliary prison officer Jacqueline Wisely was confused even further by Peter Mandelson, Secretary of State for Northern Ireland, some 14 months later. In a letter to David Wright, dated 8 May 2000, Mandelson wrote:

> You raise the question of differences in visits lists between that
> provided to LVF prisoners and the list provided to the Coroner's
> court. Only one master list for LVF prisoners is held by the

prison as the complete record of visits arranged for each particular day. The first copy of the list was issued to LVF prisoners in H6 on 24 December to indicate visits planned for 27 December. Between those dates the master list was updated to reflect additions to visits subsequently organised for prisoners. A copy of the updated master list of 27 December was the one provided by the Prison Service to the Coroner. I understand that this was explained during the Coroner's Inquest and that you took the opportunity to question the officer responsible for producing both lists.

However, assuming the visit-sheet given to the LVF prisoners is a genuine document, the Secretary of State's letter fails to answer a number of important questions.

Firstly, why were the LVF prisoners given a list containing the names of INLA prisoners? Secondly, were the INLA handed the same list, giving them prior warning that Billy Wright was receiving a visit the following day? LVF prisoners on H6 at that time maintain the list given to them was in fact a photocopy and it was more than likely that the INLA prisoners received a similar list. Furthermore, in light of the obvious and well-known tensions that existed between the INLA and the LVF within the Maze at that time, prison officer Wisely's error appears very serious indeed. Why then was no disciplinary action ever taken against her by the Prison Service? Perhaps more importantly, why have the police failed to investigate the confusion surrounding the visit-sheets when there was a doubt that a document submitted to the inquest may not have been genuine and could well have been compiled later.

Prison officer Wisely, when asked by David Wright if the only handwriting to appear on all the sheets was her own, admitted that was the case. This admission directly contradicts her earlier evidence to the inquest that alterations on the visits sheet had been made by other members of staff. The only handwriting to appear on all the visits sheets was that of prison officer Jacqueline Wisely. Therefore suspicion naturally falls on her as having compiled an additional visits sheet. However, it seems improbable that she was not directed to act as she did. The question therefore remains, who ordered the compilation of the visit-list submitted to the inquest as the LVF visits list for 27 December 1997, and why have the police failed to thoroughly investigate this matter and to question Jacqueline Wisely in relation to the compilation of the visit-sheets?

16. The Questions Remain Unanswered

Prison officer Brian Thompson told the inquest he had been on duty as 'hall guard' inside H Block 6 on Saturday, 27 December 1997. Thompson's function was to control all movement in and out of the accommodation block. The hall guard controls the two metal grilles located in the middle of the horizontal section of the block. One grille allows access to the block forecourt area the other provides access into the main area of the block known as the Circle.

Sometime between 9.15 a.m. and 9.30 a.m. Thompson said he let another officer into the block area. This officer had been ordered to drop his post in the observation tower at C and D wings (LVF wings) and report to the senior officer in H Block 6. Shortly afterwards, at around 9.30 a.m., Thompson said he let officer Raymond Hill into the block. Thompson described Hill as being 'very irate'. Hill told his fellow officer that he had been ordered to drop his post in the observation tower at A and B wings (INLA wings) and report to the prison visits area. Hill told Thompson he was going to see the principal officer (the senior officer on duty at H6) to protest his case for not dropping the A and B wing tower. Thompson told the inquest he advised officer Hill to contact the Prison Officers Association (POA) about the matter.

At around 9.50 a.m., Thompson said he heard Hill and senior officer Arthur Gallagher arguing in the Circle area. Thompson told the inquest that Gallagher stated that Governor McKee had said the observation towers he had ordered to be stood down in all the other blocks had done so without a problem. This exchange between Hill and Gallagher is significant as it appears to identify the prison official who gave the critical order to stand down the watchtower overlooking A and B

177

wings from where Wright's killers emerged to launch the murder attack. Thompson said he heard Hill tell Gallagher he was returning to the A and B wing observation tower. He then let Hill out into the forecourt area to enable him to return to the post he had left some minutes earlier.

Shortly afterwards, Thompson said he opened the outer grille to allow LVF prisoners Billy Wright and Norman Green escorted by officer Stephen Sterritt to access the transport which was waiting to take them to the visits area. At this stage, Thompson told the inquest that the white Ford Transit van used to take LVF prisoners to their visits was parked adjacent to the INLA wing. According to LVF prisoners, this was the first time their van had parked in this manner. Normally it would have been parked alongside their wing, minimising their exposure to view or the threat of possible attack by the INLA.

After Wright and Green left the block, Thompson said he was about to record their details on his block roll board when he heard shouts coming from the forecourt area. However, within seconds of Wright and Green entering the prison van the INLA killers struck. Officer Thompson's account to the inquest jury of the murder of Billy Wright was detailed and accurate. However, it was the other aspects of his evidence to the jury that raised questions about security within the Maze Prison itself.

According to Thompson, on the 24 October 1997, some two months prior to the murder of Billy Wright, he and another prison officer warned Governor Eagleston, Acting Governor Ramsden and Governor Ken Crompton (Martin Mogg's immediate subordinate) of the danger of a rooftop attack being launched within H Block 6. The meeting took place at the request of the prison management who said they were concerned about potential LVF violence. However, Thompson told the inquest that they informed the governors in strong terms that the INLA prisoners posed a greater threat and there were real fears amongst prison staff of a shooting on H Block 6. Thompson said he had pointed out that the roof areas of H6 were insecure and there was nothing to prevent the INLA from climbing over the roof and shooting LVF prisoners or from shooting at them from a cell window. Thompson said prison governors were told in the strongest terms that the LVF and INLA should not be accommodated in the same block. Significantly, Thompson and Gillam reminded prison management that an INLA prisoner, Christopher 'Crip' McWilliams, who had been transferred into the Maze in mid-1997, had been able to smuggle a gun into Maghaberry Prison earlier the same year. Thompson went on to say they had also expressed their concerns that a gun could be smuggled into the Maze during the INLA Christmas party on 15 December 1997 because the prisoners attending them were never searched, either going to or returning from the party. Thompson told the inquest that Governor Eagleston had informed him that their concerns would be reported to Maze Governor Martin Mogg, who wanted to get to grips with the overall problem. However, Thompson said that as far as he was concerned nothing was ever done about the issues he and Gillam had raised.

However, during a visit to the Maze Prison on 1 February 2000, Governor Ken Crompton denied to David Wright and Ulster Unionist MP, Jeffrey Donaldson, that the October meeting between prison management and staff had ever taken place. Management's denial of any such meeting appears puzzling in relation to comments contained in the Narey Report into the murder of Billy Wright.

In Paragraph 3.14 Narey states:

> Staff and the Prison Officers Association (POA) had voiced their concerns to prison management in the months prior to the shooting about the ease of access of H Block roofs. In particular, they told managers they had observed INLA prisoners behaving suspiciously in the exercise yards as if discussing the security fencing, watchtower and roof areas.

Thompson's remark that, 'you could feel the hatred for Billy Wright and every officer knew it' poses further concerns that senior management in the Maze did not take proactive security measures in relation to the obvious dangers that existed within H Block 6 in 1997.

However, it was his comment, 'had the alarm been raised earlier I may have been able to open the grille and allow them back in', that highlighted the significance of the order to remove the prison officer from the watchtower overlooking the INLA wings. Had the officer still been in place he would have seen the three INLA prisoners emerge from the accommodation block, enter the sterile area and raise the alarm. At that stage, it is argued, Billy Wright would have had sufficient time to return to the safety of the H Block before the gunmen reached the killing zone itself. The question of who gave the order to remove the prison officer was again raised during the evidence to the inquest of prison officer Raymond Hill.

Hill told the inquest that on the morning of 27 December 1997 he reported for duty on H6 at 8.15 a.m. and was assigned to the watchtower overlooking the INLA A and B wing accommodation and exercise yards. Hill said he collected the keys for the watchtower from the block control room and walked through the forecourt and around the top of A wing in order to reach the tower itself. Once in the tower, Hill contacted the block control room via an intercom and checked the alarm system, which was fully operational. At approximately 8.50 a.m., Hill said he received a call over the intercom instructing him to come down from the tower and report to the principal officer's post within the administration area of H6. Hill complied with the order and made his way back to the main gates of H6 where he was told by another officer that there had been a change of heart and he was to return to the watchtower.

Around 9.30 a.m., Hill told the inquest he was again contacted via the intercom system and ordered for a second time to quit his post in the watchtower. However, on this occasion Hill was ordered to report to the prison visits area and not to H6 itself.

It is clear from Raymond Hill's evidence that on both occasions the order to vacate his post in the watchtower came via the control room on H6. On the morning of 27 December 1997, two prison officers – Alan Danks and Aidan Flanaghan – were operating the block control room. Danks was responsible for manning the telephones and recording information in the control room logbook. Flanaghan's duties that morning were to monitor the intercom system and to operate the electronic locking system within the block itself. As Flanaghan was responsible for the intercom system it is logical to conclude that he received and passed on the order for Hill to quit his post in the watchtower. It is also logical to conclude that he would have known the identity of the individual issuing the instruction. However, Flanaghan made no mention of the incident in his written deposition or during his oral evidence to the inquest. Officer Hill, in his deposition to the inquest, clearly identified Flanaghan as the officer who had first ordered him to quit his post in the watchtower at 8.50 a.m. that morning.

The same logic can also be applied to the evidence of the other officer manning the control room. Alan Danks, although responsible for answering telephones and maintaining the control room logbook, makes no mention of the incident involving Raymond Hill. Nor does Danks make any reference as to whether or not he recorded the instruction to stand Hill down from his post in the control room log. Danks was able to recollect the fact that at 9.50 a.m. he had received a telephone call from an officer in the LVF visits area informing him that there were visitors for Billy Wright. Danks' deposition to the inquest also clearly states that he telephoned through to Locations and recorded in the control room logbook that Billy Wright and Norman Green had left H6 en route to the visits area. As the Prison Service have refused access to the H6 control room logbook it is not known if details of who gave the order to remove the officer from his post in the watchtower had been recorded by Alan Danks.

On receiving the second order to stand down from his post in the watchtower overlooking A and B wings, Raymond Hill contacted an official of the Prison Officers Association to complain. The official, prison officer Blundell, told Hill to sit tight while he raised the matter with the Maze duty governor. Five minutes later Blundell contacted Hill advising him that the situation was being reassessed. At 9.50 a.m. senior officer Arthur Gallagher told Hill to return to his post in the watchtower. On his way back to the tower, Hill said he noticed two vans in the forecourt area, one red, and the other white. They were both parked side by side at the entrance/exit to the hall guard area where prison officer Brian Thompson was on duty.

As he was climbing back up into the watchtower (which is some 25–30 ft above the ground) Hill said he heard a burst of gunfire – some six or seven shots – and he opened the sliding window in the tower to see what was gong on. Immediately he noticed a prisoner on the roof of A wing of H6 and pulled the alarm, which in town triggers the alarm in the block control room and the Emergency Control Room (ECR), which is centrally located within the Maze Prison. He said he then spoke to the block control room, via the intercom, and informed them: 'I have heard what sounded like gunfire and there are prisoners on the roof of A wing.' By that stage the three INLA prisoners had clambered back onto the roof of A wing, crossed it and jumped down into the sterile area returning inside the wing via the entrance yard door. Hill again contacted the block control room and asked for permission to come down from his post due to imminent danger. The request was granted and Hill made his way to the main gate of H Block, a journey of only a few minutes, where he spoke to either Governor Brian Barlow or senior officer Wiggam and told them what had happened; he identified the INLA prisoners as Christopher 'Crip' McWilliams, John Glennon and John Kennaway. Hill then went directly to the prison hospital where he received treatment for shock.

However, there are aspects of Raymond Hill's evidence that have yet to be fully explained. Firstly, why was he called out of his post in direct contravention of a local agreement between the Prison Officers

Association and prison management within the Maze, which stated that because of the close proximity of the rival factions on H6, the watchtowers on that particular block were not to be stood down? When Raymond Hill made this information known to the inquest, counsel for the Northern Ireland Prison Service immediately challenged its veracity. However, a copy of the internal agreement document was later produced in court, placing its existence beyond doubt. This in turn poses the question: why was the internal agreement broken for the first time on the morning Billy Wright was shot dead? Secondly, why have the authorities refused to reveal the identity of the officer who gave the order to stand down the officer in the watchtower? The Narey Report makes it clear that the order originated from the duty governor of the Maze. Paragraph 3.18 of the Narey Report, in accepting the existence of the local agreement, states:

> The duty governor insists he instructed the watchtowers overlooking all the H Blocks should be stood down with the exception of the H6 tower overlooking the INLA yard, but that this order had somehow been misinterpreted with the result that the H6 A and B tower was stood down. The duty governor ordered the officer to return to the tower and while he was doing so, Mr Wright was shot. As the officer entered the tower, the prisoners returned across the H Block roof to their exercise yard. The failure to have the post manned at a critical time has damaged public confidence in the Prison Service, fuelling allegations of conspiracy.

However, an opportunity to question the duty governor or to obtain clarity on the standing down of the watchtower was not afforded to David Wright and the other legal representatives, as the officer in question was not included in the list of inquest witnesses.

The conclusion by the Narey Report that had Hill been in the watchtower the murder of Billy Wright would still have gone ahead is more than surprising. Timing is critical in this instance, but had Hill been at his post in the tower and raised the alarm as soon as he saw the murderers clamber onto the roof then the murder might have been prevented. Hill, in response to a question from David Wright, made it clear that had he been in the tower he would have seen the INLA prisoners emerge from the block and enter the sterile area. Had the alarm been raised at that point in time it is more than feasible that Billy

Wright would have had sufficient time to return to the safety of the H Block itself.

The NIO assertion that Wright could not have re-entered the block because all the grilles were electronically locked when the alarm was raised is discredited by the fact that only four grilles, those leading directly into the Circle area, are electronically controlled from the ECR. The prison officers on duty within the block itself operate the remaining grilles manually.

The Northern Ireland Branch of the Prison Officers Association, in a subsequent memorandum to the Select Committee on Northern Ireland Affairs, said: 'In fact the murder of Billy Wright could have been avoided had the H6 observation tower not been stood down to allow staff to go on visits.' However, the then Secretary of State for Northern Ireland, Peter Mandelson, disagreed with this statement. In a letter to David Wright dated 8 May 2000, Mandelson said depositions made available to the Court stated that the INLA prisoners positioned themselves in such a way as to observe Billy Wright's departure from the block. Mr Mandelson's letter states that the INLA prisoners did not move out of their wing until they were sure that Wright had already emerged from the block. In an earlier chapter that particular argument has been disproved in a detailed engineer's report of the Maze murder scene commissioned by David Wright's legal team.

In February 2000, during a meeting with David Wright, the Maze Governor, Martin Mogg, questioned Raymond Hill's assertion that he had twice been called out of his post in the watchtower on 27 December 1997. Mogg told David Wright and Jeffrey Donaldson MP that Hill had been mistaken and had in fact only been stood down from his post once, at 9.30 a.m. However, Hill refuted Mogg's claim and remains adamant that he was stood down twice from the tower on the morning of the murder.

It is worth noting that following his transfer to Maghaberry Prison, Martin Mogg wrote to Raymond Hill in 1999 stating:

> I have no doubt that you were ordered down from the tower overlooking the exercise yard. The information I had at the time was that a message was passed to the Senior Officer in H6 to stand down the tower and that order was given to you and which you despite misgivings, properly obeyed.
>
> The confusion which the Narey Report refers to was in the administration building where the person who gave the instruction to H6 stated that he was told to do this by a

governor grade, whereas the governor grade claims that this was not his instruction.

The letter went on to say: 'I know from our discussions in January that you are keen to make the most of your career in the Prison Service and I wish you and your family well in this.'

Mogg's letter to Hill clearly states that the instruction to stand down the watchtower in H6 came from the administration building (AIMS) at the Maze. It also states that the order originated from an officer of governor grade. However, during his meeting with David Wright, Mogg said the order to stand down the watchtower would have been given by 'security'. As Governor of the Maze Prison, Martin Mogg would have been fully conversant with the events of 27 December 1997. As such, it is logical to conclude he would have known exactly where such a controversial order originated, therefore he has provided different versions of what happened to David Wright and Raymond Hill. Mogg would have been well aware of the identity of the duty governor for 27 December 1997. He would also have been aware of the identity of the security governor on the same date. One would expect that Governor Mogg is in possession of the information determining which one of the three governor grades on duty at the Maze between 7.30 a.m. and 5 p.m. at the weekend gave the order relating to the H6 tower.

The confusion over who gave the order to stand down the watchtower or whether the order related to H6, has never been satisfactorily resolved. Neither Martin Mogg, nor the acting security governor on 27 December and the duty governor on that date were called to give evidence to the inquest. Considering the relevance of all three individuals in relation to the events of Saturday, 27 December 1997, the decision not to call them as inquest witnesses meant that this confusion could not be resolved in open court.

The evidence of LVF prisoner Norman Green, who had been sitting beside Wright when the killers struck, also raised a number of issues which were never satisfactorily resolved because of the narrow remit of the inquest itself. Green initially raised the matter of the parking of the two prison vans used to transport the LVF and INLA prisoners to their respective visits area. Green maintained that the two vans always parked in the same position, the red van adjacent to the INLA A and B wings and the white van close to the LVF C and D wings. H6 was the only block within the Maze where prison vans were permitted to enter the forecourt area because of the threat posed to each other by the rival factions. Green told the inquest it was believed the parking of the white van close to the LVF wing minimised the risk of attack by the INLA. However, on the morning of Saturday, 27 December 1997, Green maintained the vans had been parked the other way around – the first time this had ever happened. The fact that their van had been parked away from their wing meant LVF prisoners going to visits had to walk significantly closer to the INLA accommodation. As Norman Green's description of the actual shooting incident is covered elsewhere in this book, it is not proposed to expand on that aspect of his evidence at this stage. However, it is worth noting Green's account of the actions of the two prison officers present when the shooting took place.

According to Green, immediately after the shooting he asked the escorting officer, Stephen Sterritt, if the killers had gone. At that stage, Sterritt, who had cowered in the corner of the van throughout the attack, made no reply. Instead, he simply stood up, stepped over the dying Billy Wright, who had fallen over Norman Green, and clambered out of the van. He then made his way to the safety of the air lock at the main entrance gates of H Block 6, leaving Green cradling the dying Wright in his arms. The van driver, John Parks, also fled the murder scene for the safety of the block main gates. Green remained alone and unprotected in the forecourt of H6 for several minutes before help arrived in the form of other prison staff.

Driver Parks, in response to a question from David Wright, admitted to the inquest that he had walked away from the scene of the shooting without looking back. Sterritt was excused on medical grounds from giving evidence to the inquest.

At that stage of the proceedings, counsel for the NIPS once again raised objections to the manner of David Wright's participation in the inquest. Counsel argued that the line of questioning adopted by Wright's father was an attempt to broaden the scope of the inquest rather than to decide how the deceased came to meet his death. On this occasion, Counsel persuaded the Coroner, John Leckey, to limit the scope of the inquest. Therefore the inquest format did not offer David Wright the opportunity to ask the questions that raised concerns about collusion in the murder of the LVF leader. It is clear that the inquest format is at fault and not the Coroner.

17. The Fight for the Truth

Prison officer George Patience told the inquest that on 22 December 1997, a full five days before the murder, the PTZ (Pan Tilt Zoom) overhead security camera No 3 overlooking the roof of H Block 6 had been reported defective by the senior officer on duty. Despite the importance of this camera within the Maze Prison's security operational procedures, it remained inoperative with the result that the three INLA prisoners were able to cross the roof of a wing, H Block 6, undetected. Once alerted to the attack, staff in the Emergency Control Room trained another camera, No 4, onto the roof of H Block 6. However, by that stage, the attack had taken place and Billy Wright was almost certainly dead.

Strangely, the Narey Report makes no reference to the defective security camera. It must therefore be assumed that the Narey investigation team were unaware of the problem with the camera. If that was the case, the thoroughness of Narey's investigation is called into question. However, more importantly, it also gives rise to the question: why did the prison authorities not take action to have the security camera repaired?

The deposition of senior officer Arthur Gallagher proved to be particularly interesting. Gallagher, a prison officer with 26 years' service, told the inquest he had worked on H Block 6 for six years. Gallagher said that during those six years he had come to know the LVF and INLA prisoners housed there. He went on to say that on the morning of 27 December 1997 H6 had a deficit of three members of staff, a store man and two officers from the LVF C and D wings.

At approximately 10 a.m. Gallagher said he heard a lot of yelling and shouting on the block. By this time the INLA prisoners had attacked and killed Billy Wright. However, at no time in his deposition or evidence to the jury did senior officer Gallagher refer to the events that occurred prior to the killing of the LVF leader. However, it was not the oral evidence but the content of SO Gallagher's deposition that proved to be of interest to David Wright. As a properly interested person, approved by the Coroner to participate fully in the inquest, David Wright had access to copies of all the witness statements after they had been read out in open court. On examining the deposition of SO Gallagher, it was discovered that a portion of the text, 14 lines on page 3, had been redacted.

Quite clearly the redacted portion of Gallagher's deposition confirms that PO Molloy received the call ordering the removal of the watchtower guards. The decision to redact this particular section of SO Gallagher's statement was made by the Coroner, John Leckey. This was subsequently confirmed in a letter dated 22 September 2000 from Siobhan Broderick, solicitor to the Coroner, to David Wright. The letter stated that the Coroner did not consider this information to be relevant. On the contrary, David Wright believed this information was extremely relevant and would have been of assistance to the family in determining the sequence of events in this instance. Is it not logical to conclude that Molloy, as a principal officer in charge of H Block 6, would have most certainly either known the identity of the person giving such a crucial instruction or if not, ascertained who the instruction came from? Clearly, PO Molloy is a link in the chain of events relating to the standing down of the watchtower guard and his evidence could have clarified a number of crucial issues surrounding the watchtower issue. However, despite having been in charge of H Block 6 on the morning of Wright's murder and having his name included in the list of inquest witnesses, PO Molloy did not in fact give evidence to the court. As such, none of the legal representatives nor David Wright had the opportunity to question Molloy on any matter.

The decision not to call PO Molloy as a witness was taken by the Coroner, John Leckey, during the course of inquest proceedings. Although present in court and apparently ready to testify if required, on the Wednesday of the inquest counsel for the Coroner, Jemma Loughran, told Molloy and another prison official, Governor Brian Barlow, they would not be required to give evidence.

It was only on 18 September 2000, after he had attended the Coroner's office to inspect the inquest papers, that David Wright realised the witness depositions of Barlow and Molloy were not included in the files. During the same visit, he also discovered that, although the Security Governor Stephen Davis had made a deposition, it had not been presented in court to any of the legal representatives during the course of his evidence. However, the Coroner did have a copy of the deposition as was proved by his handwritten notes added to the document in response to questions posed to Davis. A request by David Wright to have access to the Barlow and Molloy depositions was refused by the Coroner on the grounds that since they did not give evidence their depositions could not be made available for inspection. As a result, David Wright applied to the Belfast High Court on February 2001 for a judicial review of the Coroner's decision not to allow him access to the two witness depositions. Mr Wright relied on Article 2 of the European Convention on Human Rights and Articles 3 and 6 of the Human Rights Act. In light of the submissions made on behalf of Mr Wright at the judicial review proceedings, the Coroner considered the request again and decided to exercise his discretion in favour of disclosure of the witness statements of Brian Barlow and John Brian Molloy, on the grounds that the rights of David Wright under Article 2 to the European Convention on Human Rights were engaged. As a result, copies of the two disputed depositions were forwarded to solicitors acting on behalf of David Wright.

However, the papers forwarded to David Wright's solicitors were not in fact properly prepared inquest witness depositions, rather they were police witness statements, as was clearly stated at the head of each document. The statements also included the date they were made and the identity of the police officer taking the statement. Neither document had been signed, as was the case with all the other witness depositions.

The statement said to be that given by PO John Brian Molloy consisted of less than two pages. The content of Molloy's statement is extremely limited and contrasts sharply with the depositions of other inquest witnesses. Although he mentions having spoken to Governor McKee informing him of the seriousness of the situation on H Block 6 following the shooting, surprisingly Molloy makes absolutely no mention of any telephone call ordering the watchtowers to be stood down.

Brian Barlow's actual role within the Maze Prison on 27 December 1997 was as an acting governor, grade 5. As such he would not have been of sufficient status to be placed in charge of the Maze Prison on that date. He was, however, one of three governor-grade officers on duty within the prison between the hours of 7.30 a.m. and 5 p.m. By his own admission in his police statement, Barlow was in the security department at 10 a.m. when he received a telephone call from the Maze ECR stating an alarm had been received from H Block 6. In his statement, Barlow says he did not know the identity of the caller, a malaise that appears to have been endemic within the Maze Prison that particular morning. However, in the same statement Barlow states that he spoke to PO Molloy on H6 who informed him of a shooting within the Block forecourt.

Barlow's statement goes on to detail the events that unfolded within H Block 6 in the aftermath of the killing of Billy Wright. Events in which he clearly played a key role included direct dialogue with the INLA killer McWilliams, the supervision of the removal of both the weapons used in the killing and the INLA prisoners from their wings and into police custody. Elsewhere in his statement, Barlow also stated he relayed his conversation with the INLA prisoner 'Crip' McWilliams to Governor McKee, who Barlow says was in the command post. The fact that specific information was being relayed to McKee at this time by a number of officers, including Barlow and Molloy, is interesting. It would point to his seniority within the three governor grades on duty that morning. When placed alongside his location within the Maze command post it appears to indicate that McKee was in fact the duty governor and the individual in overall charge of the Maze Prison on 27 December 1997.

The non-appearance of Barlow and Molloy as inquest witnesses, along with the non-inclusion of McKee in the original witness list, meant that many questions David Wright wished to ask about the murder of his son remained unanswered. Unfortunately, the format of the inquest system in Northern Ireland is very limited and indeed has been criticised in recent European Court judgements. The European Court also recognises that due to deficiencies in the inquest system families could not get at the truth of what happened in controversial killings, such as that of Billy Wright. Furthermore, these same deficiencies have enhanced suspicions with the Wright family and sections of the Northern Ireland community that a cover-up exists in relation to the many unanswered questions surrounding the murder of the LVF leader.

This suspicion was further fuelled on 25 May 2000, when Ulster Unionist MP Jeffrey Donaldson received a response to his Parliamentary Question seeking the name of the duty governor of the Maze Prison on 27 December 1997. Junior NIO Minister, Adam

Ingram replied: 'On security grounds, I am not prepared to name the governor in question.'

Donaldson subsequently raised the matter again in a personal letter to Ingram in July the same year. Once again the minister refused to name the duty governor of the Maze.

However, the Prisoners and Young Offenders Centre Rules Northern Ireland 1995 states: 'The governor shall attend any inquest following the death of a prisoner in his custody, or arrange for an appropriate officer to do so, and shall report to the Secretary of State on the findings of the inquest.'

On 18 May 2000, David Wright wrote to the Coroner and asked why this rule had not apparently been followed in the case of his son's murder. He also asked who was the governor in charge of the Maze Prison on the day of the murder. The Coroner refused to answer these particular questions. However, four months later, the solicitor to the Coroner wrote to David Wright informing him that Governor Stephen Davis had attended the inquest. The letter creates the impression that Davis was present at the inquest in the capacity of 'an appropriate officer', although it does not say so in so many words.

Maze Security Governor Stephen Davis was the only witness called upon to give evidence to the inquest twice. Despite his two appearances in the witness box, his deposition was not handed out to the participants, as was the case with each of the other inquest witnesses. However, a subsequent search of the inquest file by David Wright unearthed the security governor's deposition containing handwritten notes taken by the Coroner in relation to Davis' response to questions asked by the various legal representatives. Although the Davis deposition consisted of a mere seven lines of evidence, his responses to the various questions put to him during the inquest takes up a full five pages. The information contained in those responses gives an interesting and somewhat startling insight into the operation of H Block 6, HMP Maze in 1997.

Stephen Davis told the inquest that the prisoners on H6, both LVF and INLA, were free to move up and down their respective wings on a 24-hour basis and during the hours of daylight had unrestricted access to the exercise yards. At night, with staff levels at a minimum, prison officers did not enter the wings or the exercise yard area because it would be dangerous to do so. In other words Davis was saying the prisoners were free to do what they liked without fear of sanction from prison staff.

The security governor told the court that the officers in the watchtower overlooking the Block exercise yards were withdrawn from their post at 8.15 p.m. daily. The exercise yards remained open and unsupervised until 10 p.m., a period of almost two hours before the turnstiles leading to them were locked. Unlike the LVF turnstile, which had to be secured manually by prison staff, the INLA turnstile was controlled by an electronic dead bolt system operated from control room. However, Davis admitted that in the past prisoners had managed to sheer the bolt by putting pressure on it. He also admitted that it would have been possible for the INLA prisoners to have cut the hole in the prison fence between the standing down of the watchtower guard at 8.15 p.m. and the locking of the exercise-yard turnstile. But Davis could not tell exactly when the hole had been cut because the fence was never inspected at any time. Indeed it was revealed that the last time prison staff had inspected the security fencing within the INLA exercise yard was in July 1997 – five months before Billy Wright was shot dead. Davis' excuse for the non-inspection of the H6 security fencing over a five-month period was put down to safety concerns for prison staff. It appears that as far as prison staff were concerned, their safety was of more importance that the secure confinement of some of Northern Ireland's most vicious paramilitary prisoners.

In response to a question from David Wright, the security governor told the inquest jury he did not know how long the hole had been in the fence, but that he knew of it immediately after the shooting. Davis denied any knowledge of a report having been made by prison staff of the possibility of a hole having been cut in the fence prior to the day of the murder. The report in question was made by a dog handler, in early December 1997, that while on night duty patrolling the perimeter fence he had heard what he described as 'rasping sounds', coming from the INLA B wing area of H6. It is also worth noting, prison authorities have stated that at the time of the incident a member of prison staff entered the INLA wings to carry out a check. It would appear that on this particular occasion there were obviously no concerns for the safety of prison staff. As previously stated, following the officer's visit to the INLA wing, three separate prison journals record that all was secure within the Maze Prison. The inadequate response to this report casts doubt on the thoroughness of the standard operational procedures within HM Prison Maze. It also casts doubts on the thoroughness of standing operational procedures within the prison itself.

However, Stephen Davis did accept that had the prison officer been at his post in the watchtower overlooking A and B wings he could have seen the three INLA prisoners in the sterile area where the hole had been cut. Davis admitted that had an alarm been raised at that point during the attack it would have given a few extra seconds' warning. However, it is most probable that those few seconds would have been even longer than Davis believed. As it would have been impossible for the three INLA prisoners to go through the hole in the fence at the same moment in time – the hole in the fence measuring just 24 in. x 27 in., they could only have gone through one at a time. The time taken to do so, combined with the time taken to remove the cut section of the fence, is estimated at between 20 and 25 seconds. Even then the three prisoners still had to run to the window, scale the wall, cross the roof, get down from it and make their way to the prison van before killing Billy Wright. It can be strongly argued that had the alarm been sounded at the time the three INLA prisoners entered the sterile area, then Billy Wright could have returned to a place of safety.

The security governor also maintained that the area where the INLA cut the security fence was a blind spot and not covered by the CCTV cameras mounted along the perimeter. He also stated that the hole in the fence was not visible from the watchtower overlooking A and B wings. That can be accepted in that nobody, except the killers, knew the wire had been cut in the first instance. As the cut section had been replaced, temporally secured with shoelaces and obscured from view, there was no visible hole in the fence, so how could it be seen? It is beyond argument that had the guard been at his post in the watchtower he would have seen the killers enter the sterile area to remove the cut section of wire. However, as he had been ordered out of his post, the alarm could not have been raised, alerting prison staff and Billy Wright to the threat of possible danger.

Significantly, Stephen Davis said before the Wright murder he was aware of the concerns raised by prison staff and the Prison Officers Association in relation to the housing of two rival factions on the same accommodation block and the vulnerability of the block roof areas. Prison staff continued to make these same representations to prison management even after the visits vans were permitted to enter the block forecourt area in an effort to minimise the risk of an attack being mounted by either of the rival factions. Davis told the inquest that there was no alternative accommodation available within the Maze Prison that would have allowed the prison authorities to rehouse either group. However, in August 1997, following disturbances on H6, LVF prisoners were removed from the Block and housed elsewhere for a period of weeks until repairs to their accommodation were completed.

Considering the tensions and threat of potential violence, which clearly existed between the LVF and INLA within H6, why did prison management not make this a permanent arrangement? Why did they deliberately ignore the concerns and warnings of prison staff and return the LVF prisoners to their wings on H6 and into the powder-keg situation that existed there at that time? The absence of a senior Maze governor from the inquest prevented any of those questions being asked and any answers being given which might have shed light on the reasons behind their decisions. Furthermore, the admissions by Stephen Davis, the Security Governor of the Maze, that INLA prisoners were free to move up and down their respective wings on a 24-hour basis and that prison staff did not inspect security fencing as they were concerned for their own welfare, undermines any claim that the Prison Service's priority was for the overall security of H6. It is noted that this situation had only been allowed to exist for a period of five months. As the Maze prison had been operational, in one form or another, for 30 years, it is clear that prison officers could have exercised control in the wings and in this area, had they so wished, as after all they had exercised control for a number of decades prior to this murder.

There was little doubt among those present at the inquest that the evidence of Governor Stephen Davis raised awkward questions for the Northern Ireland Prison Service. Admissions by Davis that fences had not been inspected for over five months, that prisoners roamed the wings as they pleased 24 hours a day, exercise yards were left unsupervised for periods of time, security locks could be sheered and that he was aware of the concerns of prison officers regarding the housing of two rival groups on H6 and the vulnerability of the prison roofs, caused considerable concern and were widely reported by the media at the time. However, the fact that the prison authorities had failed to act to redress these problems is of even greater concern.

It should also be pointed out that although he held the post of security governor at the Maze, Stephen Davis was not one of the three governor grades on duty on 27 December 1997. Like Martin Mogg, Ken Crompton and Alan Shannon he was not present during the murder of Billy Wright, but unlike the other three, he was required to attend the inquest and to give evidence twice.

18. Person or Persons Unknown

The last witness to be called, senior RUC investigating officer in the Wright murder, Detective Superintendent John Robinson Shortt, gave evidence on the third day of the inquest. Shortt said that as a result of his enquiries into the murder he had established that at 9.50 a.m. on Saturday, 27 December 1997, prison officers on duty at H6 were notified that visitors had arrived at the prison to see Billy Wright and Norman Green. However, former associates of Billy Wright have stated that his visitor arrived at the Maze reception area at 9.30 a.m. on the morning of the killing – a time which coincides with the timing of the order to remove the prison officer from his post in the observation tower overlooking the INLA wings on H6. They also state that Wright's visitor had not been unduly delayed by the standard search procedures within the prison visits area and insist that the message informing prison officers on H6 of the Wright visit had been conveyed well before the alleged time of 9.50 a.m. It would be logical to conclude that details of this particular message and the movement of Wright and Green would have been recorded in the Control Room journal on H6 which was the responsibility of prison officer Alan Danks on the morning of the murder.

In his inquest deposition, Danks does state that at approximately 9.50 a.m. he 'recorded the names and prison numbers of the two inmates who were to be taken to visits'. However, as the H6 Control Room journal has never been made available by the prison authorities for inspection it has been impossible to ascertain the precise time information on Wright's visit was conveyed by prison staff at the visits reception area to the officers on H6.

What is clear, however, is that if the information provided by all those who gave evidence to the inquest is accurate and correct, then there was considerable activity within H6 on and around 9.50 a.m. on Saturday, 27 December 1997. At that time prison officer Hill is alleged to have been disputing the instruction to remove him from the watchtower with senior officer Gallagher. Billy Wright and Norman Green were being called for visits. Other prison staff were busy removing meals trolleys from the wings and an INLA prisoner was noticed painting a wall mural within the block that had been completed days earlier. Despite the presence of so many individuals it is strange to note that few of them can agree on the exact time Billy Wright was called for a visit.

The officer on duty at the C and D wing grilles gives the time as 10 a.m. as do several other officers present in H6 that morning.

However, the driver of the LVF visits van, John Parks, says he heard Wright and Green being called for their visits some 15 minutes earlier at 9.45 a.m. Other prison staff, who state that the alarm, which was only sounded after the INLA prisoners carried out their attack, was sounded at 10 a.m., further extend the confusion over the time. In light of the obvious confusion that surrounds this particular aspect of the murder, how can the police can state with certainty that Billy Wright was called for his visit at 9.50 a.m.? Whose evidence did the police investigation team accept as being correct and whose evidence did they deem to be inaccurate or unreliable?

In response to a question from counsel for the Wright children in relation to the placing of a chair in front of the breach in the exercise-yard fencing, Detective Superintendent Shortt told the inquest he did not consider it unusual that INLA prisoners would have had chairs in their exercise yard in winter. However, taking into consideration the nature of an Irish winter, it seems highly improbable that prisoners of any political persuasion would be inclined to sit out in the open for protracted periods of time. What the police did not discover, or if they did it was not revealed to the inquest, is whether or not chairs were normally placed in the narrow confines of the area leading from A and B wing accommodation to the exercise yard. A visit to the area would suggest that any prisoner wishing to sit outside would do so in the open area of the exercise yard itself and not the restrictive location of the sterile area close to the block turnstile.

Shortt was also unable to tell precisely when the hole in the prison fence had been cut, although he did say it had to have been done before the time of the Wright visit! In response to a question from David Wright in relation to claims by prison staff that they had noticed prisoners acting suspiciously in the area where the hole had been cut and had alerted prison authorities, Shortt said no one had said anything about any suspicious activity. In relation to the time it would have taken the INLA prisoners to cut the hole in the prison fence, Shortt told the inquest that he thought this possible in an hour. He also said the INLA prisoners could have cut the hole over a period of time. Once again this aspect of the investigation remains unclear. The Detective Superintendent was also unable to state if, following the murder attack, the INLA killers had carried the weapons back over the roof and into the block area or whether they had passed them to other prisoners inside the wings via an open window. However, Shortt did say that one of the weapons, an automatic pistol, had been recovered with a round still in the breech and he would not have wanted to carry such a weapon back over the roof. The police officer said he had been unable to establish exactly when, where or how the weapons used to kill Billy Wright had been smuggled in to the Maze Prison. However, when challenged about this by David Wright, Shortt was able to state that one of the weapons, a semi-automatic pistol, had been used in a punishment shooting in September 1997. He subsequently told the inquest that it appeared the weapons had been brought into the Maze sometime between 30 September 1997 and 27 December 1997 but he could not identify precisely when.

It is also worth noting the investigating officer's remarks in relation to the time he estimates it would have taken the INLA prisoners to carry out the murder attack. Shortt told the inquest that it would have taken the INLA prisoners some 20–30 seconds to get through the hole in the fencing and into the forecourt area. According to David Wright, if this estimation is to be believed then the three INLA killers belonged in a circus act. Informed, qualified, independent, professional opinion has stated that it would have taken almost 70 seconds for the INLA prisoners to carry out this particular aspect of the murder. An opinion which questions the RUC assessment of the attack.

However, it was Detective Superintendent Shortt's closing remarks which were worth noting and call into question the situation that existed or had been created within the Maze Prison on the morning Billy Wright was shot dead. He said: 'In my opinion the murder should never have happened if the proper security measures were in place.'

The Detective Superintendent also told the inquest: 'It is my belief that other prisoners were involved, but I had no evidence to bring charges.'

This is not really surprising when it is on record that the RUC failed to arrest and interview the other 13 INLA prisoners until 28 January 1998, a full 31 days after the murder of Billy Wright. Although it is quite reasonable to anticipate that those same 13 INLA prisoners would not have cooperated with any RUC investigation, the interval between the murder and their arrest would have provided them with sufficient time to destroy any remaining evidence which might still have existed and to facilitate them getting their stories correct. Clearly the senior RUC investigating officer believed it possible that other individuals were involved in the murder of Billy Wright. Other RUC officers involved in the reconstruction of the murder thought so too. LVF prisoners have stated that when RUC officers carried out a reconstruction of the murder of Billy Wright detectives said they believed as many as seven INLA prisoners had been involved at some stage of the murder operation. In a letter to David Wright, dated 17 November 1999, Assistant Chief Constable Raymond White, in charge of Crime, said:

> The police investigation was thorough and professional with all aspects of the murder included. Unfortunately, some were not satisfactorily resolved including how the guns were smuggled into the prison and that others involved in the murder have yet to be brought before the courts.

Just a few weeks earlier Assistant Chief Constable White met with David Wright at the RUC's Knocknagoney House, Belfast, to discuss his concerns in relation to the police investigation into his son's murder. At the conclusion of the meeting, Assistant Chief Constable White assisted David Wright to put on his coat. Whilst doing so he said, 'What you need, Mr Wright, is a public inquiry.' The same statement was repeated in the presence of a witness as David Wright was leaving the building to return home.

At the conclusion of the evidence of the witnesses, the Coroner, John Leckey reminded the members of the jury about their responsibilities in relation to an inquest court. He said they were to determine who the deceased was and how and where he came by his death. Mr Leckey said it was important for the Wright family to learn the facts surrounding the death. The Coroner qualified the remark by saying that at a murder trial or in a criminal prosecution all the facts relating to a killing may not come out. However, he did stress to the jurors that the inquest procedure was not a public inquiry.

The Coroner, while highlighting the major facts of the murder, said Wright's father, David, had concerns and that these had to be dealt with.

Describing the murder of the LVF leader as a 'planned and premeditated attack', the Coroner reminded the jurors that their verdict must be a unanimous one. The jury then retired to consider its verdict.

When the jury returned to deliver its verdict it was first handed to the Coroner to read. Once he had done so, the Coroner passed the document to his legal counsel, who, having read the contents, motioned to the Coroner to leave the courtroom. After a few minutes the Coroner and his counsel returned to the court and resumed their places. Before reading out the jury's findings in open court the Coroner said he intended to pass the document containing the verdict to each of the three legal representatives and to David Wright. Addressing David Wright directly, the Coroner instructed him not to display any form of visible emotion whatsoever once he had read the findings of the inquest jury.

Once all the legal advisors and David Wright had seen the verdict, the Coroner asked counsel for the Northern Ireland Prison Service if he was happy with the verdict.

Eventually the verdict was read out in the court. It found as follows:

> We find, Mr William Stephen Wright died on 27 December 1997 as a result of a gunshot wound to the chest sustained whilst in the process of a visitor transfer from H Block 6 Maze Prison which at the time was inhabited by both LVF and INLA prisoners. His murder was carried out by three INLA inmates in an elaborate, premeditated and preplanned act. Access to the murder scene was gained by the cutting of a hole, by person or persons unknown, in an undetected and unobserved section of the security fencing.

Clearly, the members of the jury, conscious of the restrictions imposed on the findings of an inquest, had formed the same opinion as many of the others present in the courtroom that day. They too thought it possible that individuals other than the three main perpetrators had been involved in the murder of Billy Wright.

At the conclusion of the inquest, the Coroner, John Leckey, paid particular tribute to the role played by David Wright throughout the course of the legal proceedings. In remarks addressed directly to the 67-year-old grandfather, the Coroner said: 'You have acquitted yourself as an advocate most admirably, Mr Wright.'

However, despite what he was later to describe as a patronising pat on the head from the Coroner, David Wright and his family issued the following statement to the waiting media:

The family of Billy Wright wishes to express their view on the jury verdict which leaves us further from the full facts of the murder.

The inclusion of the wording by the jury, namely persons or person unknown, unobserved and undetected, remarkable in a prison of the stature of the Maze, leaves this family no choice but to once again call for a full independent and public inquiry, which if obtained will name the persons or person unknown which the jury have said exist.

Clearly, the inquest, as far as the Wright family were concerned, had raised more questions than it had answered. The complete procedure and the flaws in the inquest system had done nothing to diminish the Wright family's fear that the British authorities were deliberately suppressing many of the circumstances surrounding the loyalist leader's death. Amongst the circumstances which were causing cause for concern were:

- Why prison authorities had decided to house LVF and INLA prisoners in the same block within the Maze Prison.
- The decision to transfer two of the murderers, Christopher 'Crip' McWilliams and John Kennaway, from Maghaberry Prison to the Maze despite both being involved in a hostage-taking incident using a smuggled weapon, and despite the INLA having uttered direct threats against Billy Wright immediately following this incident.
- The failure of the authorities at the Maze to heed or act on warnings from prison staff about the insecurity of the roof area of H6 and the possibility of attack using that as access.
- The ability of the INLA prisoners to gain ready access to weapons and wire cutters and their concealment within the accommodation area.
- The failure of prison staff to inspect the INLA wings and exercise yards for a period of several months and their inability to detect a breach in the security fencing.
- That prisoners on H6 were given visiting sheets containing the names of both LVF and INLA prisoners due to take visits on Saturday, 27 December 1997.
- Why a crucial security camera had been out of action for several days at the time of the murder.
- Why a prison officer on duty in a watchtower overlooking the

INLA wings on H6 was called out of his post twice on the morning of the murder, including the time of the murder itself.
- The reason why LVF prisoners were denied access to their exercise yard on the morning Billy Wright was shot dead but INLA prisoners had access to their yard.
- Why the INLA prison visits van had been parked next to the LVF wing while the LVF bus was parked next to the INLA wing.
- The failure of the police to question INLA prisoners until four weeks after the murder.
- The refusal of HM government on security grounds to disclose the identity of the duty governor of the Maze Prison on Saturday, 27 December 1997.

These are serious questions, which as yet remain unanswered despite numerous requests for the authorities to do so. Their continued refusal to do so has only served to increase a public belief that they have something to hide in relation to the Wright killing. Furthermore, the inquest itself exposed the deficiencies in the other inquiries, which the government claimed had thoroughly investigated all aspects of the Wright killing.

It is obvious that the above and other issues remain contentious and have not yet been resolved despite the prosecution, conviction and imprisonment of the three individuals who carried out the murder, the inquest and an inquiry headed by Martin Narey. Although the Wright family and the public are not in possession of all the information collated in the course of the above investigations, it has become apparent that each of those particular mechanisms have failed to either answer or adequately address the concerns raised. In fact, in certain instances they have only served to contribute to the overall silence and confusion that continues to surround the murder of Billy Wright.

In relation to the RUC investigation, David Wright has not been allowed access to the investigation file. A request was made to the Chief Constable and subsequently declined. However, it would appear from the two statements of Barlow and Molloy, disclosed in February 2002 to David Wright by the Coroner that the RUC investigation failed to properly investigate the background to the murder, in particular the withdrawal of the watchtower guard.

The redacted portion of the deposition of senior officer Arthur Gallagher proved possible to read and it indicated that principal officer Molloy was at least present when the telephone call ordering the standing down of the watchtower post was received. However, the limited scope of the Northern Ireland inquest has meant that this particular inquiry could not proceed beyond the narrow confines of the murder itself, and wider issues were never discussed.

The issues arising from the inquest have already been outlined elsewhere in this chapter. However, the limited scope of the Northern Ireland inquest has meant that this particular inquiry could not proceed beyond the narrow confines of the murder itself, and wider issues were never discussed.

In relation to the adequacy of the Narey Report, as an investigation into the murder of Billy Wright, it must be noted that they did not speak to David Wright or to any member of his family. Furthermore, no member of the Wright family has been allowed access to the Narey team's investigation file. It has also been noted that at the time he was conducting his investigation in 1998, 26 members of prison staff were absent from work through sickness and therefore not available to be interviewed by Narey.

Chapter 3 of the Narey Report (pages 14–19) deals with the Billy Wright murder. At the very outset, page 14, Narey states:

> We are conscious that the incident is the subject of an ongoing police investigation and it would be inappropriate for us to comment in detail on the precise circumstances or persons involved. We have therefore confined ourselves to the background of the shooting and to the general issues it raises, particularly the scope for illicit items to be smuggled into the prison [see Chapter 6].

Later that same year a full inspection of HMP Maze, 23 March–3 April 1998, carried out by HM Chief Inspector of Prisons for England and Wales (the Ramsbotham Report) expressly did not deal with the circumstances surrounding Wright's murder. On page two of the report the Chief Inspector notes: 'I was not to investigate recent incidents, which had been looked into by Mr Martin Narey whose report was made available to me, or were the subject of current and ongoing investigation by the RUC.'

The Ramsbotham team did not speak to David Wright or any member of his family during the course of its investigations.

19. Injustice and Prejudice

When discussions take place on the subject of injustices, there is without doubt the belief that the individual we support or whose case we put forward is above reproach or possesses integrity. That they are pure and unsullied.

However, when the individual under discussion possesses a questionable past or is considered by the self-righteous to be less than wholesome, widespread sympathy or indeed political or public support is found to be distinctly lacking. This in turn ensures that the chances of having the injustice exacted against that individual rectified becomes almost zero.

To adopt such an attitude not only indicates a selective mind, it also clearly indicates a belief in selective justice. To adopt such a belief is prejudice. In fact it is nothing less than further injustice. After all, selective justice is no form of justice whatsoever.

Such attitudes, despite our attempts at denial, are prevalent not only in Northern Ireland, but in the Irish Republic and Great Britain at this point in time. They do little to enhance the prospects of long-term political settlement and stability being achieved in Northern Ireland in the foreseeable future.

One only has to compare the case of Billy Wright with those of solicitors Pat Finucane and Rosemary Nelson to see that prejudice in action.

All three cases raise serious and alarming issues, which should and must be addressed. They are all equally deserving of attention. However, to date, it appears that as far as the British authorities are concerned, and also to a certain extent those in the Irish Republic, the priorities lie with the nationalist concerns as opposed to loyalist ones.

There can be little doubt that the current perception of Billy Wright has contributed much to the lack of public support for a full public inquiry to be set up to examine the full circumstances of his death inside the Maze Prison on 27 December 1997. Wright was feared and despised by the nationalist and republican community in Ireland. Since his death a myth has grown up around the loyalist leader. Indeed it is possible to say that this myth has been deliberately nurtured and fed to deter any full-scale investigation into his murder. The self-appointed experts state with certainty that Wright was responsible for this murder or that terrorist attack. If so, where is the evidence to support such claims? Certain Irish Sunday tabloids find him irresistible and barely a week passes without either a picture or a reference being made to the loyalist leader. It does not matter how tenuous the link, Billy Wright is still newsworthy long after his death. Allegations against Billy Wright have multiplied since his death for the simple reason that they were unproven during his lifetime.

The present public perception of Billy Wright is such that it totally inhibits the possibility of real justice being applied to the circumstances of his death. So-called respectable people are reluctant to speak out on his or his family's behalf. They are no doubt conscious of the damage that could be done to their public, political or social status by becoming associated with such a 'notorious paramilitary'. Privately, however, there were many who quietly condoned the activities of all sections of loyalist paramilitaries.

It has been left to Wright's father, David, to carry on almost single-handedly the battle to establish how and why the LVF leader died. David Wright does not hide the fact that his son was a member of the UVF. He says: 'Billy Wright was a UVF or indeed a LVF man to the day he died.' However, being a UVF man does not deny any individual the right to justice. It also should not have denied Billy Wright any less protection and security than any other inmate of the Maze Prison in December 1997.

The support for inquiries to be held into the deaths of Pat Finucane and Rosemary Nelson contrasts sharply with the support for Billy Wright. In the case of Finucane and Nelson, the good and the great have amalgamated to bellow out the claims of collusion and state involvement. Those very same people are remarkably silent to similar claims regarding Billy Wright's murder.

United Nations representatives, United States Senators, Congressmen, Church leaders and local politicians all cry with a single voice in support of the Finucane and Nelson families. Rightly so, for they must know the truth, they are entitled to the truth and no true democrat would deny them such. However, is the family of Billy Wright any less deserving of similar concern and support when they voice allegations of state collusion?

The British and Irish prime ministers have held personal meetings with a number of families whose loved ones have died in controversial circumstances. Those families have come from within Northern Ireland's nationalist community. Both prime ministers were anxious to assure the families and the wider nationalist community that their concerns would be addressed. They moved quickly, establishing the Stevens and the Port inquiries. Already considerable progress has been made, particularly in the Finucane murder.

The Wright family has yet to meet either the British or Irish prime ministers. Number 10 Downing Street sees little benefit in such a meeting taking place. The British authorities argue that the conviction of the three INLA volunteers for the murder in October 1998 is sufficient to say that justice has been seen to be done. As far as the police are concerned, the Wright murder file is closed. The official attitude has been maintained despite the continuing number of anomalies that have come to light about the circumstances of Billy Wright's death.

Both Rosemary Nelson and Pat Finucane were murdered in open society. Billy Wright was murdered outside society, in prison. It took place within the confines of what was supposedly the most secure prison in Western Europe. The three men who killed him were also inmates of the same prison. Questions must be asked about how that happened. David Wright is entitled to ask questions and, like the Finucane and Nelson families, he is entitled to have them answered.

Although the contrast in the three murders is enormous, they have many common denominators. All three were high-profile individuals, they were brutally murdered, questions remain unanswered and there are allegations of collusion in all three murders.

Where allegations of state collusion exist, it is incumbent upon the authorities to address them, otherwise they continue to fester and create further suspicion and distrust within their respective communities. Clearly all three cases require close and independent examination. It is hoped that this can be provided by retired Canadian judge, Mr Justice Peter Cory, who has been appointed to carry out inquiries into allegations of collusion in a number of deaths, including those of Pat Finucane, Rosemary Nelson and Billy Wright. It is important to know the truth, even though the truth may be painful, and cruel and will hurt. Only then can all the families put the matter to rest.

However, independence is the key word in relation to the success of the Cory inquiries. The Northern Ireland Office, the Police Service of

Northern Ireland, the Irish authorities and the security services must not be allowed to influence the outcome of the Cory inquiries. It is also imperative that all the inquiries be treated with equality, something that has been lacking to date. No differences must be made, all are equally deserving of the truth.

It will be difficult for many to set their prejudices aside, particularly with regard to Billy Wright. Prejudice cannot be allowed to influence the right of any individual to justice. For loyalist and nationalist, justice is a basic human right. Even in death that must be applied fairly and without discrimination.

Those who have called for inquiries to be set up into the murder of individuals in civilian life range from presidents to local politicians. It is alarming that those same individuals cannot break their self-righteous silence in relation to Billy Wright's murder. How can middle-class respectable Ireland, both north and south, expect to be taken seriously, until it moves away from selective justice and embraces inclusive justice for all?

The suffering and grief of the Wright family is no less than the suffering and grief of the Finucane and Nelson families. All are equally deserving of the truth.

'It is important for republicans and indeed the British government to attack the right of the loyalist people to defend themselves. They had to be made dishonourable. To carry the label of loyalism one also had to endure the indignity of slander, innuendo and criminality' – Billy Wright.

Appendix

Northern Ireland Human Rights Commission Press Release 22 May 2002, Calling for a Public Inquiry to be Set Up into the Murder of Billy Wright

The Northern Ireland Human Rights Commission today called for an independent, international, public, judicial inquiry into the murder of Billy Wright in the Maze Prison in December 1997. It did so because, after examining closely all the facts of the case and recent case-law, it now believes that this is the process most likely to arrive at the truth as to what actually happened on the day of the murder and as to the relevant surrounding circumstances.

The Commission said that in its view the State's duties under Article 2 of the European Convention on Human Rights (made part of the law of Northern Ireland by the Human Rights Act 1998) had not been fully complied with.

Article 2 requires the State not only to protect life – especially the life of those who are held in the custody of the State – but also to investigate thoroughly and effectively cases where a person in the custody of the State has been deprived of life. In Billy Wright's case, even though there have been convictions in relation to the murder, some relevant facts have still not been established. In particular, it has not yet been established how the gun used to kill Mr Wright was brought into the Maze Prison, nor how the killers were able to gain access to the area where Mr Wright was killed without being detected.

Speaking on behalf of the Commission, the Chief Commissioner, Professor Brice Dickson, said:

> Having studied the recent decisions of the European Court of Human Rights – especially that of Edwards v UK earlier this year – and having met on two occasions with Mr David Wright (the father of Billy Wright) and his legal representatives, the Commission is now of the view that a full-scale public inquiry should be initiated so that all aspects of the murder of Mr Wright can be thoroughly and effectively investigated. The Commission is particularly motivated by the facts that Billy Wright was in the custody of the State when he was murdered and that very relevant information concerning the circumstances surrounding his murder has not yet been unearthed. We believe that Article 2 of the European Convention requires an independent inquiry in this case.

The Commission has already contacted Mr David Wright and his legal representatives to apprise them all of the Commission's position.